The Symposium and *The Phaedrus*

SUNY Series in Ancient Greek Philosophy
Anthony Preus, editor

The Symposium and *The Phaedrus*

Plato's Erotic Dialogues

Translated with Introduction
and Commentaries by

William S. Cobb

State University of New York Press

Published by
State University of New York Press, Albany

Printed in the United States of America

For information, address State University of New York
Press, State University Plaza, Albany, NY 12246

Production by Christine Lynch
Marketing by Bernadette LaManna

Library of Congress Cataloging-in-Publication Data

Plato.
[Symposium. English]
The Symposium ; and The Phaedrus : Plato's erotic dialogues / translated with introduction and commentaries by William S. Cobb.
p. cm. — (SUNY series in ancient Greek philosophy)
Includes bibliographical references and index.
ISBN 0-7914-1617-8 (alk. paper). : ISBN 0-7914-1618-6 (pbk. : alk. paper)
1. Love—Early works to 1800. 2. Soul—Early works to 1800. 3. Socrates. 4. Rhetoric, Ancient. I. Cobb, William S. II. Plato. Phaedrus. English. 1993. III. Title. IV. Series.
B385.A5C63 1993
184—dc20 92-35391
CIP

10 9 8

This work could not have been done without the encouragement and assistance of Laurie M. Crammond. I am also especially indebted to Hamner Hill, Alba Sue Johnson, and Nepeta Nubarian.

κοινὰ γὰρ τὰ τῶν φίλων

Contents

1
General Introduction

The phenomenon of erotic love,[1] the love that is originally connected with sexual desire but is able to transcend that origin and reach even the heights of religious ecstasy, is dealt with extensively in two of Plato's most impressive dialogues, the *Symposium* and the *Phaedrus*. These two dialogues deal with both the earthy origins and the spiritual heights of erotic love. The *Symposium* is a report of a series of speeches about erotic love given at a dinner party, and the *Phaedrus* is a conversation about making speeches that includes several examples of speeches on erotic love. Various aspects of erotic love are also illustrated in the dramatic action in both dialogues.

The *Symposium* and the *Phaedrus* are striking in their philosophical content as well as in their literary quality. They provide an excellent basis for discussing Platonic philosophy in general because they include substantial treatment of many of the major themes in Plato's works. They also provide an excellent basis for considering the question of how to read Plato's dialogues because they contain particularly good examples of the characteristics that have led to recent controversies about what sort of texts these dialogues are.

Plato's dialogues are traditionally divided into three groups, representing chronological divisions of Plato's writing career. Although the groupings are primarily justified by considerations of technical matters of linguistic usage,[2] the dialogues in each group share some general characteristics: 1) In the early group, the dialogues are shorter, less complex dramatically, and characterized by an apparent failure to find a satisfactory answer to the question raised in the discussion, which is usually of the "What is X?" variety. Examples of early period dialogues are the *Laches* (What is courage?), the *Charmides* (What is judiciousness?), and the *Euthyphro* (What is religiousness?). 2) In the longer, middle-period dialogues, there are positive defenses of philosophical positions and very complex dramatic structures. The *Symposium* and the *Phaedrus* fall into this period. The *Phaedo* is another excellent example of this group. It is a conversation between Socrates and his friends in the prison cell after Socrates' conviction at his trial. They discuss immortality, and

Socrates seems to conclude that the final argument they examine is a sound proof that human souls are immortal. The dialogue ends with Socrates' death from drinking poison. Other well-known middle-period dialogues are the *Republic* and the *Protagoras.* 3) In the late period, the dialogues are longer, but lack dramatic complexity, and tend to be careful analyses of relatively technical questions. For example, the *Theaetetus* examines several proposed definitions of knowledge, although it finds none of them satisfactory; the *Sophist* elaborates at great length on the definition of a Sophist, making a number of epistemological, metaphysical, and linguistic claims in passing; and the *Parmenides* examines possible interpretations of unity and plurality after raising some objections to a particular version of the doctrine of forms, the ultimate principles of reality that are the objects of knowledge in the highest sense.

The middle-period dialogues *Symposium* and *Phaedrus* have much in common. Both contain formal speeches, that is, monologues, about the nature of love. Both are characterized by a positive, affirmative tone, raising substantial philosophical issues and defending positions on them: in both, Socrates affirms certain claims about the nature of love, and in the *Phaedrus* he defends a number of claims about the requirements for making good speeches. The two dialogues are also similar in their complex richness of dramatic detail: as with other middle-period dialogues, the *Symposium* and the *Phaedrus* construct elaborate settings and depict their characters' engaging in complicated activities. The literary character of both dialogues is also striking: the *Symposium* could easily be presented as a drama, and the *Phaedrus* is full of myths and elaborately developed metaphors. These common characteristics of extended speeches about love, positively defended philosophical doctrines, and dramatic and literary richness must each be given careful consideration in deciding how to interpret these two dialogues.

The two dialogues also differ in significant ways. The *Symposium* reports a series of speeches in praise of love given at a dinner party. The speeches run the gamut from ribald comedy to sweeping scientific theory to lofty philosophical speculation, and the dialogue contains a great deal of detail about the characters who give the speeches and their interactions at the party. The *Phaedrus,* on the other hand, records a conversation between Socrates and a younger man named Phaedrus. (This same character offers the first speech about love in the *Symposium.*) After meeting and walking to a quiet place outside of town, they read a speech by Lysias, a famous orator of the time, that is an effort to seduce a young boy. Socrates offers two quite different, alternative speeches on the same theme, and he and Phaedrus then discuss what is required for making a good speech. Again, there is much detail about the interactions of the characters and the setting. Moreover, the *Phaedrus* gives much attention to the making and interpreting of myths.

SOME GENERAL ISSUES INVOLVED IN BOTH DIALOGUES

Before looking at each of these dialogues individually, a number of general questions related to the understanding of both must be considered. One major point which beginning students sometimes overlook is that these dialogues, like all the others by Plato, are works of fiction. The settings and the characters do have some historical basis—indeed, the *Symposium* and the *Phaedrus* are the source of much of our modern knowledge of the social attitudes and practices of Athenian aristocrats. Nevertheless, there is no reason to assume that these texts are reports of actual events and conversations or that any of the speeches in them were composed by anyone other than Plato (this applies even to the speech in the *Phaedrus* attributed to Lysias). Thus, the reader must keep in mind that the work is entirely by one hand and ask why the author includes what is there and why it is presented as it is. What is Plato trying to accomplish in these texts, and why does he include the various characters, settings, actions, speeches, and conversations in the way he does? The reader must avoid assuming that the contents of the dialogues are dictated by historical fact.

Another general issue that must be addressed is the status of Socrates as an exemplar of the philosopher. Until fairly recently, it was nearly universally assumed that the figure of Socrates was always presented by Plato as the ideal form of a philosopher, and of a human being. Thus, it was assumed that Socrates is not only the spokesman for Plato in the discussions in the dialogues, but that his depicted character and behavior is unqualifiedly approved by Plato. However, some contemporary scholars have challenged this assumption.

In the past, the general view has been that the *Symposium* presents Plato's own view of love in the speech of Socrates and is in part intended to exonerate Socrates from certain accusations connected with his association with the notorious Alcibiades, and that the second speech by Socrates in the *Phaedrus*, along with Socrates' conclusions in the conversation about how to make good speeches, also represent Plato's own views. However, Martha Nussbaum has argued that the *Symposium* is intended largely to criticize and reject some aspects of Socrates' behavior and the Socratic philosophy as overly attached to abstract universal principles at the expense of concern for concrete individuality. In her view the understanding of love presented by Socrates and depicted in the personal relationships of Socrates as described in this dialogue are not being affirmed by Plato, but criticized for their shortcomings.[3] Thus, the reader must not simply assume that the figure and words of Socrates in the dialogues have Plato's unqualified endorsement. (Nussbaum argues that the Socrates of the *Phaedrus*, on the contrary, does present Plato's own views.[4] She assumes there is a significant difference between the views articulated by Socrates in the two dialogues, of course.)

A further general issue that can be very distracting to contemporary, first-time readers is the treatment of homosexuality in these dialogues. In the various views that are expressed about the nature and significance of love in both dialogues, the sexual expression of love that is considered is almost always homosexual in form. Moreover, homosexual relationships are generally approved of by the speakers in the dialogues, although it is recognized that these relationships are sometimes wrong. Apparently, the usual pattern is for an older man to establish an intimate relationship with a young man who becomes his protégé, with the initiative normally coming from the older man. Thus, the benefits derived from the relationship are quite different for the two participants: educational and social advantages for the youth, and sexual pleasure and companionship for the older man.[5] This sort of relationship is presented in the dialogues as a normal part of everyday life in ancient Athens, at least among the aristocrats.[6]

It is particularly important to remember these assumptions about what is normal and appropriate in sexual relationships when trying to understand the responses Alcibiades attributes to Socrates when he describes his efforts to seduce Socrates in the *Symposium*. In this context, although such relationships can take an improper form, there is nothing improper, abnormal, or immoral about a homosexual relationship as such. In the *Phaedrus* Socrates does express some reservations about the sexual dimension of these relationships, but his remarks are more cautionary than condemnatory and must be interpreted within the context of the dialogue.

Since speeches are an important motif in both of these dialogues, an additional general issue that is important for understanding these two dialogues has to do with the Greek term for "speech," which is λόγος, *logos*.[7] The *Symposium* contains a number of speeches, and the *Phaedrus* contains three speeches and a conversation about the requirements for making a good speech. The Greek word for "speech" is *logos*, but the term *logos* cannot be translated by a single English word. I have variously used "speech," "argument," "statement," "account," "discussion," and also "reason" (in the sense of the capacity to think). The term obviously has to do with the use of language and with the activity of thinking, but just how this is being understood is not obvious from the English translations.

In its primary sense, the Greek term denotes an activity, that of using language, rather than a set of words existing as an object, such as a written speech or even language itself as an abstract entity. Moreover, as an active verb, speaking takes a direct object, that is, one does not speak *about* the world, one speaks the world. This grammatical structure suggests that speech is understood as doing something to the object one is, as we would say, speaking about. Speaking has a direct effect on its object. A useful way of understanding this is to think of speech as primarily a means of showing or displaying an object, of letting the nature of the object disclose itself, rather than of reporting one's thoughts or feelings about the object. From this point of view, talking about things can be a way of discovering something about the nature of things. That is, language can reveal more to the speaker and the listener than either brings to it.[8] This suggests an explanation for Socrates' concern for and involvement with *logos*, especially in its living form as conversation or dialogue (διάλογος, *dialogos*).[9]

The term *logos* is also sometimes translated as "reason."[10] In this sense reason is understood as the capacity to grasp the nature of something in a structured and intelligible way, just as one does in speaking (about) something. This suggests that whatever can be grasped by reason can be expressed in speech, for reason, as Plato says in *Sophist* 264a, is silent speaking. Thus, the objects of reason cannot be ineffable. This general issue regarding the nature of *logos* is particularly important for the interpretation of the *Phaedrus*. It is also an important issue in Plato's *Cratylus* and *Sophist*.

A final general issue that the reader should have in mind throughout these two dialogues concerns the term "love." The Greek term I translate as "love," following the usual practice, is ἔρως, *erōs*.[11] There can be no doubt that the term is primarily used of sexual desire, although it is used for other sorts of desire, perhaps metaphorically,[12] and in the speeches in both dialogues the sense of the term is extended far beyond sexual desire. This raises the question of how far this elevation of *erōs* can be taken as a serious suggestion, rather than a sophisticated farce. Some of the things said by some speakers in the *Symposium*, especially Socrates, might have been seen as ludicrous by an Athenian audience and could indicate an intentional parody by Plato. The greater ambiguity of the English word "love" may be misleading in this regard. There are some fantastical claims about the nature of love in Socrates' second speech in the *Phaedrus* that are surely tongue-in-cheek, though this is not incompatible with a serious intent, of course.

On the other hand, it is not clear what other Greek term the speakers could have used to engage in a serious discussion of the "elevated" sorts of attitudes and principles they here call a form of *erōs*. There are two other Greek terms that are often translated as "love" (though not in my translations of these two dialogues) namely, ἀγαπή, *agapē*, and φιλία, *philia*. The term *agapē*, which is used in the Koine Greek of the *New Testament* to refer to the peculiar love of God, in Plato's time referred to affectionate, sometimes passionate desire and does not play an important part in the discussions in these dialogues. The verbal form of this term, which I translate differently in different contexts, occurs three times in the *Symposium*: at 180b (where I translate it as "cherishes"), at 181c ("cherishing"), and at 210d ("lusting after"). The verbal form occurs five times in the *Phaedrus*: at 233e ("adore") and at 241d, 247d, 253a, and 257e ("cherish"). An adjectival form occurs at *Phaedrus* 230c ("delightful").

The term *philia* and related terms occur frequently in these dialogues, especially in the *Phaedrus*, but *philia* is closer to what we call "friendship." It is used of the relationship of mutuality and sharing between friends and between the members of a family and would not ordinarily imply sexual desire. This term and its variants, including compounds such as φιλοσοφία, *philosophia* (which, when it is not read as "philosophy," is rendered by most translators as "love of wisdom") are not translated using the term "love" in these translations, so as to avoid confusion for the reader.

The nature of love (*erōs*) is a major focus in both dialogues, and it is important for the Greekless reader to be able to see just how the term is used. Hence, every occurrence of the term *erōs* and its variants, but no other Greek word, is translated with the word 'love' and variants (except for five times as "erotic" in the *Phaedrus*).

In the *Phaedrus*, in addition to love (*erōs*), friendship (*philia*) is a major theme that is both discussed by the characters and illustrated in their interactions. Accordingly, I have consistently used the terms 'friend,' 'friendship,' and variations for every occurrence of terms related to *philia*—including compounds such as *philosophia* ("friendship with wisdom").[13] Again, the purpose is to enable the Greekless reader to follow carefully the explication of a term when it is an important focus of the dialogue.

Except for these two terms, I have not tried to maintain a rigid consistency in the translation, that is, using the same English word for the same Greek word on every occasion. This would make for an awkward and misleading translation—Greek terms do not match up perfectly with English ones. Those who are interested in careful study of Plato's use of Greek terms must learn to use the Greek text.

I should also mention that Greek does not use the term for a male human being (ἀνήρ, *anēr*) to refer to human beings in general. In the latter case, the term ἄνθρωπος, *anthrōpos*, is used. Hence, in these translations the terms 'man' and 'men' and the masculine pronouns are not being used in a supposedly gender-neutral sense. The focus in both dialogues is clearly on males and male relationships, unless it is explicitly indicated otherwise.

THE PROBLEM OF INTERPRETATIVE METHODOLOGY

In addition to the above general issues related to understanding these dialogues, some consideration must be given to the general question of how to interpret Plato's dialogues. This involves the question of what kind of texts they are and especially of how to deal with their literary and dramatic aspects. This issue of interpretive methodology in reading Plato has become a matter of considerable controversy in recent years.[14]

While it is virtually impossible to completely ignore the literary and dramatic qualities of Plato's dialogues when assessing their philosophical content, most interpreters do focus on the argumentation, especially that given by

Socrates, and assume that this represents what Plato is affirming in the dialogue. Thus, most readers assume that the views Socrates presents in his report of his discussions with Diotima in the *Symposium* and in his second speech and the discussion of the art of making speeches in the *Phaedrus* are the views Plato is defending as true.

In recent years a number of scholars have objected that this sort of approach does not give adequate attention to the significance of the literary and dramatic aspects of the dialogues. It seems implausible to treat elements that Plato uses so much effort to introduce into the texts, especially in dialogues like the *Symposium* and the *Phaedrus*, as having no significant role in shaping the philosophical content of the dialogues. However, just what the significance of the literary and dramatic aspects is for the philosophical content of the dialogues is a subject about which there is an enormous diversity of opinion.[15]

Of course, the common approach to the dialogues that focuses on the argumentation does not completely neglect literary and dramatic elements in the texts. It would be nearly impossible to ignore such things as the mythical character of the language in which Diotima's views are cast, or the role of irony in some of Socrates' claims, or the fact that the presence of Alcibiades in the *Symposium* as a young man whom Socrates could be accused of having corrupted is relevant to an assessment of Plato's intention in the dialogue.[16] Insofar as the demand is simply to pay attention to the entire text, then, this is not particularly controversial, although it might require being a little more careful about comparing statements about a single theme drawn from different dialogues. The issue is whether these literary and dramatic elements are merely supplementary to the content of the argumentation, or play a more decisive role, providing the key for interpreting the argumentation, perhaps, or a basis for claiming that the outcome of the argumentation does not really represent Plato's, or Socrates', own views. Here there is a very wide spectrum of opinion, from those who see the literary and dramatic aspects as enriching and supplementing, but not disrupting the straightforward analysis of the argumentation, to those who would claim that the literary and dramatic elements are the core of the dialogues and the argumentation is to be entirely subordinated, if not ignored, in understanding the message of the texts.

A very extreme position on this spectrum is taken by James Arieti, who argues that the dialogues should not be seen as philosophical texts at all, but as dramas in a straightforward sense. The key to understanding the dialogues in his eyes is the dramatic depiction of characters and their actions; the argumentation must be seen as subservient to dramatic necessities and not as serious efforts by Plato to develop or explore philosophical analyses and positions.[17]

Very few Plato scholars are likely to be willing to give such an extreme view any credence, but Arieti's approach does at least involve a fresh reading and can stimulate useful reflection. His interpretation of the *Symposium* is a striking example of the results of this approach. He argues that the dialogue is not a serious philosophical investigation of the nature of love. Rather it is a demonstration of the craft of theologizing. In the various speeches in the dialogue, love is personified as a divine being, and each of the speakers offers an interpretation of the nature of the god. What the drama shows us, Arieti claims, is how the depicted nature of the god in each case bears a striking resemblance to the character of the speaker who is characterizing him. In other words, the *Symposium* is a dramatic depiction of the fact that when human beings discuss the gods, they tend to make the gods in their own images. Arieti concludes that there is no reason to assume that Plato would have affirmed any of these depictions of love as "true."[18]

A slightly less radical approach, which also focuses on the literary and dramatic aspects as crucial rather than merely supplemental in interpreting the dialogues, argues that this perspective reveals that the function of the dialogues is not to present philosophical doctrines, but to stimulate readers to engage in their own analysis and reflection on philosophical issues. This way of reading the dialogues assumes that Plato's concern is more to assist his readers in learning how to think than to tell them what to think. In keeping with this pedagogical purpose, some scholars argue, Plato does not reveal, at least straightforwardly, his own views in the dialogues. Rather he presents analyses and conclusions that are all more or less problematical on purpose, hoping that readers will be caught up in the discussion and not have their own rational activity cut off by being told "the truth."[19] Another approach somewhat similar to this one argues that Plato never reveals his own views straightforwardly on the surface of the argumentation in the dialogues, but only hints at them in subtle ways. Dramatic elements are often seen as such hints.[20]

One could argue that neither Arieti's emphasis on the reading of the dialogues as drama nor the claim that Plato has a major interest in stimulating his readers to engage in philosophical enquiry is incompatible with Plato's having included argumentation in the dialogues that represents his best and most serious philosophical efforts.[21] Thus, most contemporary readers of Plato who emphasize the importance of the literary and dramatic aspects of the dialogues do not see this as involving a general denigration of the argumentation. On the contrary, they use the dramatic and literary elements to enrich and guide the analysis of the arguments.

Martha Nussbaum is a well-known exponent of this approach, in which the argumentation is interpreted in light of the dramatic and literary elements of the text. She argues, for example, that traditional analyses of the *Symposium* have been seriously flawed by a failure to realize that the dramatic and literary structure of the dialogue makes the speech of Alcibiades the key to interpreting the dialogue's message. As a result of neglecting this speech, she argues, scholars have failed to see that the *Symposium* involves a serious criticism by Plato of the Socratic way of life and love in the form of a condemnation of Socrates' otherworldliness.[22]

In such readings as this, however, it is clearly the case that the argumentation in the dialogues is being taken seriously, even when it is claimed that the dramatic and literary aspects help the reader to see that some of the argumentation is not intended to be taken in the most straightforward way as representing views Plato intends to support. On balance, therefore, attention to the dramatic and literary elements in the dialogues does not need to lead away from a concern for the argumentation in the dialogues, although it may lead to a more critical evaluation of it. Given the preponderance of the argumentation in the dialogues, it seems implausible to say that it is not the central element in the texts, although it also seems implausible to ignore the possible significance of the dramatic and literary aspects, especially of such dialogues as the *Symposium* and the *Phaedrus*.

These two dialogues are excellent ones for considering this issue of interpretative methodology. Both are exceptionally rich in dramatic and literary characteristics, and the issue of how to interpret a text, especially texts like Plato's dialogues, seems to be raised explicitly in the *Phaedrus*. I consider the implications of the discussion of this issue in the *Phaedrus* in my commentary on that dialogue, and throughout both commentaries I try to take note of ways in which one might see dramatic and literary aspects of the texts as having significance for the interpretation of their philosophical content.

The numbers and letters in the margins of the translations of the dialogues refer to sections of the pages of the Stephanus edition of the Greek text and represent the standard way of locating specific passages in Plato's dialogues. Their placement is only approximate, but is sufficiently accurate to facilitate cross-reference to the Greek texts, or to other translations, and to allow the location of passages that are referred to in secondary discussions.

2
The Symposium

INTRODUCTION

The *Symposium*, one of Plato's middle-period dialogues, is generally considered to have been composed around 385–380 B.C.E.[1] and to be one of Plato's most impressive achievements. The dialogue is constructed as a report of several speeches about love that were presented at a dinner party given by the playwright Agathon on the occasion of his winning first prize in a tragedy contest in Athens. (The actual contest occurred in 416 B.C.E.) This report is presented as being given by a man named Apollodorus to an unnamed companion some time after the event.

A number of the characters in the *Symposium* are based on well-known people. It is important for the reader to be aware of the background that would have been clear to readers in Plato's day. Besides Socrates himself, the iconoclastic, comic playwright Aristophanes is the figure we are most familiar with, through his still existing plays.[2] In Plato's day, however, no one would have been more familiar than the traitor/hero Alcibiades, whose notorious career included a youthful period during which he spent some time in the company of Socrates. At the time of Agathon's party in the dialogue, Alcibiades would have been in his early thirties.

Alcibiades was a man of enormous wealth, talent, and charm. In 415, the year after Agathon's party, he was chosen to lead the ill-fated expedition to Sicily whose disastrous loss ultimately resulted in the defeat of Athens by Sparta in the Peloponnesian War. However, the night before the expedition left, many Herms, that is, statues displaying representations of the face and genitals of the god Hermes that were placed near the doors of homes as expressions of devotion and hope for protection, were destroyed. The populace was outraged and decided that the crime was the work of Alcibiades. When Alcibiades received word that he was to return to Athens in order to be executed for this crime, he defected to Sparta instead and was of great assistance to them in their defeat of Athens. Nevertheless, some years later Alcibiades was again welcomed back into Athens as a hero, although he was not popular with some factions and was finally assassinated.

The tragedian Agathon is also known from extant records, although none of his plays have survived. Shortly after the triumph that occasions the party in the dialogue, he left Athens in order to join the court of the notorious tyrant Archelaus. Eryximachus was a famous physician of the time; both he and Phaedrus were accused of complicity in the destruction of the Herms that was blamed on Alcibiades. The other characters lack known historical bases, although there is a Pausanias of similar character in Xenophon's *Symposium.* We have no clear evidence of the existence of anyone who could be the basis of the characters Diotima, Aristodemus, and Apollodorus, although an Apollodorus appears in the *Apology* as one of Socrates' friends who offers to pay his proposed fine and in the *Phaedo* as one of those friends present at Socrates' final conversation.

The *Symposium* is not simply a series of speeches, although the bulk of the text does consist of seven monologues, by Phaedrus (178a–180c), Pausanias (180c–185c), Eryximachus (185e–188e), Aristophanes (189a–193d), Agathon (194e–197e), Socrates (201d–212c), and Alcibiades (215a–222b). Surrounding and connecting these speeches are incidents, interchanges, and editorial comments by Apollodorus that are an important part of the dialogue.

The overarching issue in the *Symposium* is, of course, the nature of love, that is, of *erōs*. Plato explores this issue through a series of speeches, but the speakers do not agree with each other and take quite different perspectives on the issue. What does Plato intend to affirm about the nature of *erōs*, and about the human condition in general, through all this? Every point raised in my commentary on the dialogue is related to that question, but a brief summation of the problem here may be useful.

While there are significant differences among the first five speakers, through Agathon, a number of points are made that seem to provide the groundwork for the final two speakers, Socrates and Alcibiades, so the reader should not neglect these early speeches. That *erōs* is initially understood to be sexual desire is obvious, and that such desire can have varied consequences and take varied forms, some of which are better than others, is emphasized. Moreover, the possibility is also raised that *erōs* has much greater significance than mere sexual desire, so that sexual desire is only a limited manifestation of something more profound: Eryximachus connects *erōs* with the most fundamental workings of the cosmos, and Aristophanes connects it with the most basic needs of human beings and sees its fulfillment as the key to human happiness. This movement toward interpreting *erōs* as the key to human being in general, and the cosmos, reaches its culmination in the views of Diotima that Socrates reports. Here *erōs* is seen as the means of actualizing the highest potentialities of human being through achieving an understanding of the ultimate principle of beauty, which is the ultimate object of *erōs*. Here is found the life that human beings are truly fit for. But what does Plato think that life is like?

There is some divergence of opinion among interpreters on this matter. Virtually everyone sees Diotima's views as the key, but not everyone understands her vision in the same way. Some see her as pointing toward some sort of mystical encounter with a transcendent reality of unspeakable beauty, while others note that she seems to suggest that *erōs* at its highest level leads to a life of producing beautiful things, especially philosophical conversations. These two views may not be incompatible. To some extent, the issue turns on how one takes Alcibiades' speech in praise of Socrates. If Plato intends it to give us a concrete example of the life Diotima is pointing toward, this provides a way of getting a grasp on what he is affirming in the dialogue. Yet Alcibiades' depiction of Socrates is somewhat ambiguous. He shows Socrates to be a man of courage, conviction, judgment, tenacity, and above all, devotion to philosophical conversation and thought, a man whose wisdom is so inspiring he should be obeyed in all things, but at the same time Alcibiades also seems to think he is arrogant and difficult, if not cold and inhuman.

So, what is Plato saying human life at its best is like? Dealing with this issue requires paying careful attention to just how Plato is depicting the life of love at its highest level, in the views attributed to Diotima, as well as in Alcibiades' stories. It also requires paying careful attention to the issues that are raised in the earlier speeches, and to the context in which the speeches are presented, that is, to the dramatic and literary aspects of the dialogue.

The grammatical structure of the dialogue is very complex. It is a conversation that reports a conversation that sometimes itself includes reports of other conversations. In order to avoid distractingly complicated patterns of quotation marks, I have greatly abbreviated their use. However, the reader can easily determine from the context what level of quotation is actually involved in individual passages. After the opening dialogue between Apollodorus and his unnamed companion, the entire text is narrated by Apollodorus.

THE DIALOGUE

APOLLODORUS: I believe I'm not unprepared for what you're asking to hear. 172a
Just the other day I was going up to town from my home in Phalerum,[3] when
someone I know, catching sight of me from some distance behind, shouted:

"Hey, Phalerian!" he called (he was making a joke[4] at the same time),
"you, Apollodorus, will you wait?"

So, I stopped and waited.

"Actually, Apollodorus," he said, "I was just looking for you as I wanted
to ask about the party at Agathon's when Socrates, Alcibiades, and the others 172b
were present for dinner. What were their speeches about love? Someone else
told me what he had heard from Phoenix, the son of Philip,[5] and he claimed
that you're also familiar with them. However, his report wasn't very clear, so
would you go over them for me? A report of the words of your companion
would be quite appropriate coming from you. But first tell me," he went on,
"whether or not you yourself were present at the party."

"The account you received wasn't at all clear," I said, "if you believe that 172c
party you're asking about was recent enough for me to have been present."

"I did indeed," he said.

"How could you, Glaucon?"[6] I replied. "Don't you know that Agathon
hasn't lived here for many years, while I've been spending time with Socrates
for less than three years, making it my purpose to know what he says or does
every day? Prior to that, I was charging around haphazardly, just as you are 173a
now, believing I was achieving something, although I was more useless than
anyone, and thinking that it would be better to do anything rather than engage
in philosophy."

"Quit teasing," he said, "and tell me when that gathering occurred."

"While we were still youngsters," I replied, "when Agathon won the
prize with his first tragedy.[7] It was on the day after he and his company celebrated his victory feast."

"Well, then," he said, "it seems it was a long time ago. But who told you
about it? Socrates himself?"

"No, by Zeus," I responded, "it was the same person who told Phoenix, 173b
an Aristodemus from Cydathenaeum, a small fellow who goes barefoot all the
time, and is a lover of Socrates (and one of the most devoted at that time, it
seemed to me). He was present at the party. However, I did also ask Socrates
about some of the things I heard from Aristodemus, and he agrees with what
Aristodemus told me."

"Then, why don't you go through it for me?" he said. "After all, the road
we're taking into town is a good one for conversation."

So, we went over the speeches as we strolled along, and as a result, as I
said at the beginning, I'm not unprepared. If I must go through them again with 173c
you, so be it. For myself, at least, aside from the question of whether it's benefi-

cial, I find any discussion of philosophy extraordinarily enjoyable, whether I
am engaging in it myself or only listening to that of others. When I hear people
talk about other things, however, especially you rich men who're involved in
business, I become bored and feel sorry for you and your companions because
you think you're achieving something when you're really accomplishing nothing. On your side, you probably believe that I'm unhappy, and I suppose your 173d
belief is true. Yet I don't think that about you, I know it for sure!

COMPANION: You're always the same, Apollodorus; you always criticize everyone, including yourself. You seem to believe that everyone is miserable, beginning with yourself—except Socrates. Where you got this nickname "the gentle one," I don't know, because in your conversation you're always so angry at yourself and everyone else—everybody but Socrates, of course.

APOLLODORUS: Ah, best of friends, is it so clear that I'm crazy and off 173e
target in thinking about myself and you in this way?

COMPANION: There's no merit in our arguing about this just now, Apollodorus. Don't do anything but what I just asked: Recite the speeches for me.

APOLLODORUS: Well, they went like this—but I'd better try to tell it to 174a
you from the beginning, as Aristodemus told it to me.

He said he met Socrates, who was coming from the baths and wearing sandals, which he rarely did, and he asked Socrates where he was going looking so beautiful.

"To dinner at Agathon's," he replied. "I stayed away from the victory feasts
yesterday, because I was concerned about the crowd, but I agreed to be there
today. I'm dressed up this way so that beauty may approach beauty. But you,"
he said, "how do you feel about going to this dinner without an invitation?" 174b

"Well," Aristodemus said that he replied, "I'll do whatever you say."

"Then come along," Socrates said, "so that we can pervert the proverb by
changing it to say: 'Good men go to the feasts of the good without an invitation.'[8] Homer not only perverts this proverb, he comes close to treating it outrageously. He makes Agamemnon a man who is extremely good at warfare,
and Menelaus a 'weak spearman.'[9] Then, when Agamemnon is celebrating 174c
the performance of a sacrifice, he has Menelaus attend the feast without an
invitation, an inferior man going to the feast of the better."[10]

Aristodemus said that when he heard this he responded, "I'm probably
not what you say I am, Socrates. Rather, as Homer has it, it's a useless person,
me, going uninvited to the feast of a wise and skillful man. So, since it's you
who's taking me, you should construct some excuse, because I won't admit
that I come uninvited. I'll say it's at your command." 174d

"Then, 'while two go along, one before the other,'"[11] he said, "we can plan what we'll say. But let's be on our way!"

Aristodemus said that after conversing in that way they set off. Socrates then became absorbed in his thoughts and fell behind as they travelled along the road, but when Aristodemus waited for him, Socrates ordered him to go on ahead. When Aristodemus arrived at Agathon's house, he found the door open. He said he felt it was somewhat awkward, for a slave from inside imme- 174e
diately came out to meet him and led him to where the others were reclining,[12] and he found them getting ready to dine. However, Agathon called out, as soon as he saw him, "Aristodemus! You've come at a good time! You must dine with us. If you've come for some other purpose, postpone it until later. I looked for you yesterday so I could invite you, but I didn't see you anywhere. But why haven't you brought Socrates with you?"

"When I turned around," Aristodemus continued, "I saw that Socrates was nowhere behind me. So, I said that I actually had come with Socrates, because he had invited me to the dinner."

"You're doing the right thing," Agathon responded, "but where is he?"

"He was coming along behind me just now, but I wonder myself where 175a
he could be."

According to Aristodemus, Agathon told a slave, "Why don't you go search for Socrates and bring him in? And Aristodemus, you recline here beside Eryximachus."

Aristodemus said that a slave brought him water to wash with so that he could recline on the couch and that another of the slaves came and reported: "Socrates is here. He has stopped on the porch next door and is just standing there. When I asked him, he didn't want to come in."

"That's odd," Agathon said, "continue inviting him and don't take no for an answer."

Aristodemus reported that he responded, "No, no! Leave him alone! It's 175b
something he often does. He can become transfixed anywhere he happens to be standing. I expect he'll come soon. Don't disturb him; leave him alone."

He said that Agathon replied, "If that's your opinion, that's what must be done. You slaves, serve the others. You always serve up whatever you wish when no one is supervising you (which I never do); so now, pretend that you have invited these other people and me to dinner. Serve us in a manner that
will make us praise you." 175c

Aristodemus said that after this they ate, though Socrates had not yet come in. Agathon kept wanting to send after Socrates, but Aristodemus wouldn't let him. And as usual, Socrates came along after not too long a time—they were hardly halfway through the meal.

Aristodemus reported that Agathon, who was reclining alone on the last couch,[13] then called out, "Socrates, recline here beside me so that by touching you I may gain the benefit of the wisdom that came to you on the porch. You
obviously found it and are holding on to it, for otherwise you wouldn't have 175d
come in."

Socrates sat down and replied, "I'd be happy, Agathon, if wisdom were the kind of thing that would flow from the one of us with more of it to the one with less when we touch each other, the way water flows through a piece of yarn from the fuller cup to the emptier. If it were that way, I'd place a very high value on reclining beside you. I suspect I'd be filled with a lot of fine 175e
wisdom from you. My own is surely as worthless and ambiguous as a dream, but yours is bright and has great promise. Despite your being so young, it shone forth brilliantly when it was manifested the other day before more than thirty thousand Greeks!"

"You're being outrageous,[14] Socrates," Agathon responded. "You and I can argue these claims about wisdom a little later, when we'll use Dionysus[15] as the judge. But for now, turn to your dinner first."

Aristodemus said that after this Socrates lay back and ate his dinner with 176a
the others. When they had eaten, they poured their libations, sang to the god, did the other customary things, and then turned to the drinking. At that point, he reported, Pausanias spoke up along these lines:

"Well now, gentlemen," Pausanias said, "what will be the most moderate way for us to drink? I can tell you that I myself am in a quite dreadful condition from yesterday's drinking, and I need some relief. I suspect most of you do, too. You were present yesterday. So, let's look for a way to drink as moderately as possible." 176b

Then Aristophanes responded, "What you say is true, Pausanias. We must, at any rate, find a way of drinking that will be easier on us. I got soused yesterday myself!"

After hearing them, according to Aristodemus, Eryximachus, the son of Acumenus declared: "What you both are saying is true, yet I need to hear something from you, Agathon. Are you up to drinking?"

"Not at all," Agathon replied, "I don't have the strength for it myself."

"Then, it seems it would be a bit of luck from Hermes,"[16] Eryximachus 176c
continued, "for me, Aristophanes, Phaedrus, and the others, if you hardiest drinkers would stop now, since we always fall short by comparison. Socrates I exempt from the account; he'll be satisfied either way, and it will be alright with him whatever we do. So, since it seems to me that no one here has the stomach for drinking much wine, I probably will provoke less displeasure when I tell you the truth about the nature of intoxication. I believe it has become clear from medical practice that intoxication is a harmful thing for human beings. I myself 176d
would not voluntarily drink too deeply, nor would I advise anyone to do so, especially when they still have a hangover from the previous day."

Aristodemus said that Phaedrus the Myrrhinousian then announced: "I customarily obey you myself, Eryximachus, especially when you speak about medical matters, and this time the others would also be well advised to do so."

When they heard this, everyone agreed not to make the present gathering 176e
a drinking bout, but to drink only as they pleased.

"Then, now that it's been decided," Eryximachus continued, "that drinking is to be as each desires and not compulsory, the next thing I propose is that we dismiss the flute-girl who just came in. Let her play for herself, or if she prefers, for the women inside. We can entertain each other today with speeches, and if you are willing, I'd also like to offer you a proposal about the topic for the speeches."

They all said that they were willing and encouraged him to make his pro- 177a
posal. So, Eryximachus continued, "The beginning of my statement is from
the *Melanippe* of Euripides,[17] for 'the story is not mine,' but Phaedrus's, that I
intend to tell. Phaedrus often complains to me, 'Eryximachus,' he says, 'isn't
it terrible that hymns in honor of each of the other gods have been written by
the poets, but none of the many poets that have existed has ever composed a
single poem or hymn of praise for Love,[18] who is such a great and ancient
god? Moreover, if you would examine the venerable wisemen who write 177b
essays praising Heracles and others, as the excellent Prodicus[19] does, it is
hardly surprising, of course, but I've actually encountered a certain book by a
wise man in which there was some astonishing praise of the benefits of salt,
and you can find many other such things that have been the subjects of trib-
utes.[20] So, they produce compositions about such things with great enthusi- 177c
asm, but not a single person to this day has ever ventured to produce a hymn
of Love in a fitting manner. On the contrary, this great god has been ignored!'
Now, it seems to me that what Phaedrus says is right, so I am eager to gratify[21]
him and to offer a contribution. Moreover, it seems to me to be appropriate for
those of us here to honor the god on this occasion. So, if it meets with your
approval, passing the time with speeches should be enough for us, and I think 177d
each of us ought to make as beautiful a speech in praise of Love as he possibly can, going from left to right. Phaedrus can lead off, since he is reclining
on the first couch and, moreover, is the father of the proposal."

"No one will vote against you, Eryximachus," Socrates responded. "I,
who say I understand nothing other than the activities of love, will surely not
protest, nor will Agathon and Pausanias,[22] nor will Aristophanes, who spends 177e
all his time with Dionysus and Aphrodite,[23] nor will any of the others I see
here. Of course, it's not fair for those of us who're reclining in the last positions, but if those who go earlier speak in a beautiful and satisfactory manner,
we'll be content. Good luck to Phaedrus! Let him begin his tribute to Love."

All the others agreed with this and with what Socrates proposed. Everyone of them made a speech on the topic, but Aristodemus didn't remember 178a
everything and I don't remember everything he told me. But I'll tell you what
seemed to me most worth remembering from each one's speech.

First of all, he reported that Phaedrus began, as I mentioned, saying something to the effect that Love is a great god, who amazes both human beings and gods for many reasons, not least because of his origins.

"He is honored as among the oldest of the gods," Phaedrus said, "and there

is definite proof of this. Of the parents of Love, no one knows or speaks, either 178b
in poetry or in prose. On the contrary, Hesiod says that there was at first Chaos

> and then,
> Full-bosomed Earth, the eternal steadfast abode of all,
> And Love.[24]

Moreover, Hesiod and Acusilaus[25] both agree that these two, Earth and Love, came into being after Chaos, and Parmenides[26] says of Love's origins:

> First among all the gods, Love was created.

Thus, it is agreed in many places that Love is among the oldest of the gods, 178c
and, as one of the oldest, he is the cause of our greatest blessings. For I can't say that there is a greater blessing right from boyhood than a good lover or a greater blessing for a lover than a darling. What people who intend to lead
their lives in a noble and beautiful manner need is not provided by family, 178d
public honors, wealth, or anything else, so well as by Love.

"So, what do I mean by this? I refer to being ashamed in the face of shameful things and inspired with a respect for honor in the face of noble things, for without these neither a city nor an individual can accomplish great and beautiful deeds. Now, I claim that if a man who loves someone is discovered doing something shameful or failing through cowardice to defend himself against some shame, he would not be as distressed at being seen in such circumstances by anyone, not his father, his companions, nor anyone else, as
he would be at being seen by his darling. We see this same response on the 178e
part of the one who is loved: He likewise is thoroughly ashamed before his lovers should he be observed engaging in something shameful. Thus, if someone could come up with a technique by which a city or an army composed of lovers and their darlings could be created, there could be no better way of organizing their city, since they would abstain from everything shameful and
would be jealous of their honor in front of each other. If such men fought 179a
beside one another, although few in number, they would succeed against practically the whole of humanity. A man who is in love would of course find it less tolerable to be seen abandoning his position or casting aside his weapons by his darling than by anyone else and would choose to die many times over before letting that happen. As for abandoning one's darling or not coming to his aid when he is in danger, no one is so base that Love could not so inspire him with virtue that he would act like the person who is by nature the most
courageous. If I may speak candidly, when Homer says that a god 'breathes 179b
strength' into certain heroes,[27] that, coming from Love himself, is what Love does to lovers.

"Moreover, only lovers are willing to die for someone else, and this is so not only with men, but also with women. Among Greeks, Alcestis, the daughter of Pelius, furnishes adequate evidence of this claim. Although her husband

had a father and a mother, she was the only one who was willing to die in his place. Because of her love, she outdid them in her filial affection and made them seem like strangers to their son, as if they were relatives in name only. When she had done this deed, her actions seemed beautiful and noble, not only to human beings, but also to the gods, so that, although many people have performed numerous beautiful and noble deeds, the gods granted her the privilege given to very few: They sent her soul back up from Hades. They
sent it back because they admired her action. So even the gods give great 179d
honor to the zeal and virtue connected with Love. However, they sent Orpheus, the son of Oeagrus, away from Hades unsuccessful, after showing him the shade of the wife for whom he had come. They refused to give her up since he seemed to be soft because he played the lyre, and he lacked the courage to die for his love, as Alcestis had, and instead managed to enter Hades alive. It was because of this that they punished him by making his death come at the hands of women.[28] It was different with Achilles, the son of
Thetis, whom the gods honored and sent to the Islands of the Blest. After 179e
learning from his mother that he would die if he killed Hector but if he did not he could return home and live out his old age, Achilles had the courage to choose to strike a blow for his lover Patroclus and not only to die for, but also
to die after the one who had already died. As a result, the gods had enormous 180a
admiration for him and specially honored him, because he had done so much for his lover.[29] Aeschylus is talking nonsense when he claims that Achilles was the lover of Patroclus.[30] Achilles was not only more handsome than Patroclus, but more handsome than all the heroes, and was still beardless because he was much younger, as Homer says.[31] Anyway, the gods do in fact give the greatest honor to this virtue that is connected with Love. However,
they are more impressed and more admiring and treat one better when the 180b
beloved cherishes his lover than when the lover cherishes his darling. A lover is more godlike than a darling, for he is inspired by a god.[32] This is why the gods gave greater honor to Achilles than to Alcestis, sending him to the Islands of the Blest.

"So, I say that among the gods Love is the oldest, the most honorable, and the most eminent, procuring virtue and happiness for human beings, both living and dead."

Aristodemus said that Phaedrus gave some such speech as this and there 180c
were some others after Phaedrus whose speeches he could not remember much of. So, he skipped them and went on to Pausanias' speech:

"This proposal doesn't seem to me to bode well for us, Phaedrus," Pausanias began, "the injunction simply to praise Love, that is. If Love were a single being, it would be fine, but as it is, there isn't just one of him. And since
there isn't, it would be more correct to say first which particular Love we 180d
ought to praise. I'll try to set this right by first explaining which Love we should praise and then offering my praise in a manner worthy of the god.

"Now, we all know that Aphrodite[33] is never separated from Love.
Hence, if there were only one of her, there would be only one Love, but since
there are in fact two Aphrodites, there are necessarily two Loves also. And
how could there not be two of the goddess? One is older, the motherless
daughter of Uranus,[34] whom we call the 'heavenly' Aphrodite, and the other is
younger, the child of Zeus and Dione,[35] whom we call the 'common'
Aphrodite. It follows, of course, that the Love joined with the latter Aphrodite 180e
is rightly called common also, and the other is called heavenly. Now, one
ought to praise all the gods; so I should try to say what has fallen to the lot of
each of these two.

"It is true of every action that doing it is in itself neither noble nor shameful. For example, nothing of what we are doing now, whether drinking,
singing, or conversing, is noble and beautiful in itself. In actions, it's the man- 181a
ner of the doing that determines the quality. When an action is done nobly and
correctly, it becomes noble and beautiful, but if not done correctly, it becomes
shameful. So, loving and Love are not in every case noble and deserving of
praise, but the loving that points us in a noble direction is.

"The Love that accompanies the common Aphrodite is truly common and
acts in an opportunistic manner. This is the one whom ordinary human beings 181b
love. In the first place, such people love women no less than boys, and they
love those they love for their bodies rather than their souls. So, they love the
most unintelligent people they can, because they are concerned only about
achieving their goal and do not care whether it is done in a noble and beautiful manner. These people seize whatever opportunities happen to come along
to engage in this activity and are indifferent as to whether it is good or the
opposite. This Love comes from the younger rather than the older goddess,
the one who in her origins shares in both the female and the male. 181c

"The Love that accompanies the heavenly Aphrodite, first of all, does not
share in the female, but only in the male—this is love for young boys. Since this
Aphrodite is older, she does not participate in outrageous behavior. Those who
are inspired by this Love are oriented toward the male, cherishing what is by
nature stronger and more intelligent. Anyone would recognize those who are
motivated by this Love in a pure way, even in the case of loving young boys. 181d
They don't fall in love with boys until they begin to show some intelligence,
which starts happening when their beards begin to grow. I believe that those
who begin to love boys at that stage are ready to be together with them for their
entire lives and even to live with them. Such lovers are not going to be
deceivers, taking on someone when he lacks understanding because of his youth
and then contemptuously abandoning him later on to run off after someone else.

"Actually, there should be a rule[36] against loving young boys, so that a lot
of effort will not be squandered on an uncertain prospect. It is unclear how 181e
young boys will turn out, that is, whether their souls and bodies will end up
being bad or virtuous. Good men willingly set up this rule for themselves, but

this sort of restriction needs to be imposed on those common lovers, just as we restrict them, as far as we can, from loving free-born women. These are 182a the people who have prompted the reproach by some who go so far as to say that it is shameful to gratify one's lovers. People who observe these men say this because they see their importunity and injustice, since whatever is done in an orderly and lawful manner surely does not justly bear censure.

"The rule about love in other cities is easy to understand, for it is simply defined, but the rule here and in Sparta is complex. In Elis and Boeotia, and 182b places where people lack skill in stating things, it is simply set down as the law that it is noble to gratify one's lovers, and no one, either young or old, would say that it is shameful. The reason for this, I suggest, is so that they will not have to make a speech in their attempt to persuade the youths to do it, since they lack skill in making speeches. In Ionia, on the other hand, and in many other places where people live under barbarians, it is shameful by law. The tyrannical rulers of the barbarians lead them to consider such gratification 182c shameful—and philosophy and exercising naked as well.[37] I suspect it does not suit the rulers to have strong ambitions develop in their subjects, nor powerful friendships and partnerships and all the other things Love so greatly enjoys engendering. The tyrants learned this from what happened here in Athens. When the love of Aristogeiton and the friendly, affectionate response of Harmodius became firmly established, it destroyed their ruler.[38] Thus, where it has been decreed that it is shameful to gratify lovers, this comes from the baseness of those who set up the rules, on the one hand from the avarice of 182d the rulers and on the other hand from the lack of manliness on the part of the ruled. Where the law declares without qualification that it is noble, this is because of the mental laziness of those who establish the laws.

"The rule that has been laid down here is far nobler, though as I mentioned earlier, not easy to understand. Note that it is said to be more noble to love openly rather than secretly, and especially when one loves the noblest and best youths, even if they are uglier than the others. Moreover, everyone encourages the lover tremendously—and not as doing something shameful. It is considered noble to succeed in this matter and shameful not to. Our custom grants to a lover who is striving for success the license to engage in surprising 182e feats to win praise, feats which, if done by someone else seeking another end or wanting to accomplish some other purpose, would reap the greatest con- 183a demnation. If someone wanted to obtain money from someone or a public post or power of some other sort and if he intended to do so by using the means lovers do in pursuit of their darlings, begging and pleading with their requests, making vows, sleeping in their darlings' doorways, and being willing to perform services for them that no slave would perform, he would be prevented by his friends and even by his enemies from doing such things. His enemies would condemn him for fawning and for behavior unworthy of a free 183b man, while his friends would admonish him and be ashamed of his actions.

However, for a lover to do all these things is attractive. He is allowed by custom to act without criticism, as if he were performing a splendid deed, and what is most extraordinary is that, as most people say, if he breaks a vow he has made, he alone will be forgiven by the gods, for a vow made under the influence of Aphrodite is not valid. Thus, both the gods and human beings 183c
have provided complete license to the lover, as our rule states.

"For this reason, one might assume that in this city it is usually considered a splendid thing to be in love or to be the affectionate friend of lovers. However, fathers assign attendants to their sons who are loved, so that they will not be allowed to engage in conversation with the lovers. The attendant's injunctions aim at this end, and a boy's own friends and companions criticize him if they see anything of this sort happening. Moreover, older people do not 183d
oppose those who object, nor do they criticize them for not speaking the truth. So, after noting these things, one might believe that such behavior is usually considered most disgraceful here, but I suggest that the fact is that this is not a simple matter. As I said at the beginning, in itself an action is neither noble nor shameful, but it becomes noble when done in a noble manner and shameful when done shamefully. Thus, it is shameful to gratify someone in a worthless manner, but it is noble and beautiful when it is a worthy person and done in a noble manner. The man who is a common sort of lover is worthless, 183e
because he loves the body instead of the soul. Nor is he steadfast, since what he loves does not endure. As the flower of the body fades, the very thing he loved 'takes flight and is gone,'[39] and his many speeches and promises are put to shame. The lover of the character of a worthy youth remains steadfast throughout his life, since he is bonded to what is enduring.

"Our custom aims at testing well and properly whom to gratify and 184a
whom to avoid. For this reason it encourages the one to pursue and the other to flee, setting up a sort of contest and putting to the test which of the two kinds the lover and the beloved are. This is the explanation of the customary belief that, in the first place, it is shameful to be captured quickly. This is so that time can pass, since time seems a good test of most things. It also explains why it is considered shameful to be captured by means of wealth or political power, either when one knuckles under if treated badly and does not 184b
hold out, or when, being offered favors in the form of money or political status, one does not disdain them. These actions do not seem steadfast and enduring, quite apart from the fact that genuine friendship does not develop from them.

"Only one path is left by our rule, then, if the darling intends to gratify his lover in a noble and beautiful manner. For our custom is this: Just as it is not considered fawning and reproachful in the case of lovers who want to be sub- 184c
servient to their darlings and act like their slaves, so also there is one and only one other voluntary servitude that is not reproachful, and that is subjection for the sake of virtue. It is usually maintained by us that, if someone wants to

serve another because he believes he will become a better person through
him, either in terms of wisdom or some other part of virtue, this voluntary
slavery is not shameful nor is it fawning. One must put both of these customs
together, the one concerning the love of boys and the one concerning philosophy and the rest of virtue, into the same rule, if one intends for it to turn out 184d
that it be a noble thing for a darling to gratify a lover.

"When a lover and his darling come together, each has a rule: The lover
is justified in performing any services he can perform for the darling who
gratifies him, and the beloved in turn is justified in providing whatever services he can for the one who is making him wise and good—assuming the
former is able to introduce the other to prudence and other virtues, and the lat- 184e
ter does want to acquire an education and other skills. When these two rules
come together as a single principle, then and only then does it come about that
a darling's gratifying a lover is a noble and beautiful thing. Otherwise, it is not
noble at all. Moreover, when one is following these rules, there is no shame in
being deceived, but in other cases, it is always disgraceful, whether or not one
is deceived: If someone gratifies a lover whom he takes to be wealthy for the 185a
sake of his wealth, it is no less shameful if it turns out that he was deceived
and he gets no money because his lover is poor. It seems he shows himself to
be the sort of person who would perform any sort of services whatsoever for
anyone whatsoever for the sake of money, and that is not noble. By the same
argument, if someone who gratifies someone whom he takes to be good for
the sake of becoming a better person himself through the friendship of a lover
is deceived, because the lover turns out to be evil and not in possession of 185b
virtue, his being deceived is nevertheless noble. This youth has demonstrated
for his part that he would eagerly do anything at any time for the sake of
virtue and in order to become a better person, and that is the noblest and most
beautiful thing of all. Thus, to gratify someone for the sake of virtue is
entirely noble. This is the Love of the heavenly goddess, and he is heavenly
and of much worth, both in public and in private matters. For he compels both
the lover himself and his beloved to care deeply about virtue. All other Loves 185c
are connected with the other goddess, the common one.

"Those are my remarks about Love, Phaedrus," he concluded, "which I
have just thrown together for you on the spot."

After Pausanias paused[40] (people who are skilled in speaking taught me
to use such phrases), Aristodemus said that Aristophanes was to speak next,
but by chance he had a bad case of the hiccups, from overeating or something
else, and couldn't talk. However, Aristophanes did say (the physician Eryxi- 185d
machus was reclining on the next couch after his), "Eryximachus, it would be
appropriate for you either to stop my hiccups or else to speak for me until I'm
able to stop them."

Eryximachus responded, "On the contrary, I'll do both. I'll speak in your
place, and when you've stopped your hiccups, you speak in mine. While I'm

speaking, if you hold your breath a long time perhaps the hiccups will be willing to stop. But if not, gargle with water, and if they're very severe, grab 185e
something you think will tickle your nose and make yourself sneeze! If you
make that happen once or twice, even if they are very persistent, they'll stop."

"You go ahead and speak," Aristophanes said, "and I'll try those things."

Eryximachus then spoke as follows: "Now then, it seems to me to be necessary, since Pausanias started off his speech well but did not complete it satisfactorily, it is, as I said, necessary for me to try to put a conclusion on his 186a
speech. It seems appropriate to me that he described Love as twofold. Not only
does he arise in human souls in response to beautiful people and many other
things as well, but he also exists in other things, in the bodies of all animals and
even in the plants that grow in the ground, in a word, in everything there is. I
think one sees from the perspective of my art, that is, medicine, how great and
marvelous the god is and how he permeates everything, both human and divine. 186b

"I will speak initially from the medical perspective because I treat that art
as preeminent. Now, physical bodies possess this twofold Love by nature,
since it is agreed that a body's health and sickness are different and indeed
opposing conditions, and dissimilar things desire and love dissimilar objects.
Hence, the Love in the healthy body is one thing and that in the sick body is
another. As Pausanias just argued, to gratify those human beings who are
good is a noble and beautiful thing, but to gratify those who are immoral is
shameful. So also, in the case of physical bodies, it is a noble thing to gratify 186c
what is good and healthy in each body and should be done (that is what is
called good medical practice), but it is shameful to gratify what is bad and
sick, and one should not do so if one intends to act in a professional manner.
In sum, the medical art is a knowledge of the activities of Love in the body in
terms of filling it up and emptying it out. The master physician is the person
who can distinguish the noble and the shameful Loves in these cases and can 186d
exchange one for the other. The physician who knows how to replace one sort
of Love with the other, how to engender it in cases where Love is not present
but needs to be, and how to remove what is there in other cases, this physician
would be a good practitioner. It is necessary to make things that are hostile to
each other in the body be friendly and love each other. Now, these hostile factors are things that are completely opposed—cold to heat, bitter to sweet, dry
to wet, all those sorts of oppositions. Our ancestor, Asclepius[41] founded our 186e
profession on his ability to instill harmony and love between such opposites,
as the poets say—and I agree with them.

"Thus, medicine, as I say, in all its aspects is governed by this god, as are
exercise, athletics, and agriculture. The same goes for music, too, as is clear to 187a
everyone from even a moment's consideration, and is probably what Heraclitus intended to say, though it's not stated very well in the words he used.
Regarding the One, he said that in its opposition to itself it is brought together
with itself, as in the attunement of a bow or a lyre.[42] Now, it is quite absurd to

say that harmony consists in opposition, or even that it results from things being in opposition. He probably intended to say instead that harmony is created in the musical art by bringing a prior opposition of high and low notes into attunement. It is clear that harmony does not come from the opposition of 187b
the high and low notes. Harmony is concord, and concord is a kind of agreement. That agreement should consist in the opposition of things that are in opposition is impossible. Things that are in opposition and not in agreement are not in harmony. Rhythm, for example, results from bringing the fast and the slow, which are at first in opposition, into agreement. As with medicine 187c
earlier, here it is music that introduces agreement between all these opposites by engendering mutual love and harmony, and, again, music is a knowledge of the activities of Love with regard to harmony and rhythm. One can easily detect the activities of Love in this construction of harmony and rhythm; there are not two kinds of Love involved here.

"Now, when one needs to make use of rhythm and harmony in human affairs, either in composition (which people call creating songs and poems) or 187d
in the correct performance of tunes and verses that have already been composed (which what we call musical education deals with), here things are difficult and a good practitioner is needed. For the same principle reappears: One should gratify decent men, as well as those who, though they are not decent, might become more so, and one should defend the Love of these men—this is the noble Love, the heavenly Love of the Muse Urania. In the case of the common Love, that of Polymnia,[43] one must be cautious about whom one 187e
engages in it with, so that one may gain pleasure for oneself but never engender immorality. It is the same as in our profession: It takes great effort to deal appropriately with the desires that are connected with the art of cooking so as to reap the pleasure without getting sick. Thus, in music, in medicine, and in every other activity both human and divine, one should be as attentive as possible regarding each of these kinds of Love. Both will be there, since even the 188a
pattern of the seasons of the year reflect their influence.

"When the elements I have already mentioned, that is, the hot and the cold, the dry and the wet, happen to arise in a proportionate manner by means of the proper Love, they realize a harmonious and sensible mixture and bring about a good, healthy season for human beings as well as the other animals and plants, and cause no harm. However, when the outrageous Love is more in control of the seasons, it causes a lot of injury and destruction. Plagues tend 188b
to develop in such situations, and many other abnormal diseases among animals and plants, including frost, hail, and blights, which develop from the greed and disorderliness of the activities of this sort of Love in the movements of the stars and seasons of the year. (A knowledge of the activities of Love in this context is called astronomy).[44]

"Moreover, all sacrifices and the matters prophecy deals with, that is, the interaction between gods and human beings, involve nothing but defending 188c

and correcting Love. Impiety tends to result when someone does not gratify
the orderly kind of Love, nor honor and respect him in every deed, but instead
gratifies the other Love, both with regard to one's parents, whether they are
alive or dead, and with regard to the gods. The role of watching over and min-
istering to these kinds of Loves has been assigned to prophecy, and, therefore,
it is prophecy that is the artisan of friendly relations between gods and human 188d
beings. It understands the activities of Love among human beings and knows
which ones tend toward that which is lawful and sacred.

"Thus, Love as a whole has very great power, indeed, he is omnipotent,
but the Love that brings about good with judiciousness[45] and justice among us
as well as among the gods, he is the one that has the greatest power, provides
us with every happiness, and enables us to associate with one another and to
be friends with the gods, who are more powerful than us.

"Now, I probably omitted many things in my praise of Love, though not 188e
intentionally, of course. If I did leave out something, it is your task, Aristophanes, to fill in the gaps. Or, if you have in mind offering your tribute in
some other manner, then offer it up, since your hiccups have ceased."

Aristodemus reported that Aristophanes then took over and declared: 189a
"The hiccups did stop completely, though not until I used the sneeze treatment on them, so that I wonder if the orderly sort of Love in my body desires
the kind of noises and tickles that sneezing involves, because they did stop
right away when I applied the sneeze treatment!"

Eryximachus replied: "Aristophanes, my good man, watch what you're
doing! Though you're supposed to be giving a speech, you're making jokes,
and forcing me to be on my guard against your speech in case you say something funny, when you could march out to speak in peace." 189b

Laughing, Aristophanes responded, "You're right, Eryximachus, let what
I said be unsaid! Don't be on your guard against me; what I'm afraid of is not
that I may say something funny (that would be a good trick and natural for my
Muse),[46] but rather that I may say something ridiculous."

"Do you think you can make me a target and get away with it, Aristophanes?," Eryximachus replied. "Put your mind to it and speak as though you
were going to be called to account, though I may perhaps decide to let you 189c
off."

"Well, now, Eryximachus," Aristophanes said, "I, of course, have in
mind a speech of a different sort from yours and Pausanias'. It seems to me
that people altogether fail to perceive the power of Love, because, if they
were aware of it, they would build the greatest temples and altars for him and
make him the greatest offerings. As it is, he gets none of these things,
although he deserves the best of everything. He is the friendliest of the gods to
human beings, for he helps people and cures them of those things which stand
in the way of the greatest happiness for the human race. I will try to explain 189d
his power to you, and you will be teachers for others.

"You must first understand human nature and what has happened to it. In
ancient times our nature was not the same as it is now, but different. At first
there were three kinds of human beings, not only two as now, male and
female, but also a third that was composed of the other two. Its name still sur- 189e
vives, but that type of being no longer exists. At one time, then, there actually
existed a kind of human being that was androgynous in form and name, being
a combination of both male and female,[47] but they no longer exist, although
the name is still used as a calumny. Now, the form of all three types of people
was completely spherical, with their backs and sides making a complete circle. They had four hands and a similar number of legs, and two faces that
were exactly alike on top of a circular neck. The two faces were turned in 190a
opposite directions on a single head that had four ears. There were also two
sets of genitals, and all the other characteristics one could infer from these
examples. They walked upright in the present manner, in whatever direction
they wanted to, and whenever they set themselves to run quickly, they would
revolve in a circle, like acrobats doing cartwheels, with their arms and legs
sticking straight out. At that time, of course, they had eight limbs to support
themselves on while they rapidly revolved.

"The reason there were these three types of humans is this: The male was
originally a progeny of the sun, the female of the earth, and the one that had a 190b
share in both was a progeny of the moon, since the moon also has a share in
both. They themselves were spherical like their parents, and their method of
travelling was also like that of their parents.

"They had terrible strength and power, as well as grand ambitions, and
they attacked the gods. Homer's story about Ephialtes and Otus[48] is about
them and their attempt to ascend the heavens in order to attack the gods. Zeus 190c
and the other gods deliberated about what they should do about them, but they
were at a loss. They did not see how they could kill them and destroy the race
with a lightning bolt, as they had in the case of the giants, since the honors and
sacrifices they received from human beings would also be destroyed. Neither
did they see how they could tolerate their outrageous behavior. Finally, after a
lot of thought, Zeus declared, 'I think I have a good idea about how human
beings can continue to exist and yet, by their becoming weaker, cease their
indecent behavior. I will cut each of them in two,' he said. 'They will be
weaker and at the same time more useful to us by becoming more numerous. 190d
And they will still be able to walk upright since they will have two legs. However, if they continue to behave outrageously and refuse to live quietly,' he
continued, 'I will cut them in two again, and they'll have to travel around on
one leg like people playing hopscotch.'[49] Having said this, he cut the human
beings in two, as people slice apples when they are going to preserve them or 190e
cut eggs with hairs. As he sliced each one, he ordered Apollo to shift its face
and its half-neck around toward the cut, so that when it looked at its own scar
the person might be more orderly. He also instructed Apollo to heal the rest of

the incision. So Apollo turned their faces around and drew the skin together
on all sides to what is now called the stomach, just as purses are pulled
together with a drawstring. He tied off the single opening he had made in the
middle of the stomach, making what people call the navel, and he smoothed 191a
out the many other wrinkles and constructed the chest, using the sort of tool
cobblers use when they smooth out wrinkles in leather on a last. However, he
left a few wrinkles around the stomach and the navel as a reminder of their
past experience.

"Now, since the natural form of human beings had been cut in two, each
half longed for the other. So, out of their desire to grow together, they would
throw their arms around each other when they met and become entwined.
Hence, they began to die from hunger and other sorts of neglect, since they
did not want to do anything in separation from each other. Whenever one half 191b
of a pair died and the other remained behind, the one that was left, whether it
happened to be a half of a whole woman (what we now call a woman) or of a
man, searched about and became entwined with someone else, and as a result
they were dying out.

"However, Zeus took pity on them and came up with another good idea.
He moved their genitals around to the front, for until then they had them on
the back side, and they fathered and conceived, not in each other, but in the
ground like cicadas. So, Zeus put their genitals around on the front side and 191c
thus made it possible for them to reproduce with each other with the male's
genitals inside the female's. For this reason, whenever a male happened to
encounter a female in their entwining, she would conceive and produce an
offspring, and if a male encountered a male, at least they would get some satisfaction from their union and they would take a break, then return to their
work and attend to the rest of life.

"It is from this situation, then, that love for one another developed in 191d
human beings. Love collects the halves of our original nature, and tries to make
a single thing out of the two parts so as to restore our natural condition. Thus,
each of us is the matching half of a human being, since we have been severed
like a flatfish, two coming from one, and each part is always seeking its other
half. Those men who are split from the mixed nature, which was then called
'androgynous,' are fond of women. Most adulterers come from this type, and 191e
those women who are fond of men and are adulteresses also come from this
type. Those women who are split from a woman, however, have no interest at
all in men, but rather are oriented toward women. This is the type lesbians come
from. Those who are split from the male pursue males. While they are boys,
since they are a slice off a male, they are fond of men and enjoy lying with men
and becoming entwined with them. These are the best of the boys and young 192a
men, and at the same time are the most manly in nature. Anyone who says they
are shameless is mistaken, for they do this, not from shamelessness, but from
courage, manliness, and masculinity, welcoming what is like themselves. There

is a definite proof of this: Only men of this sort are completely successful in the affairs of the city. When they become men, they are lovers of boys and by 192b
nature are not interested in marriage and having children, though they are forced into it by custom. They would be satisfied to live all the time with one another without marrying. This is certainly the sort of man who becomes a lover of boys, and as a boy is fond of such lovers, always welcoming a kinsman.

"Thus, whenever a lover of boys, or anyone else, happens to encounter the person who is their other half, they are overcome with amazement at their friendship, intimacy, and love, and do not want to be severed, so to speak, 192c
from each other even for a moment. These are the people who spend their entire lives with each other, though they don't know how to say what they want from each other. No one would think this is a mere union of sexual passion, as though that were the reason each enjoys and is so enthusiastic about being with the other. On the contrary, it is clear that there is something else—what, it cannot say—that the soul of each wants, though it does have a prophetic sense of what it wants and can speak of it in riddles.If Hephaestus[50] 192d
were holding his tools and standing over the pair lying there together, he might say: 'What do you people want from each other?' If they had no answer, he might continue: 'Is this what you desire, to be together as much as possible, so that you would not leave each other day and night? If you desire that, I am willing to weld and forge you into one and the same being, so that from being two you will have become one and can henceforth live as one 192e
being, both of you sharing a single life in common. When you die, you will share a death in common, there in Hades, as one being instead of two. Consider whether you would like this and would be satisfied should this happen.' We know that when they heard this, not a one would refuse, nor would they appear to want anything other than that. On the contrary, they would think they had discovered what they had really desired all along, namely, to be made one out of two by being joined and welded together with their beloved.

"The explanation of this is that our original nature was as described above and we were once whole beings. So, the name 'love' is given to the desire for wholeness. Before the current situation, as I explained, we were one 193a
whole, but now, because of our misdeed, we have been made by the god to live in a separated state, as the Arcadians were by the Spartans.[51] We are afraid that if we do not maintain good order in our relations with the gods we may be sliced in two again, so that we would have to go around like those figures that have been inscribed in bas-relief on stelae, sawn in two along the nose like halved dice. For this reason, every man must advocate continuous reverence for the gods in all things, so that we will avoid that fate and encounter good fortune, with Love as our guide and commander. No one 193b
should oppose him in any way, because whoever opposes the gods incurs their wrath. If we are friends with the god and on good terms, we will find and establish relationships with those darlings meant for us, which few do now.

(Eryximachus should not interrupt me here, making fun of my speech as
though I were speaking of Pausanias and Agathon! They probably are among 193c
those who have such relationships and are both male in nature, but I am really talking about everyone, men and women alike.) This is how the human race can become happy: We must perfect love and every man must find his own darling, thereby returning to our original nature. If this is what is best, then the nearest thing to that is necessarily the best in the present circumstances, and that is to meet up with a darling who is naturally suited to one's own outlook.

"Thus, if we are to sing the praises of the god who is the cause of this, 193d
then we must sing the praises of Love. While he benefits us most in the present moment by leading us into relationships that suit us, he provides us great hope for the future: if we show proper reverence for the gods, he will restore us to our original nature and, by healing us, will make us happy and blessed.

"That is my speech about Love, Eryximachus," Aristophanes said. "It's different from yours. So, as I asked you, don't make fun of it, so that we can
hear what each of those who are left will say, or rather each of the other two, 193e
since only Agathon and Socrates remain."

"Well, I'll do as you suggest," Eryximachus responded, according to Aristodemus, "since I did enjoy your speech. If I didn't recognize that Socrates and Agathon are terrific at the activities of love, I'd be apprehensive that they might have nothing else to say since so much has been said! However, for the moment, I remain optimistic."

Then Socrates said, "Well, you competed beautifully, Eryximachus, but 194a
if you were where I am now, or rather where I will be after Agathon gives a good speech, then you would be very apprehensive, just as I am now!"

"You're trying to put a spell on me, Socrates," Agathon responded, "so that I'll be distracted by thinking about the high expectation my audience has regarding how well I will speak."

"I would be quite forgetful, Agathon," Socrates replied, "if, having seen
the courage and self-confidence with which you went out on the stage with the 194b
actors and faced up to that audience with the intention of putting your own words on display, and having seen how you were not at all intimidated, I should now believe that you could be frightened by our small gathering of people."

"But what about this, Socrates?" Agathon said. "Surely you don't think I'm so obsessed with the theater that I don't realize that, to anyone who's intelligent, a few sensible people are more frightening than a senseless mob?"

"I would not be behaving well, Agathon," he replied, "if I thought of you 194c
as someone boorish. On the contrary, I know perfectly well that if you should meet some people you think are wise, you would care more about their reaction than about that of any mob. We, however, are not wise ourselves—we were also there at the theater and were part of that mob. But if you did happen to meet some other people who are wise, you surely would be ashamed to do

something you thought was shameful in front of them. Is that what you're saying?"

"What you say is true," he said.

"But you wouldn't be ashamed, if you thought you were doing something shameful in front of most people?"

Aristodemus reported that Phaedrus interrupted here saying, "Agathon, 194d
my friend, if you answer Socrates, he won't care whether any of our present intentions are realized, if only he has someone to engage in a dialogue with, especially if that someone is good-looking! Now, I myself enjoy listening to Socrates' dialogues, but it's my obligation to direct our praise of Love and to get a speech from each and every one of you. So, you two must first pay what is due to the god, then you can have your dialogue."

"What you say is right, Phaedrus," Agathon replied, "and nothing is 194e
going to prevent me from making a speech. There'll be plenty of opportunities to engage in dialogue with Socrates later.

"First of all, I want to say how I plan to approach the topic, then I'll give my speech. Everyone who spoke previously did not seem to me to praise the god, but rather to proclaim that human beings are happy about the good things of which the god is the cause. No one has talked about the character of the
giver of these gifts. Yet there is only one correct way to praise someone, and 195a
it holds for everyone: The subject of the speech as well as the things of which he happens to be the source should be described in detail. Thus, it is proper that we first praise Love for who he is and then praise his gifts.

"So, I say that of all the happy gods, Love (if I can say what is correct without giving offense) is the happiest among them, since he is the best and the most beautiful. He is the most beautiful for the following reasons: In the first place, he is the youngest of the gods, Phaedrus. He himself provides convincing proof of this claim in that he outruns old age, though it obviously is 195b
fast. (At any rate it catches up with us more quickly than it should.) Love naturally despises old age and will not even go near it. He is always among young people, and is young himself, for the ancient saying is correct that like always attracts like. Though I agree with Phaedrus about many things, I do
not agree about this, that Love is older than Cronos and Iapetus.[52] I say that he 195c
is the youngest of the gods, and eternally youthful, and that the ancient deeds of the gods, of which Hesiod and Parmenides speak, occurred under Necessity and not Love, if what they said is true. The castrations, imprisonments, and many other violent acts would not have occurred if Love had been there with them. On the contrary, there would have been friendship and peace, as is now the case where Love rules the gods.

"Thus, he is youthful, and in addition to being young, gentle. A poet like
Homer is needed to depict the gentleness of this god. Homer says the goddess 195d
Ate is also gentle (at least her feet are gentle), when he states:

Her feet are gentle, for it is not on the ground
That she approaches; rather she walks along on the heads of men.[53]

In this beautiful statement he seems to me to reveal Ate's gentleness, since she walks not on what is hard, but on what is soft. We can use the same proof of Love's being gentle, for he walks neither on the earth nor on the tops of our heads, which are really not soft at all, but on the contrary, he walks and dwells 195e
in the softest things there are. He establishes his dwelling place in the characters and souls of gods and human beings, though not in every soul that comes along. When he encounters a soul that has a hard character, he turns away, but when he comes upon a soft one, he dwells there. Thus, since he is always attached to the softest parts of the softest things, with his feet and everything else, he is necessarily most gentle.

"He is the youngest and the most gentle, then, and in addition his form is 196a
pliable. If he were stiff and inflexible he would not be the one who embraces everyone. Neither would he be at first unnoticed while going in and out of every soul. His gracefulness, which everyone agrees unreservedly that Love has, is a convincing proof of his shapeliness and suppleness, since there is always a conflict between Love and awkwardness. That the god lives among flowers suggests the beauty of his complexion, for Love does not rest on what is withered or without blossom in body, soul, or any other way. If a place is 196b
full of flowers and fragrance, there he will alight and remain.

"That is enough about the beauties of the god, though much is omitted; now I must speak about the virtue of Love. The greatest thing is that Love neither wrongs god or human being, nor is he wronged by god or human being. He never suffers violence, if indeed he suffers anything at all, for violence has no connection with Love. Nor does he do violence when he acts, for everyone 196c
serves Love willingly in everything, and 'the laws, the kings of the city,'[54] say that what is done in willing agreement is just. Besides justice, he partakes of the greatest judiciousness, for it is agreed that judiciousness is the control of pleasure and desire, and no pleasure is more powerful than Love. If all pleasures and desires are weaker than Love, they can be controlled by Love, and he is in control. Thus, by controlling pleasure and desire Love is thoroughly judicious. Moreover, with regard to courage, 'not even Ares can stand up against' Love.[55] Ares cannot catch hold of Love, but Love (of Aphrodite, as 196d
the story goes) can catch Ares,[56] and the one who catches is more powerful than the one who is caught. Thus, the one who controls the most courageous among all others must be the bravest of all.

"So, the justice, judiciousness, and courage of the god have been discussed; his wisdom remains.[57] To the extent that I can, I must try not to leave anything out. First of all (I in turn will honor my profession as Eryximachus did his), the god is a poet so wise and skillful that he can make others poets 196e
also. At least, everyone Love takes hold of becomes a poet, 'even were there

no song in him before.'[58] It is appropriate for us to use this as evidence that the poet Love is in general good at every creative activity associated with the Muses. What one neither has nor knows, one can neither give nor teach to another. And regarding the creation of every animal, will anyone deny that it 197a
is by the skill of Love that they are begotten and come into being? On the other hand, do we not see that the artisan who has been taught by this god turns out to be famous and illustrious, but the one whom Love does not take hold of ends up obscure? Apollo was led by desire and Love to invent archery, of course, and also medicine and prophecy, so he is a pupil of Love—as were the Muses in their invention of the fine arts, Hephaestus in 197b
blacksmithing, Athena in weaving, and Zeus in how to govern gods and human beings. It is clear from this that these activities of the gods were established when Love came into being—Love of beauty this is, for there is no Love of ugliness. Before this, as I said at the beginning, many terrible things were done by the gods, as it is said, through the rule of Necessity, but since this god was born, all good things have come into being for both gods and human beings through loving what is beautiful.

"Thus, Love himself seems to me, Phaedrus, first to be the most beautiful 197c
and the best and then the cause of that which is best and most beautiful in others. Something comes over me to speak also in verse, saying this is the one who

Produces peace among human beings,
Calm on the open sea, stillness of the wind,
And sleep abed when troubled.
He empties us of alienation and fills us with togetherness, 197d
Causes us all to join together with each other
In these sorts of gatherings, and in festivals, dances, and sacrifices,
When he becomes the leader.
He instills meekness and banishes ferocity.
He is a cheerful giver of goodwill,
And never gives hostility.
Gracious and kind, he is studied by the wise,
And admired by the gods.
Coveted by those who lack him,
He is a treasure to those lucky enough to have him,
The father of delicacy, luxury, and opulence,
Gracefulness, longing, and yearning,
Careful of the good,
And careless of the bad.
In misery, in fear, in desire, and in speech,
He is our pilot, defender, comrade-in-arms, 197e
And our bravest deliverer.
The adornment of all the gods and human beings together,

He is the best and most beautiful leader,
The one whom all men should follow,
With beautiful singing, joining in the songs he sings
As he charms the thoughts of all
The gods and human beings.

"That is my speech, Phaedrus," he said. "Let it be dedicated to the god. It's partly playful and partly serious, and as good a job as I am capable of."

Aristodemus said that after Agathon had spoken, everyone present loudly 198a
applauded the young man's remarks as reflecting well both on himself and on the god. Then Socrates, looking over at Eryximachus, declared, "Well, does it seem to you now, son of Acumenus, that my earlier apprehension was unfounded, or did I speak prophetically when I said just now that Agathon would give an astonishing speech and I would be left in the lurch?"

"One of your claims is true," Eryximachus responded. "You do seem to me to have spoken prophetically in saying that Agathon would speak well, but that you are left in the lurch, that I do not believe."

"And how, you happy fellow," Socrates replied, "could I not be in the 198b
lurch, I and anyone else whatsoever, when I have to speak after such a beautiful and elaborate speech has been given? The rest of it was not as astonishing, but that concluding section! How could anyone who heard the beauty of those words and phrases not be struck dumb by them? When I thought about the fact that I wouldn't be able to speak with nearly such beautiful words as those,
I would have left in a moment, running away in shame, if I had any place to 198c
go! His speech made me think of Gorgias,[59] so that I was struggling on like that character in Homer: I was afraid that at the end Agathon would hold up the terrifying head of Gorgias in his speech, cast it against my speech, and turn me into a wordless stone.[60] Then I realized that it was ridiculous of me to have agreed to join with you in praising Love and to have claimed that I was
terrific in the activities of Love when I knew nothing about this practice, that 198d
is, how one ought to praise things. In my simple-mindedness I thought one ought to tell the truth about the things being praised, and to begin with that. From there, then, one should pick out the finest of these points and present them in the most attractive manner. Moreover, I had complete confidence that I would speak well, since I knew the truth about how to praise anything at all.

"It seems now, however, that this is not the way to praise something in a beautiful manner. On the contrary, one should attribute the grandest and most
beautiful characteristics to the subject, whether it possesses them or not, and if 198e
the attribution is a lie, it doesn't matter. It was prescribed, it seems, that each of us should seem to praise Love, not that we should actually praise him. I believe that's the reason you twisted every statement around to apply to Love. You claimed that he is a certain sort of being and the cause of certain sorts of things so that he would appear to be the most beautiful and the best—to those

who are not acquainted with him, obviously, since I presume this would not
be effective with those who do know him. And your praise was beautifully 199a
and impressively presented. However, I didn't know this would be our
method of praising, and I did not know this when I agreed to offer my praise
in turn with you. 'The tongue uttered it, but not the heart!'[61] Well, let it go.
Still, I'm not going to offer praise in that manner—I'm not capable of doing
so! I am willing, if you like, to state the truth, and nothing else, in my own
way, and not in competition with your speeches, lest I provide a ridiculous 199b
spectacle. So, Phaedrus, consider whether you want a speech of that sort, that
is, do you want to hear the truth spoken about Love, with the terms and the
ordering of the phrases presented in whatever manner they happen to
emerge?"

Aristodemus said that Phaedrus and the others ordered him to make his speech in whatever manner he believed he ought to speak.

"One further thing, Phaedrus," Socrates continued, "you must let me ask Agathon a few questions, so that I can get his agreement to some points before I give my speech."

"Well, I'll allow it," Phaedrus replied. "Question him." 199c

Aristodemus said that after that Socrates began in this manner: "Well
now, Agathon my friend, you seemed to me to get your speech off to a good
start when you said that one must first describe what sort of qualities Love has
and then describe his accomplishments. I greatly admire that beginning. So
come, since you described everything else about who he is so beautifully and
magnificently, tell me this about Love also. Is Love a love of something, or of
nothing? I'm not asking whether Love is the love of a mother or a father (ask- 199d
ing whether Love is a mother's or a father's love would be ridiculous) but
rather it's as though I were asking about the father himself. Is a father the father
of someone, or not? Obviously, if you wanted to answer well, you would say to
me that a father is the father of a son or a daughter, wouldn't you?"

"By all means," Agathon responded.

"And the same goes for a mother, as well?"

This was also agreed to.

"Well, then," Socrates said, "answer a few more questions, so that you 199e
will have a better understanding of what I'm after. If I ask: 'What about this?
A brother, just insofar as he is a brother, is that to be a brother of someone, or
not?'"

He said that it is.

"So, he is the brother of a brother or a sister?"

He agreed.

"Then try and tell me about Love," Socrates said. "Is Love a love of nothing or of something?"

"By all means, he is of something."

"Now, remember what that is," Socrates continued, "and keep it in mind, 200a while you tell me this: With regard to that which Love is a love of, does he desire it, or not?"

"By all means, he does," he replied.

"Is it while he has this thing he desires and loves that he desires and loves it, or is it when he does not have it?"

"It seems likely that it's when he doesn't have it," Agathon said.

"Consider now," Socrates responded, "whether, instead of its seeming
likely, it is in fact necessarily the case that what desires, desires what it lacks
and does not desire what it does not lack. It seems wondrously obvious to me, 200b
Agathon, that this is necessarily so, but how does it seem to you?"

"It seems so to me, also," he replied.

"Well spoken. Now then, would someone who was large want to be large, or someone who was strong to be strong?"

"That would be impossible, given what we have agreed."

"Because the person who has these characteristics would not lack them."

"What you say is true."

"If someone who is strong did want to be strong," Socrates continued, "or
who is swift to be swift, or who is healthy to be healthy, one might suppose, in
such cases, that those who are all these things and possess these sorts of characteristics do also desire them while they have them. (I'm bringing this up so 200c
that we won't be misled.) Yet, if you reflect on these cases, Agathon, you will
see that insofar as these people have something at a given moment, they necessarily have it, whether they want it or not, and how could anyone desire to
have what they already have? Whenever someone says, 'while I am healthy, I
also want to be healthy,' or 'while I am wealthy, I also want to be wealthy,' or
'I desire these very things that I have,' we will say to him, 'My good fellow,
while you possess wealth, health, and strength, what you also want is to pos- 200d
sess them in the future as well, since at the present moment you already have
them, whether you want them or not. Consider: When you say, "I desire my
present possessions," do you mean anything other than this: "I also want to
possess my present possessions in the future as well"?' Would he agree?"

Aristodemus said that Agathon consented.

Socrates continued, "So, is this what love is of in such a case: what is not in hand and what one does not have, namely, the preservation of these things as one's possessions in the future?"

"By all means," he responded. 200e

"Then, such a person, and everyone else who desires, desires what is not in hand and not present, that is, what one does not have, what one is not oneself, what one lacks. Is this the sort of thing that love and desire are of?"

"By all means," he said.

"Come then," Socrates said, "let's agree about what's being said. First, is Love the love of something, and, second, is that something some thing that at the moment he lacks?"

"Yes," he replied. 201a

"In that case, besides these points, recall what you said Love is in your speech. If you want, I'll remind you. I think you said something like this, that the gods' actions were motivated by love of beautiful things, for there is no love of what is ugly and shameful. Didn't you say something like that?"

"I did say that," Agathon replied.

"And that was a reasonable thing to say, my friend," Socrates responded. "If that's so, could Love be anything other than a love of beauty and not a love of what is ugly?"

He agreed that it couldn't be.

"Well, wasn't it agreed that what he lacks and does not have, that is what 201b
he loves?"

"Yes," he said.

"Then, Love lacks and does not have beauty."

"Necessarily," he responded.

"But what about this? Do you say that what lacks beauty and does not possess beauty in any sense is beautiful?"

"Certainly not."

"Then, do you still agree that Love is beautiful, if this is so?"

Agathon asserted, "It seems likely, Socrates, that I didn't know what I was talking about earlier."

"Well, you did speak beautifully, Agathon," Socrates said. "But go on a 201c
bit more. Doesn't it seem to you that what is good is also beautiful?"

"It does to me."

"Then, if Love lacks what is beautiful and what is good is beautiful, he would also lack what is good?"

"I myself cannot refute you, Socrates," he replied. "Let it be as you say."

"No, Agathon, my friend, it's the truth you're unable to refute, since it's
not difficult to refute Socrates. But I'll leave you alone now." 201d

"I once heard an account of Love from a Mantinean woman named Diotima[62] who was wise and skillful in this and many other things. At one time, by having the Athenians offer sacrifices before the plague occurred, she produced a ten-year postponement of the disease for them, and she instructed me in the activities of Love. I'll try as well as I can to repeat her account for you on my own, using as a basis what was agreed to by Agathon and myself.

"As you noted, Agathon, one must first describe Love and his character,
and then his works. I think the easiest thing would be for me to proceed as the 201e
foreign woman did, describing how she questioned me at that time. I was saying to her more or less the sorts of things Agathon was just now to me: How Love is a great god and is beautiful. And she made the assertions to me that I made just now: How according to my account Love could be neither beautiful nor good."

"What are you saying, Diotima?" I replied. "Is Love then ugly and bad?"

"What a thing to say!" she responded. "Do you think that if a thing isn't beautiful, it must be ugly?"

"Most certainly." 202a

"Is someone who isn't wise, ignorant? Don't you perceive that there's something between wisdom and ignorance?"[63]

"What's that?"

"Don't you know about having correct opinions without being able to give an account of them?" she said. "That isn't having knowledge, for how could what lacks an account be knowledge? Nor is it ignorance, for how could what happens to be accurate be ignorance? Correct opinion is just this sort of thing, something in between understanding and ignorance."

"What you're saying is true," I said.

"Then, don't say that what isn't beautiful is necessarily ugly, or that what 202b
isn't good is necessarily bad. When you agree that Love is neither good nor beautiful, don't then assume that he must be ugly and bad. On the contrary," she said, "he is in between these two."

"And yet," I responded, "it's agreed by everyone that he is a great god."

"Are you talking about all those who lack knowledge," she said, "or those who know?"

"Why, all of them together."

She laughed and said, "How, Socrates, could it be agreed by those who say he's not a god at all that he's a great god?" 202c

"Who are these people?" I responded.

"You are one," she replied, "and I am one."

"How can you say that?" I exclaimed.

"Easily," she responded. "Tell me, wouldn't you say that all the gods are happy and beautiful? Or would you venture to say that some of the gods are not beautiful and happy?"

"By Zeus, not I!" I said.

"Do you say, then, that the happy are those who possess good and beautiful things?"

"By all means."

"Yet, you have agreed that Love, because he lacks good and beautiful 202d
things, desires these very things that he lacks."

"I have agreed to that."

"So, how could one who has no share in good and beautiful things be a god?"

"He couldn't in any way, it seems."

"Then, do you see," she continued, "that even you believe that Love is not a god?"

"Then, what is Love?" I replied, "a mortal?"

"That least of all!"

"But what, then?"

"Just as in the earlier cases," she responded, "he's in between mortal and immortal."

"What is he, then, Diotima?"

"A great daimon,[64] Socrates. Everything that is daimonic is between god
and mortal." 202e

"What does a daimon do?" I asked.

"It interprets and conveys things to the gods from human beings and to
human beings from the gods—entreaties and sacrifices from the one, and
from the other commands and gifts in return for the sacrifices. Since it is in
the middle it fills in between the two so that the whole is bound together by it.
All prophecy comes through a daimon, and the arts of the priests and of those
concerned with sacrifices, rituals, spells, divinations, and magic. A god does 203a
not have direct contact with a human being; on the contrary every interchange
and conversation between gods and human beings is through a daimon, both
when we are awake and in our dreams. The man who is wise and skillful in
these matters is daimonic, but the man who is skilled in any other arts or crafts
is a mere laborer. There are in fact many of these daimons of all sorts, and
Love is one of them."

"Who's his father," I asked, "and his mother?"

"It's a rather lengthy story to go through in detail," she replied, "but I'll 203b
tell it to you. On the occasion of Aphrodite's birth, some of the gods, including Resource, the son of Invention, were having a feast to celebrate. After
they had eaten, Poverty, who'd come to beg since it was such a festive occasion, was standing at the door. Then Resource, who was drunk on nectar
(wine didn't exist yet), wandered out into Zeus's garden in a stupor and fell
asleep. Poverty, because of her lack of resources, contrived a plan to have a
child by Resource, and she lay down beside him and conceived Love. 203c
Because of this, Love became a follower and servant of Aphrodite, since he
was conceived on the day of her birth, and he is also a lover of what is beautiful because Aphrodite is beautiful.

"Hence, since he is the son of Resource and Poverty, Love's circumstances are as follows: In the first place, he's always poor and far from being
gentle and beautiful, as most people believe. On the contrary, he's tough,
wrinkled, barefooted, and homeless. He always lies on the ground, since he 203d
doesn't have a bed, and he sleeps in doorways and alongside the road in the
open air. Since he has his mother's nature, he's always wedded to need. Yet on
the other hand, in keeping with his father, he's a schemer after beautiful and
good things, is brave, eager, and intense, a terrific hunter, always inventing
some device, desirous of understanding, and resourceful. He engages in the
search for wisdom[65] throughout his entire life, and is a terrific wizard, sorcerer,
and Sophist. He is by nature neither immortal nor mortal, but at one and the 203e
same time he is both flourishing and alive, while he is well-provisioned, and
then dying, but is brought to life again through his father's nature. His provi-

sions are always draining away, so that Love is never either without resources
or wealthy. He's also between wisdom and ignorance. This is the situation:
None of the gods engages in the search for wisdom or desires to become wise 204a
(because they are wise), nor does anyone else who is wise engage in the search
for wisdom. Nor, on the other hand, do those who are ignorant engage in the
search for wisdom or desire to become wise. This is precisely what is harmful
about ignorance: since the person who doesn't believe he lacks anything
doesn't desire what he doesn't think he is in need of, an ignorant person, who
is neither beautiful and good nor intelligent, considers himself satisfactory."

"So, who are those who engage in the search for wisdom, Diotima," I asked, "if they are neither the wise nor the ignorant?"

"It should be clear by now, even to a child," she replied, "that it's those 204b
who are in between these two conditions, and Love is one of them. For wisdom is a very beautiful thing, and Love is the love of the beautiful. Thus,
Love is necessarily one who engages in the search for wisdom,[66] and as a
seeker of wisdom is in between being wise and being ignorant. His birth
accounts for this, since his father was wise and resourceful, but his mother
was not wise and lacked resources.

"So, that's the nature of a daimon, Socrates, my friend. It's not at all surprising that you held the view of Love you did. From what you were saying, it 204c
seems to me that you believed Love to be the thing that is loved, rather than the
one who loves. I think that's why Love appeared to you to be so beautiful. The
beloved is in reality the one that is beautiful, graceful, perfect, and most
blessed. The one who loves has a different sort of character, which I have
described."

I responded, "Well! You are a welcome visitor, Diotima, and you state your point very beautifully. If Love is this sort of thing, of what use is he to human beings?"

"I'll try to teach you that next, Socrates," she said. "Now, Love is this 204d
sort of being and his birth was in that manner, and, as you say, he is 'of beautiful things.' But what would you say if someone were to ask us, 'What is love
of beautiful things, Socrates and Diotima?' Or, more clearly, 'the one who
loves, loves beautiful things, but for what does he love them?'"

I said that it was for them to become his own.

"That answer requires an additional question," she continued. "What will this person have, if beautiful things become his own?"

"I cannot provide a ready answer for that question," I replied.

"Well," she said, "suppose one were to replace 'beautiful' with 'good' 204e
and then ask: 'Come, Socrates, the one who loves, loves good things, but for
what does he love them?'"

"For them to become his own," I replied.

"And what will this person have, if good things become his own?"

"That," I said, "I am better prepared to answer: That person will be happy."

"Because happy people are happy through possessing good things," she 205a
continued, "and there's no need to ask beyond that, 'What does the person
who wants to be happy want?' This seems to be a final and complete answer."

"What you say is true," I replied.

"Do you think that this yearning, this love, is common to all human beings, and that everyone wants good things to be their own forever? What would you say?"

"As you say," I replied, "it's common to all."

"Then why is it, Socrates," she asked, "that we don't speak of everyone
as loving, if in fact everyone does always love these very things? Why do we 205b
speak instead of some people as loving and others as not?"

"I wonder about that myself," I replied.

"But you shouldn't wonder," she said. "We separate off one particular form of love and call it 'love,' giving it the name of the whole. We also misuse other names in such ways."

"Can you give me an example?" I asked.

"Here's one: You know that there are various kinds of creativity,[67] since
every time something that did not exist comes into being creativity is responsible. The productions of every art and craft are the result of creativity, and all 205c
of their practitioners are creative people."

"What you say is true."

"Nevertheless," she continued, "you know that these practitioners are not all called creative people. On the contrary, they have various other names. Yet from the whole of creativity the one part that deals with music and verse was set aside and is referred to by the name of the whole. This latter alone is called creativity, and those engaging in this part of creativity are the people who are called creative."

"What you say is true," I said.

"Well, that's the way it is with love, also. In general, every desire by 205d
everyone for good things and for happiness is 'all-powerful and treacherous
Love.'[68] Yet those who turn to him in his diverse forms (whether in connection with making money, with fondness for athletics, or with philosophy), are
not spoken of as loving, nor are they called lovers.[69] Rather, those who go
after one particular form of love, and zealously pursue it, have the name of the
whole, love, and they are spoken of as loving and are called lovers."

"You're probably telling the truth," I responded.

"A certain speech claims," she continued, "that lovers are those who seek
their other halves, but my account states that love is of neither the half nor the 205e
whole, unless, my friend, it happens to be good, since people are willing even
to have their hands and feet cut off if they think they're harmful to them. I don't
think people hold on to something that is their own unless one calls that which
is personal and one's own 'good' and what belongs to another 'bad.' People
don't love anything other than what is good. Does it seem otherwise to you?"

"Not to me, by Zeus," I replied. 206a

"Well, then," she said, "can we simply say that people love what is good?"

"Yes," I replied.

"But what about this?" she asked. "Shouldn't we add that they love for the good to be their own?"

"We should add that."

"And not only to be their own," she continued, "but to be such forever?"

"We should add that also."

"In short, then," she said, "love is of the good's being one's own forever."

"What you say is most true," I responded.

"Given that that is what love always is," she continued, "in connection 206b
with what sort of behavior and what activity on the part of those pursuing the good would their zeal and effort be called love? What is the function of love? Can you say?"

"I would not be so impressed by you and your wisdom, Diotima, if I could," I responded, "nor would I be coming to you in order to learn those very things."

"Then I'll tell you," she said. "It is giving birth in beauty both in body and in soul."

"The services of a prophet are needed to determine what you mean," I said. "I don't understand."

"Then, I'll speak more clearly," she said. "All human beings are preg- 206c
nant, Socrates, both in body and in soul, and when we come of age, we naturally desire to give birth. Yet one cannot possibly give birth in ugliness, only in beauty, because the union of a man and a woman, that is, birth, is a divine affair. Pregnancy and procreation instill immortality in a living, mortal being,
and these things are impossible in what lacks harmony. And ugliness is 206d
disharmonious with everything divine, while beauty is harmonious. Thus, Beauty is involved in procreation as the Fate and the Goddess of Childbirth. This is why, when something that is pregnant comes close to something beautiful, it becomes gentle and relaxes in the delight of procreation and giving birth. When it comes near something ugly, however, it recoils and turns away, frowning and distressed. It shrinks back and does not bring forth, but instead painfully continues to carry the foetus it contains. Thus, in someone who is
pregnant and bursting with life, there is great excitement in the presence of 206e
what is beautiful because it is freed of the great labor pains it had. So, Socrates," she declared, "love is not of the beautiful, as you think."

"Then, what is it of?"

"It is of procreation and giving birth in beauty."

"Well!" I replied.

"By all means, it is!" she said. "Now, why is it of procreation? Because

procreation is eternal and immortal, insofar as anything can be such in a mortal being, and, given what we've agreed, one necessarily desires immortality 207a
along with the good, since love is of the good's being one's own forever. On
the basis of this account, love is necessarily also of immortality."

So, she taught me all these things when she was making her arguments
about the activities of love, and one time she asked, "Socrates, what do you
think is the cause of this love, this desire? Don't you see how terribly it affects
all the wild animals, both those that run on the ground and those that fly, when
they desire to procreate? Do you see how they are all stricken and affected by 207b
the activities of love, first in intercourse with each other and then in taking
care of their young? And how ready the weakest among them are to fight the
strongest for the sake of their offspring, and even to die for them? Do you see
how they will exhaust themselves by starving in order to feed their young, and
would do anything else for them? One assumes that human beings do these
sorts of things on the basis of reason,[70] but what causes wild animals to be so 207c
affected by the activities of love? Can you say?"

I again said that I didn't know, and she replied, "Then, how do you
expect to become terrific at the activities of love, if you don't comprehend
these matters?"

"But that's why I've come to you, Diotima, as I explained earlier,
because I know I need to be educated. So, tell me the explanation of these
things and of any other affairs connected with the activities of love."

"Then," she replied, "if you believe that by nature the object of love is
what we have several times agreed it to be, you won't be surprised by my
answer. My claim here is the same as in the former case: mortal nature seeks 207d
as far as possible to be eternal and immortal, and it is only in this way, by producing offspring, that it is able to do so, through always leaving behind
another, a young one, in place of the old. It is also on this basis that each individual living being is said to be the same individual during its lifetime. For
example, as one develops from childhood to old age one is said to be the same
person, although one never has the same elements in oneself even though one
is called the same person. On the contrary, one is always undergoing renewal
while losing some element of one's hair, flesh, bones, blood, and all parts of 207e
the body generally. This is so not only with regard to one's body, but also
with regard to one's soul. One's habits, characteristics, opinions, desires,
pleasures, pains, fears, none of these ever stays the same in anybody; some
are coming into being while others are passing away. Yet even more odd than
these points is the fact that not only do bits of knowledge come and go for us 208a
(we are never the same even in terms of our knowledge), but each single bit of
knowledge also undergoes the same experience. What is called studying
exists because knowledge goes away. Forgetting is the departure of knowledge, and study saves the knowledge by reimplanting a new memory in place
of what has gone away, so that it seems to be the same knowledge. Everything

that is mortal is preserved in this way, not by being the same in every way forever, like what is divine, but by having what is old and departing leave behind 208b
another like itself that is new. By this means, Socrates," she continued, "a mortal thing participates in immortality, both in terms of its body and in all other regards. An immortal thing operates in a different way. So, you shouldn't be surprised when everything, by virtue of its nature, values its own offspring. In every case, this zeal, this love is in pursuit of immortality."

When I heard her account I was astonished. "Well!" I said, "wisest Diotima, can it be true that things really are this way?"

In the manner of those perfect Sophists, she responded, "You know it, 208c
Socrates![71] When, if you will, you look at people's fondness for fame, you may be surprised by their irrationality, unless you keep in mind what I have said and consider how terribly inflamed they are by a love of becoming a famous name and 'laying down immortal glory for eternal time,'[72] and how they're ready to face every danger for this—even more than for the sake of their children, to squander their money, to endure any pain, and even to die. 208d
Do you think," she continued, "that Alcestis would have given her life for Admetus,[73] or that Achilles would have sought out death after Patroclus died,[74] or your own Codrus would have sought to be the first to die for the sake of his sons' kingdom,[75] unless they thought there would be the immortal memory of their virtue that we now have? That's a long way from being the case," she said. "On the contrary, I believe all these people engage in these famous deeds in order to gain immortal virtue and a glorious reputation, and the better people they are, the more they do so, because they love immortality. 208e

"Now, those who are pregnant in body are more oriented toward women and are lovers in that way, providing immortality, remembrance, and happiness for themselves for all time, as they believe, by producing children. Those who are pregnant in soul however—for there are people who are even more pregnant in their souls than in their bodies," she continued, "these people are 209a
pregnant with and give birth to what is appropriate for the soul. What, then, is it that it is appropriate for the soul to bring forth? Good sense[76] and the rest of virtue, of which all poets are procreators, as well as those artisans who are said to be inventors. But much the most important and most beautiful aspect of good sense," she said, "is that which deals with the regulation of cities and households, the name of which is judiciousness[77] and justice.

"Whenever someone who has been pregnant in his soul with these things 209b
from youth, and who is reaching adulthood and coming into his prime, desires to give birth and produce offspring, he goes around, I believe, searching for something beautiful, with which he can produce offspring. He can never produce offspring with something that is ugly. Hence, since he is pregnant with these things, he eagerly embraces beautiful bodies rather than ugly ones, and should he happen upon someone who has a beautiful, well-bred, and naturally gifted soul as well, he embraces the combination with great enthusiasm and

immediately engages in many conversations with this man about virtue, about
what a good man should be like, and what he should make it his business to do; 209c
thus, he sets out to educate him. When he attaches himself to someone beautiful, I believe, and associates with him, he gives birth and brings forth what he
was pregnant with before, both while in that person's presence and while
remembering him when he's absent. Together with him he nurtures the offspring produced, so that such men have much more to share with each other and
a stronger friendship than that which comes from rearing children, since they
share in the rearing of children who are more beautiful and more immortal.

"Everyone would prefer to bring forth this sort of children rather than
human offspring. People are envious of Homer, Hesiod, and the other good 209d
poets because of the offspring they left behind, since these are the sort of offspring that, being immortal themselves, provide their procreators with an
immortal glory and an immortal remembrance. There are also, if you like,"
she continued, "those children whom Lycurgus left behind in Sparta as the
saviors of Sparta and even, one could say, of all Greece.[78] You also honor
Solon because of the laws that are his offspring, and there are other men in
many places who are honored for other reasons. Among both Greeks and bar- 209e
barians are men who have produced many beautiful works, bringing forth
virtue of every sort. Many shrines have been dedicated to men because of this
sort of children, but none at all because of their human offspring.

"These are the activities of love, Socrates, into which you could probably
be initiated. I don't know whether you are the sort of person for the final rites 210a
and mysteries, for which these former things are the preparation, if one can let
go in the right way. So, I'll speak," she said, "and I'll not curtail my enthusiasm. Try to follow as well as you can.

"The person who is going to approach this matter correctly," she
declared, "must begin while young to turn toward beautiful bodies, and at
first, if he is correctly led by his guide, to love a single body and to bring forth
beautiful conversations in that situation. He must then realize that the beauty
of any particular body is akin to the beauty of every other body, and that if it 210b
is necessary to pursue beauty of form, it is quite mindless not to believe that
the beauty of all bodies is one and the same. When he comprehends this, he
must become a lover of all beautiful bodies, and he will despise that vehement
love of a single body, thinking it a trivial matter.

"After that he must believe that the beauty of souls is more valuable than
that of the body, so that if someone who has a decent soul is not very attrac- 210c
tive, he will be content to love him, to take care of him, and with him to search
out and give birth to the sort of conversations that make young men better. As
a result, he will be compelled to study the beauty in practical endeavors and in
laws and traditions and to see that all beauty is related so that he will believe
that the beauty connected with the body is of little importance.

"After practical endeavors he must be led to examples of knowledge in

order that he may see in turn the beauty of knowledge and no longer look
upon what is limited to an individual case as being very beautiful, like a 210d
house-slave who is enthralled by what is paltry and of little account, lusting
after the beauty of a young boy or of some particular person, or of a single
practical endeavor. On the contrary, after turning toward the great sea of
beauty, he studies it and gives birth to many splendidly beautiful conversations and thoughts in a magnanimous philosophy, until, as he becomes more
capable and flourishes in this situation, he comes to see a knowledge of a singular sort that is of this kind of beauty.

"You must try," she continued, "to pay attention to me as closely as you 210e
can. The person who has been instructed thus far about the activities of Love,
who studies beautiful things correctly and in their proper order, and who then
comes to the final stage of the activities of love, will suddenly see something
astonishing that is beautiful in its nature. This, Socrates, is the purpose of all
the earlier effort.

"In the first place, it is eternal; it neither comes into being nor passes 211a
away, neither increases nor diminishes. Therefore, it is not beautiful in one
respect while ugly in another, nor beautiful at one time while ugly at another,
nor beautiful with reference to one thing while ugly with reference to something else, nor beautiful here while ugly there, as though it were beautiful to
some while ugly to others. Moreover, the beautiful will not appear to this person to be something like a face or a pair of hands or any other part of the body,
nor will it appear as a particular statement or a particular bit of knowledge,
nor will it appear to exist somewhere in something other than itself, such as in
an animal, in the earth, in the sky, or in anything else. On the contrary, it
exists as itself in accordance with itself, eternal and uniform. All other beauti- 211b
ful things partake of it in such a way that, although they come into being and
pass away, it does not, nor does it become any greater or any less, nor is it
affected in any way. When someone moves through these various stages from
the correct love of young boys and begins to see this beauty, he has nearly
reached the end.

"In the activities of Love, this is what it is to proceed correctly, or be led
by another: Beginning from beautiful things to move ever onwards for the 211c
sake of that beauty, as though using ascending steps, from one body to two
and from two to all beautiful bodies, from beautiful bodies to beautiful practical endeavors, from practical endeavors to beautiful examples of understanding, and from examples of understanding to come finally to that understanding which is none other than the understanding of that beauty itself, so that in
the end he knows what beauty itself is.

"Here is the life, Socrates, my friend," said the Mantinean visitor, "that a 211d
human being should live—studying the beautiful itself. Should you ever see it,
it will not seem to you to be on the level of gold, clothing, and beautiful boys
and youths, who so astound you now when you look at them that you and many

others are eager to gaze upon your darlings and be together with them all the
time. You would cease eating and drinking, if that were possible, and instead
just look at them and be with them. What do we think it would be like," she
said, "if someone should happen to see the beautiful itself, pure, clear, 211e
unmixed, and not contaminated with human flesh and color and a lot of other
mortal silliness, but rather if he were able to look upon the divine, uniform
beautiful itself? Do you think," she continued, "it would be a worthless life for
a human being to look at that, to study it in the required way, and to be together
with it? Aren't you aware," she said, "that only there with it, when a person 212a
sees the beautiful in the only way it can be seen, will he ever be able to give
birth, not to imitations of virtue, since he would not be reaching out toward an
imitation, but to true virtue, because he would be taking hold of what is true?
By giving birth to true virtue and nourishing it, he would be able to become a
friend of the gods, and if any human being could become immortal, he would."

"This, then, Phaedrus and the rest of you, is what Diotima said, and I was 212b
persuaded. Now, since I am persuaded, I also try to persuade others that one
could not easily find a better collaborator with human nature for acquiring this
than Love. That's why I say that every man must honor Love, and I myself
honor the activities of Love, practice them industriously, and encourage others
to do so. Both now and always, I praise Love's power and courage to the
extent of my ability. So, Phaedrus, if you will, consider this account my hymn
of praise, delivered for Love, though if you would prefer to call it something 212c
else, call it that."

Everyone applauded after Socrates concluded his speech, except for
Aristophanes, who tried to say something about how Socrates referred to his
own speech in his remarks. Suddenly, there was a loud noise of what sounded
like festive drinkers pounding on the courtyard door, and they heard the sound
of a flute-girl. Agathon then called out, "Why don't you servants see what that
is? If it's someone we know, invite him in, and if it isn't, say that we've 212d
already finished and are no longer drinking."

Almost immediately they heard Alcibiades'[79] voice in the courtyard (he
was extremely drunk and shouting loudly) asking where Agathon was and
demanding that they lead him to Agathon.[80] So, with the flute-girl and several
of his companions supporting him, they led him before them, and he stood at
the door, crowned with a thick wreath of ivy and violets and wearing a great 212e
many ribbons on his head.

"Greetings, gentlemen!" he said. "Will you accept a quite excessively
drunk man as a fellow imbiber? Or should we just leave after crowning
Agathon, which is the reason we came? I wasn't able to come myself, yesterday," he said, "but I'm here now with these ribbons on my head so that I can
make a crown for the head of the wisest and most beautiful of us all from my
own head, if I may speak in that way. Are you laughing at me for being
drunk? You may laugh, but I nevertheless know quite well that what I'm say-

ing is true. But tell me right now, will you do what I propose? Will you 213a
imbibe with me or not?"

They all called out loudly and insisted that he come in and recline with them, and Agathon beckoned him over. So, he went in, assisted by his companions. He was taking off his crown of ribbons as he entered, so that they were covering his eyes, and he didn't notice Socrates. He sat down next to
Agathon, in between Socrates and the latter (Socrates had moved over when 213b
he saw him). And as he sat down beside him, he embraced Agathon and put a crown of ribbons on his head.

Then Agathon said, "Take off Alcibiades' sandals, boy, so that he can recline with us as a third."

"By all means," Alcibiades responded, "but who is this third fellow drinking with us?" He turned around then and saw Socrates, and when he saw him he leapt up and said, "Oh Heracles, what is this? Is this Socrates? You're
lying here in ambush for me again, aren't you? And suddenly showing up 213c
where I least expect you to be, as you often do. Why have you come now? And why are you reclining on this couch? How is it you're not beside Aristophanes or someone else who's an intentional jokester, but instead have somehow found a way to recline beside the most beautiful man in the room?"

At this point Socrates responded, "See here, Agathon, will you defend me? My love for this fellow is not an insignificant affair. Since the time I fell
in love with him, it has been impossible for me to glance at or have a conver- 213d
sation with a beautiful person, not even one, or else he treats me in an amazing manner out of resentment and jealousy. He rails at me and can scarcely restrain himself from hitting me! So watch out, lest he do something right now. Try to adjudicate between us, or if he begins to get violent, defend me, as I am very frightened by this fellow's madness and loving friendship."

"Wait!" Alcibiades replied. "There is no reconciling you and me. On the
contrary, I'll be getting even with you for those remarks later on. But for the 213e
moment, Agathon," he continued, "give me some of those ribbons, so that I can also crown the amazing head of this fellow. Then he won't complain to me that I've made a crown for you, but not for him, although in the arena of words he triumphs over every human being, and not only just recently as you did, but all the time." Then he took the ribbons, crowned Socrates, and lay down on the couch.

When he was settled, he said, "Well, gentlemen, you seem sober to me. Now, that can't be permitted. You must drink! We've agreed to that. So, I choose as the person to lead the drinking (until you've imbibed enough)—myself! Bring me a large mug, Agathon, if there is one. But wait, that's not necessary. Boy," he said, "fetch me that wine cooler over there." (He saw that
it could hold more than two quarts.) After this container was filled, he first 214a
drank it off himself and then ordered it refilled for Socrates. At the same time he said, "With Socrates, gentlemen, my ploy won't succeed. No matter how

much anyone orders him to drink, he drinks it and still never gets drunk." So, when the boy refilled it, Socrates drained it.

Then Eryximachus said, "What are we doing, Alcibiades? Aren't we going to say anything over the cup or sing something? Are we going to just 214b guzzle it down like we were dying of thirst?"

Alcibiades replied, "Ah, Eryximachus, the best son of the best and most judicious father. Greetings!"

"Greetings yourself," Eryximachus said, "but what are we going to do?"

"You should give the orders, Eryximachus, because we ought to obey you, 'since a medical man is worth many others.'[81] Prescribe whatever you like."

"Then listen," Eryximachus replied. "Before you came in, we decided that each of us would make the most beautiful speech he could in praise of Love, going in turn around to the right. Now, all the rest of us have already 214c given our speeches, but since you haven't spoken (though you have been drinking!), it's fair that you should have to give a speech. After you've spoken you can make whatever demand you like of Socrates, and he can do the same to the person on his right, and so on for the rest."

"That's a good suggestion, Eryximachus," Alcibiades responded, "but it wouldn't be an equal match to put a drunken man up against the speeches of people who are sober. Anyway, you blessed fellow, were you persuaded by any of the things Socrates was just saying? Do you realize that everything is 214d just the opposite from what he said? Whenever I praise someone around him, whether it's a god, another human being, or anyone, it's this fellow who can't restrain himself from hitting me!"

"What a thing to say!" Socrates responded.

"By Poseidon!"[82] Alcibiades said. "Don't you deny it! I can't praise anyone else when you're around."

"Then do what you're saying," replied Eryximachus. "If you like, praise Socrates."

"What do you mean?" Alcibiades responded. "Do you think that's what I 214e should do, Eryximachus? Should I attack the man and have my revenge right here in front of all of you?"

"Here now!" Socrates exclaimed. "What do you have in mind? Are you going to praise me in a manner that will make me a laughingstock? What're you going to do?"

"I shall tell the truth. Will you allow that?"

"Of course, I'll allow that," he replied. "In fact, I command you to tell the truth!"

"I won't hesitate to do so," Alcibiades said, "and you should do this: If I say anything that's not true, interrupt me, if you like, and say that I'm mistaken about that. I won't say anything that's false if I can avoid it, but if I do get things out of order in my recollecting, don't be surprised. It isn't easy for 215a a man in my state to produce an account of your odd behavior in a fluent and orderly manner.

"Now, this is the way I will attempt to praise Socrates, gentlemen, by
means of images. He'll probably think that it's to make him a laughingstock,
but the image aims at truth. It's not a joke. I would say that what he's most
similar to are the Sileni[83] that sit in the statue-makers' shops,[84] the ones arti- 215b
sans make that hold shepherd's pipes or flutes,[85] which when pulled apart are
found to have statues of gods inside. Moreover, I would say that he's especially like the Satyr Marsyas.[86]

"That your form is similar to theirs, Socrates, you yourself can't deny.[87]
Moreover, listen to some other ways you're like them. You behave outrageously, don't you? If you disagree, I'll provide witnesses. And you're a
flute-player, aren't you? In fact, you're a more amazing one than Marsyas. He
used instruments to bewitch human beings with the power that emanated from 215c
his mouth, as do those who play his tunes today. (I claim the tunes Olympus[88]
played were those of Marsyas, since he was Olympus' teacher.) Thus, if a
good flute-player, or even a poor flute-girl, plays his tunes, the tunes by themselves can possess people, and, because they are divine, they disclose the people who are ready for the gods and for initiation into the mysteries. The only
way you differ from him is that, while you do the same thing he does, you do
it using plain words without instruments. At any rate, whenever we hear any- 215d
one else talking, even a very good orator, no one takes any interest, but when
someone hears you (or someone else repeating your arguments, even if he's
quite a poor speaker), whether it's a woman listening, a man, or a lad, we are
astounded and possessed.

"I myself, at any rate, gentlemen, if I wouldn't seem to be totally drunk,
would tell you under oath how much I have been influenced by this man's
words and even now I am still affected by them. For, when I hear them, my
heart pounds and the tears flow—even more than among the Corybantes[89]— 215e
from the effect of this man's words. And I see a good many others who are
affected the same way. I believe that Pericles[90] and other good orators I have
heard spoke well, but I was not affected like this. My soul didn't clamor or get
angry about my servile state. However, I have been put in that position many
times by this Marsyas here, with the effect that it seemed to me that I ought 216a
not to live the way I have. (You can't say this isn't true, Socrates.) And even
now, I know in my heart that if I would open my ears, I wouldn't be able to
resist, but would be affected the same way. He forces me to agree that though
I have many faults I neglect my own needs and busy myself with the affairs of
the Athenians. So, I forcibly stop up my ears and run away, as from the
Sirens,[91] so that I won't grow old just sitting there beside him.

"Socrates is the only human being in front of whom I have experienced 216b
what no one would believe possible for me—a sense of shame in front of someone—though I only feel shame in front of him. I know in my heart that I cannot

refute him and so I ought to do what this man commands, but then I go away, a slave to the honor given by the masses. So, I desert him and escape, and whenever I see him, I am ashamed because of what we had agreed on. Many times I would gladly have seen the end of his existence among human beings, but if 216c
that ever came to pass, I well know that I would be even more distressed, so that I don't know how to deal with this man. Thus, I myself, and many others, have been affected in these sorts of ways by the flute-playing of this satyr.

"And now you'll hear from me just how similar he is to those I've likened him to and how amazing the power he has is. None of you understand him, and you know it! However, I will make clear who he is, as I've begun to do. You can see that Socrates is lovingly fixated on beautiful young men, is 216d
always around them—in a daze, and furthermore that he is ignorant about everything and knows nothing. So, isn't this bearing of his like that of the Sileni? Of course it is. He's put on this external appearance just like the statue of Silenus, but when his interior is opened up, he is more filled than you would think, gentlemen and fellow imbibers, with judicious good sense. You have to realize that he doesn't care at all whether or not someone is beautiful. On the contrary, no one would believe how little regard he has for such mat- 216e
ters and for whether one is wealthy or has anything else the multitude values as contributing to happiness. I'm telling you, he believes all those sorts of possessions to have no value at all and that we are worthless as well, and his entire life is occupied with being ironic and playing games with people. I don't know whether any of you have seen the glorious figures inside him when he is serious and opens up. I did see them once, and they seemed to me to be so divine, golden, splendid, and amazing, that, to put it briefly, whatever 217a
Socrates commands must be done.

"I believed he was seriously attracted to my youthful good looks, which I considered a gift from Hermes and amazing good luck, since by gratifying Socrates I would provide myself with the opportunity to hear everything he knew. (I did think my youthful good looks were quite wonderful.) So, with that in mind, on this occasion I dismissed the attendant in order to be alone with him. Before this it had not been customary for me to be alone with him without an attendant. 217b

"Now, I must tell you the whole truth, and you give me your undivided attention, Socrates. If I say anything that's false, correct me!

"Well, gentlemen, I was completely alone with him, and I thought he would talk to me right away in the way a lover talks to his darling when they are alone, and I was delighted. However, nothing at all of that sort occurred! On the contrary, he conversed with me just as he customarily did, and when we had spent the day together, he went away and left me. After that, I began inviting him to exercise with me, so that something might be accomplished 217c
that way.[92] So, he exercised and wrestled with me many times when no one was present, and what can be said? Nothing worked for me!

"Since I was achieving nothing this way, it seemed to me that I should set upon the man with a direct assault and not give up, now that I had taken on the project. However, I had to know what the situation was. So, I invited him over for dinner, just like a lover guilelessly laying snares for his darling. He didn't yield to me in this very quickly, but nevertheless in time I persuaded him. 217d
When he came the first time, he wanted to leave right after he had eaten, and that time out of shame I let him go. The next time I planned ahead, and after we dined I kept the conversation going until late at night. When he wanted to leave, I suggested that it was late and pressed him to stay. So, he lay down on the couch next to mine, where he had eaten, and no one else was sleeping in the room besides us.

"Now, I would have no trouble speaking in front of anybody thus far in 217e
my account. From here on, however, you wouldn't hear me giving it, except for the fact that, first of all, as the saying goes, wine makes for truth when the servants are absent—or when they're present, and that it also appears unjust to me, though I am praising him, to conceal Socrates' contemptuous deed. Moreover, the experience of the man who was bitten by the snake is also relevant here. They say he wouldn't tell anyone about this experience except those who had themselves been bitten, because only they could comprehend 218a
and be understanding of all the things he did or said because of the pain. Now, I have been bitten by something more painful than a snake and in the most painful place one can be bitten, in the heart or the soul or whatever it should be called. I have been struck and bitten by the arguments in his philosophy, which take hold more savagely than a viper when they seize the soul of a not untalented youth and make him do and say anything whatsoever. I am looking at Phaedrus, Agathon, Eryximachus, Pausanias, Aristodemus, Aristophanes, 218b
and all the others—and should one mention Socrates himself? Every one of you has taken part in the madness and Bacchanalian frenzy of philosophy, which is why all of you get to hear this, since you will forgive what was done then and what is being said now. But you slaves and anyone else who is uninitiated and uncivilized, cover your ears very tightly!

"So, gentlemen, after the light had been put out and the slaves had gone, it seemed to me that I shouldn't be coy with him, but just state freely what I 218c
was thinking. So, I nudged him and said, 'Socrates, are you asleep?'"

"Of course not," he replied.

"Then, do you know what I think?"

"What, exactly?" he said.

"You seem to me," I asserted, "to be the only person worthy of being my lover, yet you appear to be hesitant about courting me. Now, my view of the situation is this: I believe it would be quite thoughtless of me not to gratify you in this regard—and in any other, if there is anything you need from my property or that of my friends.[93] Nothing is of greater concern to me than my 218d
becoming the best person I can, and I think no one could be a better partner

for me in this than you. I would be much more ashamed in front of people of good judgment for failing to gratify such a man as yourself, than I would be in front of the masses, who lack good judgment, for gratifying him."

After he heard this, he spoke with his quite excessive though characteristic irony: "Alcibiades, my friend, you may not in fact be so stupid, if what you claim about me turns out to be true and there is some power in me by means 218e
of which you could become better. You must see in me a beauty that is extraordinary, and quite different from your own good looks. If, having detected this, you're trying to partake of it with me and to offer beauty for beauty, you shouldn't think you can obtain more from me in return for less. You're attempting to acquire true beauty in exchange for apparent beauty, 'gold for bronze.'[94] Well, you blessed fellow, look closer lest you fail to notice that I 219a
am not what you think. The vision of the mind begins to see keenly when that of the eyes starts to lose its edge, but you are still a long way from that."

Upon hearing this, I said, "As for myself, what I've said differs not at all from what I think; they're the same. Thus, you yourself must decide what you believe would be best for you and me."

"My!" he replied, "you state that well. After considering this and other matters in the coming days we'll do what appears to us to be best." 219b

"After I had made my statement and heard his reply, and as it were let loose my arrows, I thought I had smitten him. So, I stood up, and not letting him say anything further, I put my own cloak over him, since it was winter. Then I lay down, getting under his own worn garment, threw my arms around this truly daimonic and amazing man, and lay there the entire night. (And you 219c
can't say that I am lying about this, Socrates!) After I had done these things, he acted far better than I had; he disdainfully laughed at my youthful good looks, in a quite outrageous manner—and this was about something I thought was of real importance, gentlemen of the jury (for you are a jury, judging Socrates' arrogance, and you know it!). By every god and goddess, I swear I 219d
got up after having slept with Socrates in a way that had no more significance than sleeping with a father or an older brother.

"Now, what do you think ran through my mind after that? I believed I had been dishonored, but I also admired his nature—his judiciousness and his courage. In terms of good sense and strength, I had happened upon a person of a sort I would never have expected to encounter. As a result, while I could never get angry enough to deny myself his company, I was never able to find a way to win him over either. I knew perfectly well that he was far more invul- 219e
nerable to any sort of bribery than Ajax was to the sword,[95] and in the case of that which I thought would capture him all by itself, he escaped from me. So, I was destitute, enslaved by this man as no one has been by anyone else.

"All these things had happened to me earlier, and then later on we both participated in the campaign in Potidaea,[96] during which we ate our meals together. Now in the first place, in terms of dealing with hardships, he not

only outdid me, but everybody else as well! When we had to do without food
because we had been cut off somewhere (the sort of thing that happens on a
campaign), there was no comparison between his endurance and that of 220a
everyone else. Moreover, when there were feasts, he was the only one who
really enjoyed them, and although he never wanted to drink, when he was
compelled to do so he outlasted everyone—and what is most amazing of all,
nobody has ever seen Socrates drunk! (Though I expect this latter claim is
going to be tested in the near future!)

"Furthermore, in terms of his ability to withstand the cold (and those win-
ters were awful), he did some other astonishing things. One time there was a
most terrible frost, and everyone either did not go outside or, if anyone did go 220b
out, he wrapped up in an amazing amount of clothes, encasing his feet in felts
and sheepskins after putting on shoes! Yet this man ventured out in those conditions wearing only the sort of cloak he customarily wore and walked around
barefooted on the snow and ice with more ease than the others in their shoes!
The soldiers were suspicious that he was being condescending toward them.
And these things really happened! 220c

"'And yet this further deed the mighty man dared and did'[97] while on that
campaign that is worth hearing. He was reflecting on something and he stood
there from early morning considering it, and since no solution occurred to
him, he didn't leave, but continued to stand there seeking one. By the middle
of the day, people were taking notice, and were amazed, saying to each other
that Socrates had been standing there thinking about something since early
morning. In the evening, some of the Ionians[98] who had finished eating finally
carried their bedding outside, since it was then summer, so that they could
sleep where it was cool and watch him at the same time to see if he would 220d
stand there all night. And he did stay there until dawn when the sun was coming up. Then, after he had offered a prayer to the sun, he departed.

"And if you'd like to hear how he behaved in battle, it's appropriate to
render him his due in this regard as well. In that battle for which the generals
awarded me the prize for valor, Socrates, and no one else among the men,
actually saved me! He wouldn't abandon me after I was wounded and rescued 220e
my armor as well as myself. I demanded at the time that the generals give the
prize for valor to you, Socrates, so you can't blame me for that situation, nor
can you say that I'm lying. On the contrary, when, out of regard for my position, the generals were planning to award the prize to me, you were more
eager than the generals themselves for me to get it instead of yourself.

"Furthermore, gentlemen, Socrates was a sight to see when the army was
retreating in flight from Delios.[99] I happened to be there on horseback, but he 221a
was on foot in hoplite's armor. As the men were scattering in every direction, he
and Laches were retreating together.[100] By chance, I came along, and when I saw
them I immediately exhorted them to have courage and said that I would not
desert them. I had a better view of Socrates that day than at Potidaea, because I

was on horseback and was less afraid for myself. In the first place, he carried himself with more self-confidence than Laches. Then it seemed to me that he 221b was tramping along there just as he does around here, 'holding his head high and glancing from side to side,' to use your phrase, Aristophanes.[101] He was carefully looking around at both friends and enemies, so that it was clear to everyone near and far that this man would defend himself very vigorously if anyone were to attack him. Which is why both this fellow and his companion escaped safely. For, when people behave like that in battle, they're almost never touched. On the contrary, people chase the ones who've taken off in headlong flight.

"Now, there are many other amazing feats one can refer to in praising 221c Socrates. However, while with regard to some of his individual achievements one could probably say similar things about others, as a person, there is no other human being like him, neither among the ancients nor among those who exist now. That's what merits the greatest astonishment. Even with such a man as Achilles, one could make a comparison with Brasidas[102] and others, and in turn with Pericles there are Nestor and Antenor,[103] and even others. One can make comparisons of this sort for everybody else, but this man is so 221d odd, both himself and his words, that even after searching one would never find anyone like him, either among those existing now or among the ancients, except perhaps if one were to compare him and his arguments to those I'm speaking of, not human beings, but the Sileni and Satyrs.

"Furthermore (I left this out at the beginning), his arguments are most like those Sileni that can be opened up. If anyone is willing to listen to Socrates' arguments, they at first appear to be quite ridiculous. They're cov- 221e ered over on the outside with words and phrases that are like the hide of an outrageous Satyr, for he talks about donkeys and pack-asses, about blacksmiths, cobblers, and tanners, and throughout it all he appears always to be saying the same things, so that an inexperienced and ignorant person would take everything he says as a joke. However, anyone who sees his arguments 222a opened up and gets inside them will find in the first place that they are the only arguments that make sense and then that they are the most divine, that they contain within themselves many marvelous images of virtue, and that when they are fully expanded they deal with everything that a person who wants to be good and beautiful needs to consider.

"That, gentlemen, is what I offer in praise of Socrates. I also mixed in with what I told you the things I object to, the times he treated me outrageously. Moreover, it's not just me that he has done these things to. There are also Charmides, the son of Glaucon, and Euthydemus, the son of Diocles,[104] 222b and quite a few others whom this man deceived by acting more like a darling than a lover so that they adopted for themselves the role of the lover! I am speaking especially to you, Agathon, lest you be deceived by this fellow in that way. So, be careful and learn from our experiences and not, as the saying goes,[105] like an infant,[106] learn things only through your own experience."

Some of the group laughed at Alcibiades' frankness in saying this, 222c
because he seemed still to be in love with Socrates. Socrates then remarked, "You seem sober to me, Alcibiades. Otherwise you wouldn't have attempted, by means of such an elegant and roundabout cover-up, to disguise your intent in saying all those things, and then tack it on at the end as though you were just adding an afterthought and hadn't said everything for the purpose of pro-
voking a quarrel between Agathon and me. You think that I ought to love you 222d
and not anybody else, while Agathon is to be loved by you and not by a single other person. You don't fool me! Why, that Satyr and Silenus ploy of yours was patently obvious! Agathon, my friend, don't let him gain anything by this, and be on guard so that he won't be able to make you and me quarrel."

Agathon then said, "Well, Socrates, you may well be telling the truth. I
base that judgment on the fact that his reclining between you and me has the 222e
effect of separating us. So, he's not going to gain anything by it; on the contrary, since I want to, I am going to recline beside you."[107]

"By all means," Socrates replied. "Recline here on the other side of me."

"By Zeus!" Alcibiades exclaimed. "What I do suffer from this person! He thinks he ought to get the better of me at every turn. Well, if nothing else, you astonishing man, let Agathon recline between us."

"But that's impossible!" Socrates responded. "Since you have already praised me, I in turn must praise the person on my right. Thus, if Agathon reclines on the other side of you, won't he be praising me again, rather than being praised by me? Let it be, you daimonic fellow, and don't be jealous of
the lad's being praised by me, for I very much desire to laud him." 223a

"Oh, my!" said Agathon. "There's no way I'll stay where I am now, Alcibiades. On the contrary, I will most certainly move over if I'm to be praised by Socrates."

"That's it," said Alcibiades, "the usual situation. With Socrates here, it's impossible for anybody else to take up with the beautiful ones. And now how easily he finds a persuasive argument, so that this beauty here will be reclining beside him."

Then, while Agathon was getting up to go recline beside Socrates, a crowd 223b
of revellers suddenly came to the doors. When they discovered the doors were open because someone was going out, they trooped right in and reclined among those who were already there. Everything was in an uproar, there was no order anywhere, and everyone was forced to drink a great deal of wine.

Aristodemus said that he believes Eryximachus, Phaedrus, and some
others left then, but he passed out and slept for quite a while, since the nights 223c
were long at that time of year. He woke up toward morning when the roosters were crowing, and when he awakened he saw that some were sleeping and others had gone home, except for Agathon, Aristophanes, and Socrates, who were still awake and drinking from a large bowl, passing it around to the right. So, Socrates was engaging them in conversation. Aristodemus said

he doesn't remember other parts of the argument, since he had missed the beginning and was also sleepy, but he said that the chief point Socrates was 223d
forcing them to accept was that the same man could know how to compose both a comedy and a tragedy and that a skillful tragedian could create comedies. They were being forced to go along, although they were getting drowsy and hardly following it. Aristophanes fell asleep first, and by the time morning came Agathon had also.

Having seen them to sleep, Socrates then got up to leave, and Aristodemus followed him as usual. When Socrates arrived at the Lyceum[108] he washed up and then spent the rest of the day as he usually did, and after a routine day, he went home to rest in the evening.

3
Commentary on the Symposium

The commentary presupposes a basic familiarity with the text of the dialogue and with the topics discussed in the general introduction above. My intention is to encourage the reader to focus on the entirety of the text and to open up the reader's reflection on the dialogue by commenting on various issues and interpretations. I am particularly concerned to bring out the possible significance of dramatic and literary aspects of the dialogue and to suggest how a consideration of such factors can impact on the interpretation of the philosophical content of the dialogue. I try to initiate the task of working out the implications of and adjudicating between rival interpretations, but the fulfillment of that task belongs to the conversation with the dialogue that this commentary is designed to stimulate. Thus, the commentary is not designed to fulfill or complete the dialogue, but to return the reader to the dialogue with a renewed enthusiasm and appreciation for the richness and complexity of Plato's text.

APOLLODORUS AGREES TO REPORT ON THE FAMOUS PARTY: 172A–173E

The dialogue begins with a brief conversation that leads to a lengthy description of a long past conversation. This brief "present time" dialogue at the beginning of the text raises a number of interesting questions.

It is striking that the opening remark by Apollodorus is directed to an unnamed companion (172a). It is to this unnamed companion that Apollodorus recounts his story of Agathon's dinner party and the speeches on love given there, after explaining why he is well rehearsed for such a recitation. Perhaps the use of the second-person pronoun without an explicit reference is intended to draw the reader into the conversation.

Apollodorus indicates that he was not at the party, but was told about it by Aristodemus, who accompanied Socrates to the party. However, Apollodorus says that he did check some of the details with Socrates himself. One could see this passage as evidence of an intent to establish the historical accuracy of the report that follows,[1] but the report as a whole seems too carefully crafted for this to be plausible.

This complicated introduction to the dialogue is a curious conceit by Plato. One effect of it is to direct the reader's attention to the lives of the speakers during the years since the banquet:[2] Alcibiades' notorious career has run its course; Agathon has befriended a vicious tyrant; Phaedrus and Eryximachus have been exiled. Only Socrates and Aristophanes remain in Athens. (We know nothing of Pausanias, if there was such a historical character.) Perhaps Plato intends for the reader to take the later careers of these men into account in weighing their views of love. In other words, the suggestion may be that an inadequate grasp of love has disastrous political consequences.[3]

One other possible significance of the delay between the party and the present report of it could be to illustrate the process of immortality as Socrates describes it in his speech in the dialogue. See especially the references to producing beautiful things both when in the presence of the loved one and "while remembering him when he's absent" (209c) and to the beautiful "children" left behind by people like Homer and Solon (209d). Plato is certainly capable of such self-reflexivity in his dialogues.

Another striking element in this opening section is the companion's mentioning of Apollodorus' nickname (173d). He suggests that there is something paradoxical about the fact that Apollodorus is called "gentle" because his manner is in fact rather violent. This theme of an unexpected connection between gentleness and violence plays an important role in the characterization of love in the dialogue.[4]

SOCRATES' ARRIVAL AT THE PARTY: 174A–176A

After inviting Aristodemus to accompany him to Agathon's dinner party, Socrates gets caught up in thought and lets Aristodemus arrive ahead of him (174d). Aristodemus reacts as though this were not an unusual occurrence, and Alcibiades later recounts a similar occasion of Socrates' getting lost in his reflections (220c–d). There is nothing to suggest that this is anything more than an unusually intense example of Socrates' normal thinking processes. There is no reason to see this incident as involving some sort of mystical transcendence of normal reasoning.[5]

We also find in this passage a good example of Socratic irony in the response to Agathon's request to share in the wisdom Socrates has gained while lost in thought just before he arrived at the party. Socrates' claim that his own wisdom is "as worthless and ambiguous as a dream" while that of Agathon is "bright and has great promise" is obviously not sincere (175e). Whether Socrates is equally ironic in other assertions in the dialogue, such as his claim to know the truth about love (177d, 199b), is more difficult to judge.

THE PARTY CHOOSES TO GIVE SPEECHES IN LIEU OF DRINKING: 176A–178A

After they all finish eating, Pausanias asserts that the hard drinking of the previous evening has left him in no shape to indulge again this evening, and, in a fine display of mutuality, everyone agrees to forgo serious drinking, although this resolution is abandoned at the end of the evening under the influence of a crowd of revellers who crash the party (223b). Socrates does not participate in this discussion, but Eryximachus mentions that it won't matter either way to Socrates (176c). This prepares the reader for the final scene in the dialogue, where Socrates drinks everyone under the table and leaves to carry on his normal daily routine, apparently suffering no effects from the heavy drinking at the end of the evening. This theme of Socrates' transcendence of ordinary human limitations appears several times in the dialogue, especially in Alcibiades' story about Socrates. It adds a certain otherworldliness to his character and furthers the association between the character of Socrates and the daimonic Love described in his speech. This theme could also be seen as suggesting that the Socratic way of life is an unrealistic extreme, inappropriate as a human ideal.[6]

Eryximachus then suggests that they entertain themselves by taking turns giving speeches in praise of the god of Love, an idea he claims to have gotten from Phaedrus' complaint about the absence of such praise in the works of the poets.[7] Everyone again agrees, and Socrates participates in this discussion with a quite surprising remark. He says that he will certainly not object to this proposal because "I understand nothing other than the activities of love" (177d). This claim to know something[8] is not typical of the image of Socrates in the dialogues, although it is not unprecedented. For example, he claims at *Meno* 98b to know that knowledge and correct belief are different. Socrates will reaffirm this claim at the end of his speech (212b).

James Arieti argues that Eryximachus' reference at 177b to a work praising the benefits of salt is of considerable importance for understanding the speeches that are coming.[9] It was a common device for rhetoricians to show off their ability to construct convincing arguments by defending absurd conclusions.[10] Defenses of Helen were particularly popular topics for this exercise. In a similar vein, one could make grandiose claims for the importance of trivial matters, such as the mentioned treatise that extravagantly praised the virtues of salt, an ordinary, everyday substance. Arieti argues that this prepares the reader to see the speeches about love as similarly extravagant hyperbole, this time in praise of an ordinary, everyday activity, namely, sex. He emphasizes that the normal meaning of *erōs* is sexual desire and concludes that Plato does not intend the reader to take *any* of the speeches praising it, especially that of Socrates, seriously. Instead, Arieti claims, the reader is to see these speeches as examples of human efforts to describe the gods, that is, of theologizing, and what they reveal is that human beings make the gods in their own images (a view expressed by the earlier philosopher Xenophanes).[11]

This passage also contains the first reference to the order of the speakers (177d), an issue that comes up several times. Aristophanes speaks out of order (185c–d), and there is much ado about the issue when Alcibiades finishes his speech (222e). One question is whether the order is hierarchical, with an ascent to the profundity of Socrates' speech.[12] Those who take this approach usually do not treat Alcibiades' speech as part of the series, and Alcibiades' speech does differ from the others in several ways, of course: the scene is dramatically changed before he gives his speech, and its object ostensibly is to praise Socrates rather than the god Love.

Including Alcibiades' speech in a hierarchical interpretation opens interesting questions. It could suggest that the image of Socrates that Alcibiades provides is the highest manifestation of the true nature of love. On the other hand, Nussbaum, who argues that the placement of Alcibiades' speech at the end shows that the interpretation of the dialogue must take it very seriously, sees it as correcting the one-sided otherworldliness of Socrates' speech.[13] Vlastos agrees that the Socrates of Alcibiades' speech is not the Socrates who reports Diotima's views. He sees Alcibiades' Socrates as the historical Socrates, whose views are radically incompatible with those of the Platonic Socrates who affirms the conclusions of Diotima.[14]

All the speeches do seem to echo each other in various ways, directly and indirectly.

PHAEDRUS GIVES THE FIRST SPEECH: 178A–180C

Phaedrus offers a rather naive and apparently conventional (in Athenian terms) depiction of the nature of love. Love is seen as entirely positive in its effect, inspiring virtue in those who have it. He ascribes to the traditional myth, found in Hesiod, of Love and Earth (*Erōs* and *Gaia*) as the original progenitors of everything else and repeats several well-known stories of virtuous activity inspired by love.

It is striking that, while he tends to speak of love as manifested in the homosexual relation of an older with a younger man, he does use a woman, Alcestis, and her love for her husband as one of his examples, even comparing her favorably to Orpheus, whose love for his wife was found lacking. The status of women in this context is an issue that appears several times in the dialogue, though what Plato intends by it is unclear. The possibility that he means to challenge the dominant male chauvinism of his day is highly debatable. (See the commentary on Socrates' speech below.)

THE SPEECH OF PAUSANIAS: 180C–185C

Pausanias begins by distinguishing between a heavenly and a common form of Love and by making the interesting suggestion that actions in themselves are neither good nor bad, but become so by virtue of the manner in which they are performed (180d–e). The primary action he has in mind is sex, of course. The inferior kind of Love is careless of the quality of its object, being directed toward people of both sexes as well as toward people of lesser character (181a–b). It also is opportunistic. The superior kind of Love is interested only in young males, is careful in choosing worthy darlings, and is enduring (181c–d). Pausanias suggests that it is the excesses of the common sort of Love that have led to the general disapproval of young men gratifying the desires of their older lovers (182a). This is the first hint in the dialogue of the existence of social disapproval of homosexuality.

Focusing exclusively on homosexual relations, Pausanias discusses the different customs regarding love in different communities, providing sociological studies in place of the literary allusions of Phaedrus. He sees states where homosexuality is either accepted without any restrictions or totally prohibited as characterized by a lack of skill in making speeches (with which to seduce young men) in the first case, and in the other, a lack of virtue (primarily "manliness"—the literal meaning of ἀνδρεία, *andreia*, a Greek term that is often translated as "courage") (182b–c). Neither of these, Pausanias claims, recognize the twofold nature of Love, that it is both good and bad.

The Athenian custom, however, is quite complex, Pausanias asserts (182d ff.). While extoling such relationships as a good thing, many hindrances are put in the way of those who seek to establish them. This is justified by the intention of preventing the abusive forms of common Love and of guaranteeing that loving relationships are properly heavenly, that is, designed to promote virtue. In such cases, Love is of enormous benefit, both to the individuals involved and to the community.

Plato has Pausanias construct a very elaborate analysis of this complex situation concerning homosexual love. It is tempting to assume that he is articulating a defence and explanation of actual practice in Athens, or at least, providing an idealized view of practice among the elite. On the other hand, the speech may also be read as an example of self-serving cleverness on the part of a man who enjoys this kind of relationship.[15] Pausanias' speech does conclude with an emphatic emphasis on the nobility of a young man's actually gratifying the desires of his lover. His justification for this is that it is "for the sake of virtue" (185b), but while the youth is supposed to receive training in virtue from his older lover, the lover seems to have nothing to gain from the relationship other than sexual pleasure (184d). The behavior of Socrates as reported by Alcibiades (219c) seems to stand in marked contrast to Pausanias' view, and the second speech by Socrates in the *Phaedrus* contains a strong caution against engaging in such gratification. While it is clear that homosexuality (or bisexuality) was practiced in classical Athens, and with some degree of public approval, Plato's treatment of this practice in the *Symposium* and the *Phaedrus* is somewhat ambiguous, although the practice is never straightforwardly condemned.

ARISTOPHANES GETS THE HICCUPS: 185C–E

This amusing incident fascinates everyone who reads the *Symposium.* But does it have any significance beyond offering a bit of comic relief after Pausanias' analysis of social customs? Perhaps Plato intends to ridicule Aristophanes, whose caricature of Socrates in his comedy *Clouds* may have offended him. Alternatively, the satire may be directed at Eryximachus, as the famous physician is reduced to giving medical advice of a rather trivial sort. A third possibility is that the satire is directed at Pausanias. The latter view takes the suggestion that Aristophanes' hiccups may have been "from overeating or something else" (185c) as involving a hint that the "something else" was being fed up with bad speeches. All three views have been held by various ancient and modern readers of the dialogue, and all three could be correct.[16] It seems likely that the hiccups would not be the result of excessive drinking, since the party had agreed not to overindulge. If so, it must be bad speeches that Aristophanes has had an excess of.[17]

At any rate, the reader should visualize what is going on during Eryximachus' speech that follows. Aristophanes holds his breath until he explodes and starts hiccuping again. Then he gargles, no doubt loudly, but still continues to hiccup. Finally, he makes himself sneeze several times. This counterpoint to Eryximachus' speech is in fact surprisingly relevant to the content of what Eryximachus is saying. The basic principle of Eryximachus' theory is that harmony results from the bringing together of opposites, yet in this homely application of his theory, it is precisely the bringing together of similars that restores harmony. The quiet restraint of holding his breath should have worked if Eryximachus' theory were correct, yet it is the application of one violent motion to another that is successful. After this, the reader is not surprised when Aristophanes offers a radically different view of things from that of Eryximachus.

ERYXIMACHUS OFFERS A COSMIC THEORY: 185E–188E

Eryximachus begins by adopting Pausanias' notion that Love is twofold (186a), although he immediately moves beyond the realm of the human and social on which Pausanias focused, and by the end of his speech he has submerged this duality into a single source to which (or to whom, since he still speaks of Love as a divine being) as a whole he attributes all the power in the world and from which he claims all good things come (188d). He starts with an analysis of the medical profession as simply a mastery of the workings of *erōs* in the body, which he explains as involving the handling of opposing things so as to bring them into harmony (186b–e), a view held by the

Pythagoreans. This principle of a harmony of opposites he then generalizes as the basic principle in all of nature, mentioning in some detail such examples as music and weather patterns (187a ff.).

To some extent this speech probably includes a parody of traditional philosophical theories of the natural world. It is especially reminiscent of the views of the fifth-century philosopher Empedocles, who also spoke of *erōs* as the force of attraction between the fundamental elements of natural things, though he added strife as the opposing force that drives things apart.[18] At the same time it effectively prepares the reader for the speculations about Love as an ultimate principle of reality in the views Socrates attributes to Diotima. The next speech forms a dramatic contrast to the dry, "scientific" character of Eryximachus' encomium.

ARISTOPHANES' COMIC MYTH: 189A–193D

Aristophanes begins by thanking Eryximachus for his hiccup remedy (189a). The latter's response of complaining that Aristophanes is making jokes may suggest that Plato intends for the reader to see Eryximachus as recognizing that Aristophanes' treatment of his hiccups has resulted in a ridiculing of his own view.

The great comic myth of human origins that Aristophanes now presents is one of the most enjoyable parts of the *Symposium*. Dropping the dualistic view of Love that Pausanias introduced, he tells one of the best-known stories in all of Plato's dialogues. There is no reason to assume that anyone other than Plato himself is the author of this tale, which seems to mimic effectively the style of the great comic playwright.[19]

The notion of the three types of original humans (189d),[20] male, female, and a mixture of the two, leads naturally to the suggestion that in their modern, divided forms three types of sexual relationships will occur, homosexual, lesbian, and heterosexual. There is much greater evidence of homosexual relations in ancient Athenian society, but this reference at 191e may suggest that lesbian relationships were also accepted as normal. In the rest of his story, Aristophanes' refers only to same-sex relationships between males. He continues the general tone of the *Symposium* by treating heterosexual relationships as of inferior worth, associating them with adultery (191d–e), and suggesting that homosexuals only engage in marrying women and having children because of social pressure (192b). However, he does qualify this one-sided view at one point, when he is talking about the good things that happen to proper lovers, by claiming that he is "really talking about everyone, men and women alike" (193c). Nevertheless, he concludes that homosexual relationships are clearly the best, as is shown by the fact that "only men (that is, 'males'—the term for a male human being [ἀνήρ, *anēr*] is not used in a gender-neutral sense in Greek) of this sort are completely successful in the affairs of the city" (192a). It is interesting that many of the metaphors of unity that Aristophanes uses in describing the desires of lovers are still used by us today.

The moral of Aristophanes' tale is that love is "the desire for wholeness" (192e). Although he focuses on the wholeness of sexual union, the idea is easily expanded to other levels. The suggestion that a certain lack characterizes the human situation and motivates us to reach out toward various potential objects of satisfaction prepares us for the view that Socrates will report later. Aristophanes emphasizes that this search for wholeness must be in the context of proper respect for the gods, whose ability to affect human lives in dramatic ways has been shown in his myth. He concludes with the comment that only two speakers are left, Agathon and Socrates. The reader knows that a third will appear.

AN EXCHANGE BETWEEN AGATHON AND SOCRATES: 193E–194E

Agathon's philosophical inadequacies are effectively displayed in this brief exchange with Socrates. Socrates first points out that Agathon has labelled all the speakers at his dinner party as "senseless" by calling the entire audience of his play such (194a–b), and then catches him in a mindless platitude that implies he would have no qualms about doing something shameful as long as it was not witnessed by anyone who knew better (194b–c). This latter point contains the suggestion that Agathon is now going to be judged by a more discriminating audience than he was at the theater. The reader is prepared for the worse from Agathon's speech, and we are not disappointed. Agathon concludes this exchange with a remark that has a poignant ring, since the dialogue was written after Socrates' death: "There'll be plenty of opportunities to engage in dialogue with Socrates later" (194e).

AGATHON'S "BEAUTIFUL" SPEECH: 194E–197E

Agathon's speech is striking for its elaborate, poetic style and its superficiality of content. He begins by asserting that the earlier speakers only described the gifts of the god and failed to depict his character (194e). He promises to correct this oversight. In a rather pat description of Love's character, Agathon declares that the god Love is both beautiful and virtuous. His beauty consists in his being youthful, gentle, pliant, and graceful. His virtue consists in his neither doing nor suffering any wrong and in his being completely nonviolent. He also possesses the four cardinal virtues of justice, judiciousness, courage, and wisdom. The catalogue of Love's gifts to humankind, with which Agathon follows this ebullient description of his nature, amounts to little more than saying that Love is the source of all good things. Throughout, the language is effusive and full of metaphors, but, although the rest of the party is enthusiastic in its response, Socrates will quickly show how superficial all of this verbiage is.[21]

As noted earlier, James Arieti claims that the dramatic function of these speeches is to display how people tend to characterize the gods in their own images. This self-referential character is especially obvious in Agathon's speech. One can easily believe that he has himself in mind as he lists the characteristics of the god: youthful, handsome, graceful, wise, superior to all in his skill as a poet, etc.

Agathon's claim that Love has absolutely nothing to do with violence (195c–e), but is remarkable in his gentleness, reminds the reader of the theme of the relation between these two characteristics that was introduced in the remark about Apollodorus' nickname at 173d. Agathon's view here contrasts sharply with that just presented by Aristophanes, and is also rejected in the speeches that follow.[22] Insofar as Socrates is presented in the *Symposium* as the personification of *erōs*, it is noteworthy that he is characterized as fully capable of violence in Alcibiades' description of his actions, and it is obvious that he suffered violence of the most extreme sort. Yet, at the same time, he is shown as capable of great gentleness in his dealings with Alcibiades.

SOCRATES ASKS WHETHER BEING TRUTHFUL MATTERS: 198A–199C

This brief interlude seems to mark a significant change in the tone of the text. Socrates not only sharply criticizes the earlier speakers, he also explicitly claims that he is now going to state the unvarnished truth about the nature of love (199a–b). Of these two actions, the latter is the more surprising in terms of the usual depiction of Socrates in the dialogues.

Socrates associates Agathon with the famous Sophist Gorgias (198c), whose rhetorical style is known to us from several surviving speeches and who is attacked directly in the *Gorgias* and indirectly through his student Meno in the *Meno*, and Plato seems to be imitating the style of Gorgias in Agathon's speech.[23] Saying that Agathon's speech, and by implication those of the other speakers as well, is more concerned to make a good impression than to tell the truth, Socrates declares that this is not the correct way to offer praise—another matter he explicitly claims to know about (198d). He then asserts that he will simply tell the truth about love, which he, fortunately, knows. He gets permission from Phaedrus to begin by questioning Agathon (199b–c).

It is certainly understandable that many readers assume that Plato is indicating here that what follows expresses his own best understanding of the issue at hand. However, it is also possible to see this assertive dogmatism on the part of Socrates as an ironic move appropriate for this character in this dramatic context. From this second interpretive perspective, Plato's intent is seen as being to put the reader on guard to expect that in what follows there will be a consummate example of the Sophist's art. Socrates accuses the other speakers of simply ascribing the best possible characteristics to the subject to be praised, regardless of what the subject is really like. Perhaps he will now do exactly the same thing, only with much more effective rhetorical skill, so that the hyperbole will actually seem plausible.

In trying to decide between these two interpretative approaches, the reader must keep in mind the entire text, and especially the final section with the speech of Alcibiades. Is the character of Socrates in this dialogue one which Plato intends the reader to identify and agree with, or does Plato intend to reveal the approach to life and love represented by this character as seriously deficient? The answer to this question must take into account the role of this interlude.

SOCRATES QUESTIONS AGATHON: 199C–201D

In this passage Socrates gets Agathon to admit that the main premise of his speech, namely, that the god Love is beautiful and good, is not correct and that he therefore did not know what he was talking about (201b). Socrates' argument, which he later says he learned from Diotima (201e ff.), is straightforward. Love is the sort of thing that requires an object. Just as one cannot simply be a father or a sister, but must be the father or the sister *of someone*, so one cannot just love, period. One must love something. Hence, love is always "of something" (199c–e). Moreover, the something is necessarily something that one does not have (200a). Here Socrates makes explicit the fact that love is basically a type of desire (ἐπιθυμία, *epithumia*) (200e) and therefore shares the character of all desire of being for something that is lacking. It makes no sense, he says, to speak of desiring something that you already have. The only way you can relate desire to what you already possess is to think of desiring to continue possessing it in the future, a condition which, of course, is lacking in the present (200b–e). Now, since love is obviously of what is beautiful and good,[24] it follows that love does not already possess beauty and goodness (201b).[25]

Agathon admits his error with surprisingly good grace, and in this is not like the typical recipient of a Socratic refutation (201b–c). This may only indicate that he is not very concerned about the issue of truth, however, and is well satisfied by Socrates' admission that he did speak beautifully (201c). It would not be unprecedented for Plato to portray a poet as unconcerned with truth, as every reader of the *Republic* knows.

Agathon might have tried to use Socrates' point about people desiring things they already possess to save his claim. He could claim that the god is beautiful and good and desires to remain so. Thus Love could be "of the beautiful," in the sense of desiring to remain so, and still already be beautiful. That he does not make use of this move that Socrates offers him, with several repeated examples, is further evidence of his lack of genuine interest in discovering the truth about love.

In his later discussion Socrates effectively covers this possibility by adding the point that love is the desire to possess the beautiful "forever" (205a, 206a). If the fact that the logic of Socrates' analysis here leaves open the possibility of Love's being beautiful were acknowledged, it would make the initial analysis he attributes to Diotima much more complex. The crucial notion of being in between, which is introduced by seeing Love as lacking beauty and hence in between the beautiful and the ugly, could still be developed, but not with the simple effectiveness Socrates achieves in the text. This passage is an interesting example of Plato's pointing toward a more complex level of argumentation, in this case by means of Socrates' emphasis on this point about the sense in which you can desire what you already have, but not exploring it in the text.[26]

Socrates concludes with yet another assertion that what he is saying is the truth, although the phrase "it's not difficult to refute Socrates" makes his remark ambiguous (201c). Some would find here a hint or challenge from Plato to the reader, implying that he is aware of problems in the views he has Socrates defend.

SOCRATES REPORTS WHAT HE LEARNED FROM DIOTIMA: 201D–212C

In assessing the account of love that Socrates presents, the first issue the reader must confront is that of the significance of the fact that he attributes the account, which he defends as true, to a woman. It is very rare for Socrates to be depicted as the philosophical inferior in the dialogues,[27] but this situation is made even more surprising here by having his superior be a woman. It is clear that ancient Athenian men assumed that women were inherently inferior in terms of rational capacity.[28] Whether one takes Plato's suggestions about allowing women to be among the philosophical rulers of the proposed state in the *Republic* as ironic or serious, it is obvious that he assumes that such proposals will be shocking to his audience.[29] Several interpretive responses to the presence of Diotima are possible.

The reader could see this dramatic device as a means of striking a blow against Athenian male sexism, making Plato something of an ancient feminist.[30] This view seems especially plausible from the perspective that finds in Socrates' account of love here the view that Plato himself intends to affirm. If Plato intends the reader to take what Socrates presents as true, then it seems reasonable to suggest that the format of presentation is intended in an equally serious manner. This could also suggest that the story has an actual historical basis.[31]

Another possibility, which is more ambiguous as to its implications for how one understands Plato's intentions regarding the view of love Socrates presents, is that Plato has Socrates attribute this account to a woman because the fundamental metaphor used in the account, that of pregnancy and birth, is more appropriate in the mouth of a woman. It is certainly striking that an event that is unique to women is used as the basis for illuminating a phenomenon that is presented as the key to the satisfactory fulfillment of human existence in a context where the focus is on men. One could argue that it is more appropriate to the dramatic context to have this approach attributed to a woman rather than to Socrates himself.

However, thinking about the dramatic context suggests a third possibility, and this one would seem to imply that the account that Socrates gives is not to be taken as Plato's best effort at a statement of his own view of the truth. This possibility is that Plato is making use of the common attitude toward women to indicate that what follows will lack rational rigor, that is, it will be an account that is excessive, lacking balance and judiciousness—"just what you would expect from a woman."[32] In other words, attributing the account to Diotima is a comic device that implies that Socrates' repeated claims to be interested only in telling the truth are all ironic. It is hard to imagine the group of men gathered at this party not snickering at Socrates' suggestion that he has learned from a woman what he presents as the most important thing one could know. As with any comic passage, this would not eliminate the possibility of there being serious content in the account, but it would suggest that the account must be carefully interpreted so as to distinguish the hyperbolic elements.

Another factor in assessing the significance of the role of Diotima, that counts against the claim that Plato is signalling that this account is not to be taken seriously, is the fact that women served as oracles for the gods at divine sanctuaries such as that at Delphi, and there are a number of elements in Socrates' account that associate it with an initiation into the mysteries, another context in which women would have special status. This consideration might suggest that what follows is to be seen as a message from the god, a source that Socrates takes very seriously in the *Apology*. Moreover, there is some evidence that there was such a prophetess of some repute in the fourth century in Mantinea.[33]

The upshot of all this is that the figure of Diotima adds a very complicated challenge to the interpretation of the *Symposium*.[34]

In his recapitulation of his conversation with Diotima, the first point Socrates reports is the introduction of the notion of the in-between (202a). Diotima's argument uses an analogy with the fact that there is a middle ground between wisdom and ignorance, namely, having a true opinion but not *knowing* that or why it is true (202a), in order to suggest that Love is a kind of being that is in between a mortal human being and an immortal god (202d). This middle-way being is called a "daimon." The Greek term is δαίμων (*daimōn*), which refers to a more than human being and can be used as a synonym of the term for "god," θεός (*theos*), although it is often used of beings who have a lower status than the gods and a closer connection to humans, such as human souls in Hades. Socrates refers to the mysterious voice or sign that sometimes tells him not to do things as daimonic.[35] Plato here introduces a special interpretation of the role of the daimon, of whom Love is only one (203a), that presents an interesting picture of the cosmos.

The key sentence in this regard is "Since [the daimon] is in the middle [between gods and human beings] it fills in between the two so that the whole is bound together by [or through] it" (202e). A striking point in this statement is the clear affirmation of the fundamental unity of the cosmos. The apparent separation of the realms of the gods and of human beings is overcome by the workings of the daimonic; the heavenly realm is not wholly transcendent and closed to direct human access in this life.

This view contrasts with the image sometimes found in the dialogues that suggests that human beings, at least while on earth, have no access to the heavenly realm, an image that creates an epistemological problem if the forms, the true objects of knowledge, are lodged in the heavenly realm. An example of this latter image is found in the discussion of recollection in the *Meno* at 81a–86c and the *Phaedo* at 72e–77a, where a special sort of recollection is offered as a solution to the problem, and in the judgment myths in the *Phaedo* at 107d–115a and the *Republic* at 614b–621b, as well as elsewhere. This problem would not arise in Diotima's cosmos, especially if there were a daimon associated with knowledge of the forms, perhaps Logos (speech)—but this suggestion is rather speculative. Nevertheless, it is striking that the first function of the daimon that Diotima mentions is that of interpreting the words of human beings and gods so that they can communicate with each other. This cosmic image must not be forgotten when interpreting Diotima's later remarks about the "heavenly staircase" (211c) and when considering just how "separated" the forms are in Diotima's view. The suggestion that love binds things together also reminds the reader of Aristophanes' speech, of course.

Diotima next develops this notion of Love as a being in between through a story about the birth of the god.[36] The characterization of Love as the offspring of Resource (Πόρος, *Poros*) and Poverty (Πενία, *Penia*) presents a figure whose characteristics are very reminiscent of those of Socrates himself. This parallel between Socrates and the god of Love can also be seen as preparing the reader for Alcibiades' later depiction of Socrates as a lover and raises the important interpretive question of whether the figure of Socrates in the dialogue is being presented as an ideal personification of Love.[37] This question is most appropriately dealt with in the context of Alcibiades' speech, though it needs to be kept in mind while considering Diotima's view as well.

Diotima begins her explication of the uses of love[38] by asking Socrates why people love beautiful things, it having been granted earlier that love is of the beautiful (204d). Socrates responds that people love beautiful things because they desire them to become their own (204d), and she leads him to see that this means that one loves beautiful (or good) things in order to be happy, "because," she says, "happy people are happy through possessing good things" (205a). This notion that love is basically a desire to *possess* beautiful things will later be rejected as an inadequate view. However, Diotima uses this assumption to make a number of important initial points.

The first point is framed as a linguistic one. Diotima has identified the love of beautiful things as the desire to possess them, and that has been shown to be the desire to be happy. Socrates readily agrees that this is common to all human beings (205a). Diotima asks how one is to explain, then, the fact that all people are not called lovers (205a). She explains it as an example of using a general term to refer to only one of its specific instances, giving as an illustration the restriction of the term "creative," which literally applies to any activity that produces something that was not there before, to apply only to the production of music and verse and not to any other productive crafts (205b–c).

This little wordplay serves to emphasize the universal character of the claim that Diotima is making about love. She is interpreting it as the fundamental drive of all human activity, the basic motivating force of human being: "In general, every desire by everyone for good things and for happiness is 'all-powerful and treacherous Love'" (205d). This universalization of love gives the discussion a profound turn; from here on the topic is the fundamental nature of human being and the basic structure of all human activity, rather than only one aspect of human life. Moreover, this universalization recalls Eryximachus' speech, and Diotima immediately makes a reference to Aristophanes' story, which also makes love the central motivation in human existence (205d–e).

Diotima now adds to the earlier analysis of what it means to love beautiful/good things the claim that people not only want to possess such things as their own, they also want them to be their own "forever" (206a). This point suggests an expectation of immortality, and Diotima uses it to introduce the basic metaphor of her analysis and to challenge the earlier assertion that love aims at possession of the beautiful.

The key metaphor Diotima uses startles and puzzles Socrates, and she repeats it and explains it at some length. The Greek phrase, which occurs at 206b and at 206e, is τόκος ἐν καλῷ (*tokos en kalō*). Τόκος (*tokos*) means "birth." 'Eν (*en*) is a preposition that is very similar to the English term 'in.' Καλῷ (*kalō*) is the adjective "beautiful," in the form appropriate for the object of this preposition. Thus, the phrase is literally "birth in beautiful," but this is misleading, as well as ungrammatical, in English. In Greek, as in English, the singular adjective can be used for a general abstraction or collection, as we say, "You have to take the good with the bad." Hence, *kalō* can be translated as "beauty," which enables us to bring out the adverbial force of the prepositional phrase "in beauty." The preposition here indicates manner rather than location, as when we say, "He lives in poverty," or as in Shelley's line, "She walks in beauty." *Tokos* refers to the productive activity of giving birth, and Diotima applies it to both men and women, as we do in English when we use the term 'birth' metaphorically. The basic metaphor, then, is that of giving birth in a beautiful manner, which can imply that the surroundings and product of the birth, as well as the event itself, are beautiful. Compare the idea of painting, or engaging in any other productive activity, in a beautiful manner. The rest of Diotima's remarks, as reported by Socrates, can be read as an explication of this metaphor.[39]

The first point she makes, as she repeats the metaphor at 206e, is that this view of love interprets it, not as a desire to *possess* beautiful things, but as a desire to *create and produce* "in beauty." She adds the term 'procreation' (γέννησις, *gennēsis*), which usually refers to the father's role in the generation of a child or to the general activity of producing something. This leads to a profound transformation of the understanding of human being, since the fundamental nature of human desire and activity is now seen as involving productivity rather than acquisition.[40] The significance of this shift from possession to creation is sometimes overlooked by interpreters.[41] Diotima concludes this section of her remarks by saying that this procreative activity is eternal and immortal, insofar as anything that is a part of mortal beings can be immortal.

According to Socrates' report, the next issue that Diotima brings up, beginning at 207a, is that of the cause of one's engaging in the activities associated with love. She refers to such activities among nonhuman animals as including not only intercourse and the nurturing of offspring, but even parents' sacrificing their lives for their young. She suggests that we assume that human beings do such things "on the basis of reason" (207b), but why do wild animals do them? The implication that the description of the motivation of action which follows does not apply to "rational" beings is immediately corrected, as Diotima explicitly applies her analysis to human beings (207d). The final implication, therefore, is that love and reason are not in some sort of conflict. Diotima's explication of the "activities of love" is an explication of activity in accordance with reason.

Diotima asserts that this procreative activity, that includes caring for its products, is to be explained as the mortal creature's pursuit of immortality (207d). In fact, she affirms, it is only through creating and leaving behind something new that a mortal creature can have a share in immortality; for as mortal beings we are always changing, and no part of us, either in the body or in the soul,[42] is immortal (207d–208b).

This apparent denial of human immortality by Diotima has caused much perplexity among those interpreters of the *Symposium* who assume that Socrates is here presenting Plato's own view and that this view will be consistent with views defended by Socrates in other dialogues written in the middle period, especially the *Republic*, the *Phaedo*, and the *Phaedrus*, all of which include arguments for immortality.[43] The denial of human immortality seems to be repeated at the end of Diotima's remarks when she says that the person who gives birth to true virtue will "become a friend of the gods, and if any human being could become immortal, he would" (212a)—the implication being that the hypothetical possibility cannot be fulfilled.

A common way of avoiding the apparent conflict with other middle-period dialogues on this issue is to claim that the denial of immortality in the *Symposium* applies only to the "mortal" being, that is, the being that is a combination of body and soul.[44] However, this seems a bit strained, since no one would argue for the immortality of the human being insofar as the being includes the body. Moreover, Diotima seems to explicitly apply her claims of mortal limitation to the soul at 207e. One could see this point in Diotima's remarks as an indication that her views do not, in fact, represent those Plato himself would defend, or as showing that Plato does not always defend the same views.[45]

Diotima concludes this section of her analysis with her first clear description of the life of the person who gives birth in beauty, that is, the life of a person who follows the path of Love. This depiction of the ideal lover is not rejected in what follows. She says that a person who is pregnant in soul, and not just in body, gives birth to what is fitting for the soul, that is, "good sense and the rest of virtue" (209a). And "much the most important and most beautiful aspect of good sense is that which deals with the regulation of cities and households, the name of which is judiciousness and justice" (209a). This kind of lover seeks a beautiful person with whom to produce offspring (209b). Finding such a person, the lover "immediately engages in many conversations with this man about virtue, about what a good man should be like, and what he should make it his business to do; thus, he sets out to educate him" (209b–c).[46] It is important to focus on the fact that this ideal lover is very much engaged in the world, practicing the virtues of ordinary life, ordering cities and households and engaging in useful conversations. The object of his love is not out of this world.

Diotima now says, according to Socrates' report, that all the things she has taught him up to this point are a preparation for the final initiation,[47] which takes the form of an elaborate metaphor of ascending a staircase that leads to the highest form of love (210a ff.). Here the reader finds the union of the divine and the mortal through the daimonic power of Love. This passage is one of the most famous in the Platonic corpus. It is important to read it within its context, and especially in connection with the earlier parts of Diotima's speech and with the speech of Alcibiades.

Virtually all interpreters treat this passage as propounding serious philosophical claims. Nussbaum follows Vlastos in finding in it the presentation of a view of love that takes the object of love to be the universal, rather than the particular individual, a view of love that she condemns herself and argues that Plato is rejecting in this dialogue.[48] Bury takes it as Plato's affirmation of a religious mysticism that focuses on the contemplation of a transcendent, divine reality.[49] Our first task is to examine the text as straightforwardly as possible.

Diotima describes a series of ascending forms of love, using the metaphor of a staircase (210e ff.). From an appreciation of physical beauty, one ascends first to an appreciation of the beauty of practical endeavors and social practices and then to an appreciation of the beauty of knowledge and understanding in general. In the final step of the ascent, Diotima says, "after turning toward the great sea of beauty, [the initiate] studies it and gives birth to many splendidly beautiful conversations and thoughts in a magnanimous philosophy, until, as he becomes more capable and flourishes in this situation, he comes to see a knowledge of a singular sort that is of this kind of beauty" (210d). Here, the initiate "come[s] finally to that understanding which is none other than the understanding of that beauty itself, so that in the end he knows what beauty itself is" (211c). Two questions immediately arise: What is the nature of this beauty that is the ultimate object of love, and what is it like to love it? Diotima responds to both of these questions.

As to its nature, Diotima speaks of it in some of the loftiest language Plato uses anywhere in regard to the forms, the ultimate objects of knowledge. She describes it as "the divine, uniform[50] beautiful itself" (211e). In more detail, she says that it is eternal and unchanging, beautiful in itself and not in connection with or on the basis of its relation to other things so that it might be only relatively beautiful (211a). In fact, other things are beautiful by partaking of or participating in it (211b), using Plato's usual metaphor for the relationship of particular things to the forms, but this does not in any way affect the beautiful itself. It does not have the appearance of a physical object or exist in a physical thing (211a). Moreover, it does not "appear as a particular statement or a particular bit of knowledge" (211a).[51]

The interpretation of this sort of language and of Plato's discussions of the forms throughout the dialogues is controversial, but a number of things seem to be suggested by this passage. In the first place, it seems very clear that the ascent to the final level does not lead to a transcendence of knowledge or reason. Diotima explicitly speaks of this achievement as "a knowledge of a singular sort" (τινὰ ἐπιστήμην μίαν τοιαύτην, *tina epistēmēn mian toiautēn*, 210d) in which the lover achieves an "understanding[52] which is none other than the understanding of that beauty itself, so that in the end he knows[53] what beauty itself is" (211c). This leaves open the question of what sort of knowledge this is, but the text seems clear in asserting that it does not involve going beyond the reach of human understanding.

The only problem about this point is that Diotima also seems to deny that beauty itself can be an object of knowledge. She says at 211a that this thing "that is beautiful in its nature" (210e) "will [not] appear as a particular statement [τις λόγος, *tis logos*] or a particular bit of knowledge [τις ἐπιστήμη, *tis epistēmē*]." The last two Greek words are included, in a different grammatical form, in the phrase translated above as "a [particular bit of] knowledge of a singular sort." Thus, this phrase for what Diotima says *is* possible refers to "a particular bit of knowledge," and yet she says a few lines later that beauty does not appear as such. Since it seems likely that Plato has not accidentally included a contradiction in the text here, one searches for an explanation.

One possibility is to focus on the additional qualification added to the description of the bit of knowledge that is possible, namely, that it is a knowledge "of a singular sort" (μίαν τοιαύτην, *mian toiautēn*) and to ask what sort that might be. Since the denial that beauty itself will appear in a particular bit of knowledge occurs in a context where Diotima is denying that beauty itself can be identified with any particular things in the world, it seems reasonable to assume that she is saying that no statement by anyone at any time about the beauty *of some particular thing* will capture the nature of beauty as such. This would leave open the possibility that the knowledge referred to earlier as that which the ideal lover has of beauty itself will consist, not in a statement about the beauty of a particular thing, but in a statement of a general principle. This is not surprising. We do not expect the statement of a general principle to consist in a list of particular cases; indeed, Socrates regularly objects in various dialogues to efforts to define general terms in that way.[54] So, we can conclude that the nature of the beautiful as such *is* open to rational understanding and can be stated as a general principle.[55]

This still leaves the question of what sort of thing the beautiful itself is, beyond its being an object of knowledge. This is a question about the metaphysical status of the forms, of course, and the poetic language of this passage leaves that question largely unanswered. Since beauty itself is depicted as an available object of knowledge and particular beautiful things are such by "partaking" of it, the form is at least accessible to human beings and the world. It is not, in some literal sense, an otherworldly object. The ascent of the staircase does not lead one out of this world.

Vlastos argues that this passage in the *Symposium* presents the forms as things that are separated from the world in just the sense that Aristotle objects to,[56] that is, the forms are radically transcendent and hence not directly accessible from within this world.[57] It seems more plausible to me to say that Vlastos (along with Aristotle) is taking literally language that is intended metaphorically. As I argue in the next paragraph, it is possible to read this passage as advocating precisely the sort of "separation" of the forms that Aristotle himself affirms, namely, their separation in *logos*.[58]

It is striking that Diotima seems to suggest that the lover will come upon this object at the top of the staircase through becoming capable in conversation/argument/speech (λόγος, *logos*) (210d).[59] Perhaps the forms are to be understood as some sort of linguistic phenomena, structures implicit in language that are made manifest through dialogical examination by those who have mastered the art of speech. This would be consistent with the depiction of Socrates as devoted to conversation and to speeches.[60] This point is emphasized by Alcibiades in his characterization of Socrates. However, all that can be said with confidence on the basis of this passage is that Diotima's analysis suggests that the form of beauty is not to be identified with any particular objects nor with any statements about particular objects, that the form is eternal and unchanging, that the form is discovered in and through conversation, and that seeing it will transform one's life.

This brings us to the second question raised above: What is it like to love/know the beautiful itself? The essential question is whether the life of the lover who has been initiated into "the final rites and mysteries" is different from that Diotima has already described as the life of the one for whom loving the beautiful is participating in the creative process of birth in beauty. Diotima raises this question explicitly: "What do we think it would be like, if someone should happen to see the beautiful itself, pure, clear, unmixed, and not contaminated with human flesh and color and a lot of other mortal silliness, but rather if he were able to look upon the divine, uniform beautiful itself? Do you think it would be a worthless life for a human being to look at that, to study it in the required way, and to be together with it?" (211d–212a). And she answers the question immediately: "Aren't you aware that only there with it, when a person sees the beautiful in the only way it can be seen, will he ever be able to give birth, not to imitations of virtue,...but to true virtue...?" (212a). It is striking that Diotima explicitly connects this discussion of the vision of the beautiful itself with the metaphor of birth in beauty and the life of virtue. Here again, then, the image is that of an intensely engaged life in the world, concerned with ordering cities and households and creating useful conversations. The staircase of love does not lead one out of this world.[61]

One reason some readers find Diotima pointing in this passage toward some sort of religious vision of a transcendent reality and a life of withdrawal from the world in mystical contemplation may be partly the result of a misleading reading of a key Greek term in this passage, namely, the verb θεᾶσθαι, *theasthai*. In this passage the verb is often translated as "to contemplate," but this can be misleading in English. I prefer to translate the term in this context as "to study." The initial impact of Diotima's use of the term at 211d is quite different for most readers under the two translations. She says,

"Here is the life, Socrates, my friend, that a human being should live—studying/contemplating the beautiful itself." When reading "contemplation" in the context of such lofty poetic language, the reader may be tempted to think of an attitude involving a state of passive religious awe. The Greek term does refer to looking at something as an interested and, often, admiring observer, but it is a rational activity, not a mystical vision.

Diotima uses the term earlier in describing the ascent of the staircase. At 210c she says that after moving beyond the love of bodies and souls, the initiate "will be compelled to study/contemplate [θεάσασθαι, *theasasthai*] the beauty in practical endeavors and in laws and traditions and to see that all beauty is related so that he will believe that the beauty connected with the body is of little importance." This seems to refer to an active process of analysis and understanding, not a "transporting" vision that leaves the viewer speechless. There is more emphasis on rapt admiration in the second occurrence of the verb in 211d, where Diotima suggests that those still stuck at the lowest level of love want "to gaze upon [θεᾶσθαι, *theasthai*] your darlings and be together with them all the time." However, the verb occurs again in Alcibiades' speech where it is clear that the reference is to an *understanding* appreciation. Alcibiades has no trouble describing what he is "contemplating": "Socrates was a sight to see [θεάσασθαι, *theasasthai*] when the army was retreating in flight from Delios....I had a better view [ἐθεασάμην, *etheasamēn*] of Socrates that day than at Potidaea" (220e, 221a). The verb also occurs at 190E in Aristophanes' tale. In describing the dissection of the original, spherical human beings, he says that Zeus "ordered Apollo to shift its face and its half-neck around toward the cut, so when it looked [θεώμενος, *theōmenos*] at its own scar the person might be more orderly." Thus the usage of the term in the *Symposium* does not support reading Diotima's remark as pointing toward a mystical experience that transcends the grasp of reason and speech, that is, of *logos*. Nor, of course, does the general character of her description of the life of the lover at the highest level.

The question of whether the ascent to the beautiful itself is a one-way climb is also related to this question of what the life of the person who has made the ascent is like. Although some interpreters have claimed that the lower stages are transcended in a final and permanent way,[62] it seems more likely that the lower stages continue to be recognized as genuine, though limited, manifestations of beauty and hence to be appreciated for the beauty they contain. This is much more compatible with the depicted behavior of Socrates, who is surely being presented as one who has completed the ascent, and with Plato's emphasis on the fact that the person who has seen the beautiful itself will produce true virtue. The initiate's understanding of beauty itself makes possible correct judgments of the beauty of the lower objects, including sexual relationships, conversations, practices, laws, and so on.[63]

The final comment Diotima makes concerning a person who sees the beautiful itself is that "by giving birth to true virtue and nourishing it, he would be able to become a friend of the gods, and if any human being could become immortal, he would" (212a). The hypothetical seems to be counterfactual, that is, it assumes that no human being can in fact "become immortal." This interpretation would be consistent with what seems the most plausible interpretation of her rejection of immortality earlier at 207d–208b. However, the Greek text can be read as merely suggesting that the possibility is one that is rarely actualized, although it is not clear how to understand such an idea. At any rate, the syntactical ambiguity of this passage prevents using it to support the claim that Diotima is not denying immortality in the earlier discussion.

Socrates concludes his speech by again affirming that he is persuaded that Diotima's account of love is true (212b).

THE ARRIVAL OF ALCIBIADES: 212C–215A

With the entrance of Alcibiades, who is roaring drunk, the atmosphere at the party changes dramatically. In the context of the dialogue, Alcibiades is no longer a youth, but he has not yet engaged in the notorious deeds that so tarnished his image. By the time the dialogue is written, however, Plato's readers are well aware of Alcibiades' checkered career. His assistance to the Spartans in their triumph over Athens, as well as his conviction for the destruction of the Herms which prevented him from leading the Sicilian expedition, had caused him to have the reputation of an irreligious traitor, even though he had been later welcomed back to Athens by some. It seems clear that the general view of him was quite negative when Plato was writing and that Socrates was subject to much criticism for his involvement with him when Alcibiades was a youth. Alcibiades could be considered the prime example of a youth whom people could blame Socrates for having corrupted, and it is often argued that one of the goals of the *Symposium* is to portray Socrates' innocence of that charge.[64] In the context of the *Symposium*, however, Alcibiades is a popular, if somewhat scandalous, figure. Obviously admired by the crowd at the party, he acts as a person accustomed to being the center of attention—and to having his own way. His speech in praise of Socrates is the final speech of the *Symposium*.

In the description of his entrance and agreement to give a speech about Socrates (212c–215a), a number of interesting points are made. Alcibiades arrives at the party with the intention of presenting Agathon with a crown of ribbons to commemorate the latter's winning the prize for his tragedy (212e). He is surprized to find Socrates there, sitting beside Agathon in the place of honor (213a–b). His response is to crown Socrates also, noting that while Agathon has triumphed in his recent contest of words, Socrates is always doing so (213e). This emphasis on Socrates as a master wordsmith is an important aspect of Alcibiades' characterization of him.

Alcibiades also reminds us of the claim made earlier about Socrates' capacity as a drinker (214a); here too he triumphs over all human beings, as is illustrated in the final scene of the dialogue (223c–d). One could also find in this outburst of drunken revelry in the dialogue the introduction of the aspect of madness that will be connected with love in the *Phaedrus*. This element becomes more explicit in Alcibiades' description of Socrates and the effect Socrates has on him. In a famous image at 218b he compares the impact of Socrates' arguments to the bite of a snake that will not turn loose and speaks of "the madness and Bacchanalian frenzy of philosophy."

Finally, when Alcibiades has backed into being obliged to give a speech praising Socrates (214d–e), there is an emphasis on the claim that what is about to be said is the truth. Socrates orders Alcibiades to tell the truth about him, and Alcibiades promises to do so, telling Socrates to interrupt him if he says anything that is not true (214e). During his speech, it is explicitly noted that Socrates does not protest against anything Alcibiades says (217b).[65] Thus, as with the reported conversation with Diotima, one could claim that there is an emphasis within the dialogue on the special importance of Alcibiades' speech. And what we get in that speech is considerably more than some amusing anecdotes about Alcibiades' encounters with Socrates. Socrates is presented as the living personification of Love,[66] even though Alcibiades himself does not fully understand the meaning of this. The depiction of the life of Socrates in the stories Alcibiades tells should be compared with the description of the life of love in Socrates' report of Diotima's views. Since Socrates is depicted as affirming that both pictures are true, one assumes that they will illuminate each other, and they do.[67]

ALCIBIADES PRAISES SOCRATES: 215A–222B

Alcibiades begins his speech with a brief characterization of Socrates, based on a comparison of him to the Satyrs, especially the famous flute-playing Satyr, Marsyas (215a–c). Speaking under the influence of the god of wine, Dionysus, Alcibiades shows Socrates to be capable of inducing in his hearers a response that goes far beyond mere intellectual assent to convincing arguments. He compares the bewitching power of Socrates' words to the magical power of a divine flute-player, and the response of listeners to the frenzied excitement of religious enthusiasts (215c–216c). Alcibiades confesses that, although he feels the enormous attraction of Socrates and believes that "whatever Socrates commands must be done" (216e), he himself nevertheless turns away, a slave to the desire for popular fame (216b).

By this confession Alcibiades, in effect, clears Socrates of any blame for his own wrongdoing, but Plato may also be warning the reader to be cautious of accepting Alcibiades' interpretation of Socrates uncritically. The association of Socratic dialectic with the Bacchic enthusiasms of the Corybantes may be a bit startling (215e), but this association of what we may think of as religious inspiration and enthusiasm with Socratic rational enquiry is common in the dialogues.[68] It appears in the *Phaedrus*, and the role of religious inspiration in the work of Socrates is focused on in the dialogue *Theages*. Moreover, Socrates explicitly appeals to religious motivation in his defense of himself in the *Apology*. Perhaps Plato does not think of this element of the religious as something antithetical to the rational. The appeal of the beautiful occurs at many levels, not just at the level of intellectual analysis.

The shortcomings of Alcibiades' understanding of Socrates seem most evident in the story he tells of his attempt to seduce Socrates (217a ff.). In this amusing and revealing anecdote, Alcibiades is frustrated by what he takes as Socrates' refusal to make love to him (219c). However, this simply shows that Alcibiades is still operating on the lowest level of Diotima's staircase, while Socrates is at the highest level, engaging in the creation of beautiful conversations—and trying to assist in the beautification of Alcibiades' soul.

Alcibiades then tells several stories of the deeds of Socrates (219e ff.): his courage in battle, his ability to out-drink everyone without getting drunk, his imperviousness to cold, his power of concentration, his humility and delight in the success of others, his constancy in defeat. Indeed, Alcibiades argues, Socrates is not only an outstanding man, he is so outstanding that he is entirely incomparable (221c–d). Thus, the only comparison one can make is not to human beings, but to the Satyrs (221d).

As he returns to the image with which he began his speech, Alcibiades also returns to his emphasis on Socrates as wordsmith. To the ignorant, he says, Socrates' discussions may appear ridiculous with their homely analogies, but those who can open them up "will find in the first place that they are the only arguments that make sense and then that they are the most divine, that they contain within themselves many marvelous images of virtue, and that when they are fully expanded they deal with everything that a person who wants to be good and beautiful needs to consider" (222a). Throughout his speech, Alcibiades shows Socrates, the ideal philosopher, the ideal personification of Love, and the ideal human being, as intensely engaged in the world, involved in relationships and activities that produce beautiful effects, and, above all, creating beautiful and useful conversations. The lover who reaches the top of Diotima's staircase does not depart from this world; the beautiful itself is found and studied in the production of its worldly manifestations.

THE END OF THE DINNER PARTY: 222C–223D

The conclusion of the dialogue begins with a playful exchange between Socrates, Agathon, and Alcibiades over the order in which they will sit on the couch they are sharing (222e–223b). The controversy is related to the original instruction from Eryximachus that after Alcibiades had spoken he could command Socrates to do whatever he liked and Socrates could do the same to the one on his right (214c). The situation is complicated by continuing charges of jealousy and rivalry, especially between Socrates and Alcibiades for the attention of Agathon. Socrates interprets Eryximachus' instruction to mean that he should praise whoever is sitting on his right (222e), and he uses the enticement of this praise to persuade Agathon to sit on his right while Alcibiades remains on Socrates' left, thus winning the battle for Agathon's attention (223a–b). Alcibiades complains that Socrates continues to triumph over him in the game of love—a remark whose significance is much more profound than Alcibiades himself realizes (223a).

After this demonstration of the practical value of having achieved the highest levels of love, and of the fact that reaching the highest levels does not mean one is unappreciative of the beauties focused on at the lower levels, the party is disrupted by the invasion of a crowd of revellers and disintegrates into a rowdy drinking party (223b). Aristodemus reports that he slept for a time and when he awoke he observed a final conversation between Socrates, Agathon, and Aristophanes (223c–d). Socrates, the only one who is not ultimately overcome by disorder, was persuading them that the same person could compose both comedies and tragedies,[69] but Aristophanes and Agathon soon fall asleep. As morning comes, Socrates sets out for the Lyceum where he spends a normal day, engaging, one assumes, in beautiful conversations, before returning home in the evening to rest (223d). The dialogue ends with a mundane image of the personification of Love engaged in the world of ordinary life, but in his usual extraordinary way.

4
The Phaedrus

INTRODUCTION

The *Phaedrus* presents a complex conversation between Socrates and Phaedrus, a younger man who is also a key figure in the *Symposium*. The dialogue contains three speeches, one ostensibly by the famous rhetorician Lysias, which is read by Phaedrus, and two invented by Socrates for the occasion. Lysias' speech and the first by Socrates are in praise of the advantages of establishing a liaison with a nonlover rather than a lover.[1] Socrates' second speech praises the merits of a lover. After the three speeches are presented, there is a lengthy discussion of the art of making speeches. The *Phaedrus* is usually included among the middle-period dialogues, though whether it was composed before or after the *Symposium* cannot be determined with any certainty.[2]

The dialogue situates the conversation as occurring around 410–405 B.C.E.[3] Socrates is depicted as an older man, and Phaedrus as younger, but not a youth. The Athenian orator Lysias, whose speech plays a large role in the dialogue, had a high reputation in the ancient world. Several of his speeches are extant. Whether the speech attributed to him in the *Phaedrus* was actually from his hand or written by Plato in Lysias' style is a subject of some controversy.[4] The dialogue refers to many other prominent figures in ancient Athens. Especially striking is the reference at the end of the dialogue (278e) to Isocrates, a contemporary of Plato who was a famous teacher of rhetoric and a strong critic of Plato and Socrates as impractical visionaries. There are also a large number of references to the gods in the *Phaedrus*, and several myths are told.

In a special way, this dialogue presupposes a distinctive feature of ancient Athenian society, namely, the prominence of the teaching and practice of rhetoric. As any reader of Plato's *Apology* knows, Athenian justice was decided by large juries. The one Socrates faced contained 500 members. Moreover, the assembly of the citizens had a great deal of power and often served as the ultimate authority in the community. In such a society, the ability to speak persuasively was the key to personal prominence and political success, and teachers of this skill were highly regarded and richly rewarded. A number of these teachers and the things they taught are discussed in this dialogue.

The overall structure of the *Phaedrus* is fairly simple: Socrates and Phaedrus meet and decide to go to a quiet place outside of town to read a speech by Lysias. In response to Lysias' speech Socrates gives two speeches of his own. He and Phaedrus then engage in an extended discussion of the art of making speeches. A simple outline would be:

1. Introduction: 227a–230e
2. The Speeches about Love: 230e–257b
   - A. Lysias' speech: 230e–234c
   - B. Socrates' first speech: 237a–241a
   - C. Socrates' second speech: 243e–257b
3. The Art of Making Speeches: 257b–278b
4. Conclusion: 278b–279c

THE DIALOGUE

SOCRATES: My friend Phaedrus! Where are you going and where have you 227a
come from?

PHAEDRUS: From Lysias,[5] the son of Cephalus, Socrates, and I'm going for a walk outside the walls because I sat there for a long time, from early morning, in fact. And since I obey that associate of yours and mine, Acumenus,[6] I take walks along the country roads, for he says they are less exhausting than laps around the exercise tracks. 227b

S: Well, he's right in saying so, my friend. So it seems Lysias was in town, then.

P: Yes, at Epicrates' place, the house that used to be Morychus's, near the temple of Olympian Zeus.[7]

S: How did you spend the time? Or is it obvious that Lysias was entertaining you with a feast of his speeches?

P: You shall hear, if you have the leisure to come along and listen.

S: What! Don't you think that I'd make hearing how you and Lysias passed the time something that, as Pindar says, "is even more important than business?"[8]

P: Lead on, then. 227c

S: Please speak.

P: Actually, Socrates, it's appropriate that you should hear it because the speech with which we were passing the time was, well, erotic, in a way.[9] Lysias has actually written out an attempted seduction of a handsome boy—but not by a lover! That's what's so impressive! He says that one should gratify[10] the one who does not love rather than the one who does.[11]

S: Ah, the noble fellow! If only he would write that one should gratify a poor man rather than a rich one, and an older man rather than a younger one, and so on for the many other things that are characteristic of me and of most
of us. Then his speeches would indeed be urbane and beneficial to the general 227d
public. Of course, I'm so eager to hear it that if you walk as far as Megara[12] on your stroll, I won't be left behind by you, even if you come right back after you reach the wall, as Herodicus[13] recommends.

P: My dear Socrates! What are you saying? Do you expect an amateur
like me to recite from memory, and without disgracing Lysias, what that 228a
cleverest of current writers composed at leisure over a long period of time? That's way beyond me, although I'd rather be able to do that than come into a large fortune.

S: Oh, Phaedrus! If I don't know Phaedrus, I have forgotten myself, yet
neither of these things is true. I know very well that, while listening to Lysias'
speech, this fellow didn't hear it only once, but urged Lysias to speak and
repeat it many times, and Lysias was gladly persuaded to do so. However, this
wasn't enough for him, and finally, seizing the manuscript, he went over the 228b
parts that he liked best. After sitting and doing this since early morning, he
grew tired and went for a walk, as I suspect, by the dog,[14] knowing the speech
by heart, unless it was very long. He was setting out on a walk outside the
walls to practice it. Then, when he met someone who is obsessive about listening to speeches, he was delighted to see him because now he would have
someone with whom to share his Corybantic revels,[15] and he urged him to
lead the way. When the lover of speeches begged him to speak, he became 228c
coy, pretending he didn't want to speak, though he intended to do so in the
end, even if he had to force himself upon an unwilling audience. So, Phaedrus, require him to do right now what he'll soon be doing in any case.[16]

P: By far the best thing for me, surely, is to speak in whatever way I can, since you don't seem at all likely to let me go until I speak somehow or other.

S: Well, your surmise about me is quite true.

P: Then this is what I'll do. Actually, Socrates, I didn't really learn his 228d
exact words by heart, but I'll go through the general sense of all his points
about how the one who loves differs from the one who does not, going
through them in order beginning with the first.

S: After you first show, dear friend, what you're holding in your left
hand under your cloak! I suspect you have the speech itself. If that's so,
believe this of me, that though I am of course your friend, if Lysias himself is 228e
here, I have no intention of making myself available for you to practice on.
Come on, show it.

P: Stop! You've dashed my hope of using you for a rehearsal, Socrates, but where do you want us to sit while we read?

S: Let's turn aside here and go along the Ilissus; then we can sit down in 229a
a quiet spot wherever you like.

P: It's fortunate, it seems, that I happen to be barefooted; you, of course, always are.[17] So, it will be easiest for us to wade in the stream getting our feet wet, which won't be unpleasant, especially at this hour at this time of year.

S: Then lead on, and look for a place where we can sit down.

P: Well then, do you see that very tall plane-tree?[18]

S: What about it?

P: There's shade there and a moderate breeze, and grass to sit on or, if 229b
we'd like, to lie down on.

S: Please lead the way.

P: Tell me, Socrates, isn't it from somewhere along here on the Ilissus that Boreas is said to have abducted Oreithuia?[19]

S: So they say.

P: Was it from right here? The water certainly seems delightfully pure and sparkling, a suitable spot for young girls to play.

S: No, the place is some two or three hundred yards farther along, where 229c
we cross over to the district of Agra.[20] There's an altar to Boreas[21] at the spot.

P: I haven't really noticed. But tell me, Socrates, before Zeus, do you believe this mythical tale to be true?

S: If I disbelieved it, as the wise do, I wouldn't be odd.[22] In that case,
being wise, I might say that while she was playing with Pharmaceia[23] a puff of
wind[24] pushed her off the nearby rocks, and that when she came to her end in
this manner she was said to have been carried off by Boreas. Or else it was
from the Areopagus,[25] for the story is also told that she was abducted from 229d
there rather than from here. I myself, Phaedrus, believe that such things, while
amusing, are the work of a man who is exceedingly clever and industrious but
not at all fortunate for no other reason than that after this he must account for
the form of the Centaurs and then for that of the Chimaera, and then a crowd of
such creatures floods in upon him, Gorgons and Pegasuses and a great number
of other inexplicable and odd creatures of which strange things are said.[26] If 229e
someone who disbelieves in these things is to bring forth a plausible account of
each of them, using a sort of rustic ingenuity, he'll need a great deal of leisure.
I myself have no leisure at all for such business, and the reason for that, my
friend, is this: I'm not yet able, in accordance with the Delphic[27] inscription, to
know myself, and it seems ridiculous to me to investigate things that don't con- 230a
cern me while still lacking that knowledge. So, I leave those matters alone, and
being persuaded by what is traditionally maintained about them, I investigate
(as I was saying just now) not those things but myself, as to whether I happen
to be a beast more complex and agitated than Typhon,[28] or a gentler and sim-
pler animal, possessing by nature a divine and un-Typhonic lot.

But, my friend, in the midst of our conversation, isn't this the tree that you were leading us to?

P: That's so; this is it. 230b

S: By Hera,[29] it is a beautiful resting place! This plane-tree is very wide-spreading and tall. The height and thick shade of the chaste tree[30] are also

splendid, and since it's in full bloom, it will make the place very fragrant. Moreover, the spring flowing from under the plane-tree is very pleasant, with quite cold water, to judge by my foot. From the figurines and statues it seems
to be a place sacred to some of the Nymphs and Achelous.[31] Furthermore, if 230c
you please, the fresh breezes of the place are lovely and exceedingly sweet, reverberating with the shrill summer chorus of the cicadas. However, the most exquisite thing of all is this grassy slope whose gentle rise makes a quite comfortable and natural place to rest one's head while lying down. You are an excellent guide for the visiting stranger, Phaedrus my friend!

P: And you, you surprising man, appear to be the oddest person. You really seem to be a visiting stranger being guided around, as you say, and not
a native. You seem to me to be acting as though you never go out across the 230d
frontier and in fact as though you don't even go outside the city walls!

S: Forgive me, you most excellent fellow, for I'm a friend of learning. The countryside and the trees don't want to teach me anything, but the people in town do. Yet you seem to me to have found the prescription[32] to bring me out. Just as people lead hungry animals by shaking a branch or some fruit in front of them, it appears that by holding manuscripts of speeches out in front
of me you can lead me all around Attica and anywhere else you wish. Now 230e
that we've arrived at this place, I intend to lie down, and you, when you've taken whatever position you think easiest for reading, read.

P: Listen, then.

You understand my situation, and you have heard how I think it would be to our advantage for this to happen. Because I am not your lover, I deserve not
to be disappointed in what I request. When lovers' desires cease, they regret 231a
their earlier generosity, but for nonlovers there never comes a time when they find it appropriate to change their minds. Nonlovers are as generous as they can be, not out of compulsion, but willingly, for they make their plans in terms of what is in their own best interest.

Furthermore, when those who love consider their earlier generosity and the way their own interests have been managed badly because of their love, and when they also take into account the trouble they have had, they believe
that they long ago repaid those they love for their kindness. But those who do 231b
not love cannot make this excuse of neglect of their own interests because of their condition, nor count up past troubles, nor make accusations about quarrels with their relatives. Hence, since these evils are removed, nothing remains for those who do not love but to do eagerly whatever they think will gratify the recipients of their attention.

Furthermore, if lovers are highly regarded because they say they are the 231c
greatest of friends to those they love and that they are prepared to be hated by

others for their words and their deeds in order to please those they love, it is easy to see, if they are telling the truth, that those whom they fall in love with later will matter more to them than their earlier loves; and it is clear that, if their later loves suggest it, they will treat the earlier ones badly.

Moreover, how reasonable is it to trust such a matter to someone who has an affliction that no experienced person would even attempt to cure? They 231d
themselves agree that they are more mad than sane and that they know their intentions are wrong but cannot control themselves. So, how could they believe, when they return to their senses, that the decisions they made in that condition were well taken?

In fact, if you choose the best of your lovers, the best will be from a small group, but if you choose the one most suitable to yourself from among the others, it will be from a large group. There is a much greater hope of there 231e
being someone worthy of your friendship in the large group.

Now, if prevailing convention makes you fear that you will be criticized if people find out, consider that lovers, since they believe others take them to 232a
be as worthy of emulation as they themselves do, are likely to get carried away in telling stories and will boastfully[33] proclaim to everyone that their efforts have not been in vain, but those who do not love are in control of themselves and will choose what is best rather than a public reputation.

Furthermore, many people will inevitably see and hear about lovers following those they love around and making this their business, so that whenever they are seen talking to each other, people will assume that they are 232b
together because their desire either has been or is about to be satisfied. However, no one even tries to criticize nonlovers for being together, since they know that one may have to talk with someone because of friendship or for some other pleasant purpose.

In fact, if you are afraid because you believe that it is difficult to hold a friendship together and that, while in other circumstances a quarrel would be a misfortune shared in common by both sides, when you have given away 232c
what you value most a quarrel would come as a great loss to yourself, then it would be reasonable for you to fear lovers more. Many things upset them, and they think that everything that happens is done to injure them. That is why they prevent those they love from associating with others, for they fear those with property, lest they surpass them in wealth, and those who are educated, lest they be superior in intellect. And they are on their guard against anyone 232d
who has acquired any other advantages. Then, if they persuade you to incur the hatred of these men, they leave you without any friends. On the other hand, if you are more sensible than they and consider your own interests, you will find that you have aroused their animosity. However, those who happened not to love, but have obtained what they want through merit, would not be jealous of those associating with you, but would detest those who do not want to do so, believing you are not appreciated by the latter, but are benefit-

ted by associations with the former. Thus, there is a much greater hope that 232e
friendship rather than animosity will come to you from the affair.

In fact, many lovers will desire your body before they know your character or become acquainted with your circumstances, so that it is unclear to them whether they will still want to be friends after their desire ceases. But in
the case of those who are not lovers, who were friends with each other before 233a
they did these things, their friendship is not likely to be diminished by the things they are fortunate enough to receive from the affair; on the contrary, such things remain as memorials of what is to come.

In fact, it will be better for you to be under my influence rather than that of a lover. They commend whatever you say and do, even when it is less than
the best, partly because they fear incurring your animosity and partly because 233b
their judgment is impaired by their desire. For this is how love manifests itself: it makes those who are unsuccessful treat as grievances things that do not cause distress in others, and it compels those who are successful to commend things that ought not even to be considered pleasant. So, rather than emulating them, those they love really ought to pity them. If you accept my proposal, my primary concern in associating with you will not be present
pleasure, but future benefit, since I am not the slave of love but my own mas- 233c
ter. I will not be provoked to violent hostility over trivial matters; on the contrary, major problems will make me only a little angry, and that slowly. I will forgive unintentional slights and try to prevent intentional ones. Such things guarantee that a friendship will last a long time.

If it has been put to you that friendship cannot be significant unless one happens to be in love, you must consider that in that case our sons would not
be very important to us, nor our fathers and mothers, nor would we have faith- 233d
ful friends who have not been acquired through that sort of desire but on the basis of other concerns.

Furthermore, if one ought to gratify those who are most in need, then it would be appropriate for you to be generous, not to the best people, but to the most needy, for they will be most grateful since they have been relieved of the greatest sufferings. In fact, it would also be appropriate for you to invite to
private parties, not your friends, but beggars in need of a meal, for they will 233e
adore you, follow you around, and hang around your front door. They will be most delighted and grateful and will pray that you receive many blessings. Perhaps, however, it is appropriate to gratify, not those with the greatest need, but rather those who are best able to return the kindness; not those who are
merely in love with you, but rather those who are worthy of the affair; not 234a
those who will enjoy your youthful good looks, but rather those who will share their possessions with you when you are older; not those who, when they have been successful, will boast of it to everyone,[34] but rather those who out of modesty will tell no one; not those who court you zealously for a short time, but rather those who will be steadfast friends throughout their entire life;

and not those who, when their desire ceases, will look for some excuse for breaking up with you, but rather those who will display their own excellence when your youthful good looks have passed. 234b

So, remember what has been said and bear in mind that their friends admonish lovers for engaging in bad behavior, but not even a relative has ever admonished those who do not love for making bad decisions about their own interests on that account.

Perhaps you will ask me, then, if I am advising you to gratify everyone who does not love you. I do not believe that a lover would urge you to think that way about everyone who loves you. Your kindness would not be so much 234c
appreciated by the recipient in that case, nor would you be able to hide your relationship with the one from the others, if you should wish to do so. No harm at all should come from this sort of affair; it should benefit both parties.

So, I think that what has been said is sufficient, but if you believe that anything has been omitted, and want more, just ask.

P: What do you think of the speech, Socrates? Isn't it superb, both in terms of its language and in other respects?

S: It does have an unearthly[35] power, my friend, so that I was astounded 234d
by it. I felt that way because of you, Phaedrus. As I looked at you, you seemed to me to be set aglow by the speech as you read. Since I believe you understand such things better than I do, I followed your lead and joined your divinely inspired self in Bacchanalian ecstasy.[36]

P: What! Does it seem a joking matter?

S: Why, do you think I'm being playful rather than serious?

P: Not at all, Socrates; but tell me truly, before Zeus the god of friend- 234e
ship, do you think that anyone else among the Greeks could speak more ably or fully on the same subject?

S: What's this? Should you and I praise the speech as one in which the author has said what he ought to have, rather than merely because each of his expressions has been precisely crafted in a clear and well-turned manner? If we should, we must agree to do so on for your authority since, on account of my negligence, that aspect of it escaped my notice. I paid attention to it only as an example of rhetoric, and in that regard I would think that Lysias himself 235a
wouldn't consider it satisfactory. In fact, it seemed to me, Phaedrus, unless you disagree, that he repeated the same things two or three times, as though he didn't find it very easy to say much about the subject or perhaps wasn't really interested in it. Indeed, he appeared to me to be indulging in youthful extravagance, showing off his ability to say the same thing in two different ways, both stated in the best possible manner.

P: You're talking nonsense, Socrates. That's the greatest thing about the 235b speech: it omits nothing that ought to be said about the subject, so that no one could ever speak on this topic in a more complete or more admirable way.

S: You won't persuade me of that. If I should agree, just to please you, wise men and women who have spoken and written about these matters in the past will refute me.

P: Who are these people? Where have you heard something better than 235c
this?

S: I can't say just now, but I'm sure I've heard better from someone, perhaps from the beautiful Sappho or the wise Anacreon[37] or even from some prose writers. On what grounds do I say this? Somehow, you divine fellow, the fullness of my heart makes me feel I could say some things about this subject that would be different and not inferior. Now, I am well aware that I've not thought them up by myself; I know my own ignorance. So, I assume
they're the remains of others' efforts that poured in while I was listening and 235d
filled me up like a jug, but through stupidity I've forgotten where and from whom I heard them.

P: An excellent proposal, most noble Socrates! Don't tell me, even if I demand it, where or from whom you heard these things, but just do what you're suggesting. You've promised that you'll offer different points than those in the manuscript that are better and no fewer in number; and I promise you that, for my part, like the nine Archons, I'll put up a golden, life-sized
statue in Delphi, not only of myself, but of you also. 235e

S: You are a dear friend and truly golden, Phaedrus, if you think I'm saying that Lysias has completely missed the mark and that I could say something entirely different from what he says. I don't think that could happen even with the poorest writer. For example, regarding the subject of his speech, do you suppose that anyone could argue that one should gratify the one who
does not love rather than the one who does and omit praise of the good sense 236a
of the one and condemnation of the foolishness of the other, which are inevitable points, and say something different instead? I think such points must be allowed and the speaker be forgiven for using them. Of such things, we should praise not the invention, but the presentation. In the case of points that are not inevitable, and are difficult to invent, we should praise both their presentation and their invention.

P: I agree with what you're saying. Your point seems reasonable; so this
is what I'll do. I'll allow you to use the assumption that the lover is more mad 236b
than the nonlover, but for the rest, when you state a greater number of points than those of Lysias, that are different and better than his, your statue shall stand beside the offering of the Cypselids at Olympia.[38]

S: Have you taken me seriously, Phaedrus, because in order to tease you I attacked your darling?[39] Do you really think I'm actually going to attempt to say something different and of greater ingenuity, than the output of his wisdom?

P: As to that, my friend, I've got you in the bind you had me in earlier. You certainly must speak as best you can, lest we be compelled to perform the 236c
tedious role of comedians engaging in repartee. Be careful, and don't deliberately force me to say, "Socrates, if I don't know Socrates, I have forgotten myself," or "he wanted to speak but he became coy." Instead, take note that we're not going to leave this spot until you state what you said was filling your heart. We're alone in this isolated place, and I'm stronger and younger. Given all these circumstances, "hark what I am saying"[40] and don't choose to 236d
speak under duress when you could speak voluntarily.

S: But, Phaedrus, you lucky fellow, I'll be a laughingstock if I, an amateur, improvise on the same subject in competition with an accomplished author.

P: You know the situation. Stop putting on airs. I can say something that will very nearly compel you to speak.

S: Then you shouldn't say it.

P: I shouldn't, but I shall; and my speech will be an oath. I swear to you—by what, by which god? Or do you prefer it be by this plane-tree here? Well, then, I swear that unless you deliver your speech in the presence of this 236e
very tree, I will never show you or report to you another speech by anyone, not a single one!

S: Alas! You bloody wretch! What an effective means you've discovered for compelling a man who's a friend of speeches to do what you command.

P: Then why do you twist and turn so?

S: Not any more, since you've sworn that oath. How could I survive without that sort of banquet?

P: Speak then! 237a

S: Do you know what I'm going to do?

P: In what regard?

S: I'm going to speak with my head covered, so that I can rush through my speech as quickly as possible and, by not looking at you, avoid faltering through being ashamed.

P: Just speak! Do whatever you like otherwise.

S: Lead on then, clear-voiced Muses—whether you have the name clear-voiced because of the quality of your song or because of the race of Ligurians[41] who are adept in the arts of the Muses. Take hold with me of the tale this excellent fellow here forces me to tell, so that his associate, who seemed wise to him before, will now seem even more so. 237b

There once was a boy, or rather a young man, who was very handsome and had a great many lovers. One of them, a crafty fellow who loved him no less than the others, had convinced the boy that he did not love him. And on one occasion when he was courting him, he tried to convince him of this very point, that one ought to gratify the one who does not love in preference to the one who does, and he spoke as follows.

For those who intend to consider something successfully, my boy, there is only one way to begin in every case. They must know what it is they are deliberating about, or they will inevitably miss the mark entirely. Most people 237c fail to realize that they do not know what things really are. So, since they assume they know, they do not establish mutually agreed upon definitions at the beginning of their enquiry, and as they proceed the result is what you would expect: they agree neither with themselves nor with each other. Now, let's not allow ourselves to suffer what we are condemning in others. Since the question before us is whether one should enter into a friendship with one who loves or with one who does not, let us agree on a definition of love, as to what sort of thing it is and what power it possesses, and make our enquiry as 237d to whether it brings benefit or harm with this held in view for reference.

It is clear to everyone that love is some sort of desire. Moreover, we know that even those who are not lovers desire beautiful things. How then are we to distinguish the one who loves from the one who does not?

We must note that there are two sorts of ruling or guiding principles in each of us, which we follow wherever they lead. One is the innate desire for pleasure, and the other is an acquired judgment that aims at what is best. These two principles in us are sometimes in accord, and sometimes they are at variance. Sometimes one prevails and at other times the other. When judg- 237e ment guides us by reason[42] toward what is best and is strong enough to prevail, we call that judiciousness. When desire rules in us and drags us toward pleasure in a manner contrary to reason, its rule is called *hubris*.[43] But *hubris* 238a has many names, for it has many parts and takes many forms, and whichever of these forms happens to dominate gives its name to the person who has what is called by that name—an acquisition without honor or merit. For example, when the desire for food prevails over rational judgment as to what is best as well as over other desires, it is called gluttony and gives the corresponding 238b name of glutton to the person who has it. When the desire for strong drink becomes the tyrant and leads the person who possesses it toward drink, it is obvious what name he is called, and with regard to other such desires and the related names for people who have them, it is quite clear that whenever one of the desires dominates it is appropriate to be called by its name.

The point of all that has been said up to now is already rather obvious, but everything is probably clearer when stated than when not. The irrational desire that leads us toward the enjoyment of beauty and overpowers the judgment that directs us toward what is right, and that is victorious in leading us 238c toward physical beauty when it is powerfully strengthened by the desires related to it, takes its name from this very strength and is called love.[44]

Well, Phaedrus, my friend, does it seem to you, as it does to me, that I've been seized by a divinely inspired passion?

P: Certainly, Socrates, some sort of unusual fluency has seized you.

S: Then hear me in silence. This place really does seem divine; so if, as I present my speech, I often seem to be possessed by the Nymphs, don't be sur- 238d prised. Already I'm close to speaking in the dithyrambic style.[45]

P: What you say is very true.

S: It's you who are responsible for this. But hear the rest of it; perhaps what threatens can be averted, although that's a matter for a god—we must return to the boy in our speech.

Well, you most fortunate fellow, what it is that we are to deliberate about has been stated and defined. Keeping that in view, let us talk about what remains, namely, what benefit or harm is likely to come from the lover and the 238e nonlover to the one who gratifies them.

Anyone ruled by desire and enslaved by pleasure inevitably makes his beloved as delightful to himself as possible, and to someone who is sick, all lack of opposition is pleasant, while superiority or equality is offensive. So, a lover will not tolerate a darling who is superior or equal to himself, but always 239a makes him inferior and deficient by comparison; and the ignorant is inferior to the wise, the cowardly to the brave, the incompetent speaker to the orator, the slow to the quick-witted. A lover is bound to be pleased when such intellectual defects and more besides develop or exist by nature in the one he loves, and he will try to induce more in him lest he be deprived of his immediate pleasure. In fact, a lover is inevitably jealous and causes great harm by pre- 239b venting many advantageous associations with others that would greatly facilitate his beloved's growing into manhood, and the greatest harm will be caused by preventing that association which would make his beloved supremely wise. This happens to be philosophy, the divine friendship with wisdom, which a lover inevitably keeps his darling away from for fear of becoming an object of contempt. He will also contrive other ways to keep him ignorant in every regard and dependent on his lover for everything, so that the beloved will be most pleasant for his lover, but most damaging to himself. With regard to intellectual matters, then, a man who is in love is in no way a 239c profitable guardian and companion.

We must next consider the condition and care of the body as to how someone who is compelled to pursue pleasure in preference to good will take care of that when he becomes one's master. He will be seen to pursue someone who is soft rather than tough, who was not reared in clear sunshine but in mottled shade, who is unacquainted with manly toil and dried sweat, but accustomed to a soft, unmanly way of life, who uses artificial cosmetics to 239d
cover his lack of a natural complexion, and all the other practices that go along with these, which are obvious and not worth further enumeration. We can go on to other things after making a single statement in summation: this is the sort of body that, in war and in other important crises, inspires confidence in one's enemies and apprehension in one's friends—and even in one's lovers themselves.

We may leave that as obvious, but we must talk about what's next in order, namely, what benefit or harm to us the company and guardianship of the 239e
lover will bring in regard to our possessions. It is evident to everyone, and especially to a lover, that he would pray above all that his beloved be bereft of those who are for him the most friendly, most well-intentioned, and most divine, for a lover would welcome his beloved's being deprived of father and mother, relatives and friends, since he believes they will cause difficulties and 240a
raise objections to his most delightful relationship with his beloved. Moreover, he will believe that someone who has property, whether gold or other possessions, will not be as easily caught nor, when caught, as easily managed. As a result it is altogether inevitable that a lover will be jealous of the property his darling possesses and rejoice at its loss. Furthermore, a lover would pray that his darling be without wife, children, or home as long as possible, since he wants to enjoy his beloved's sweetness all by himself for as long as possible.

There are also other evils, but some divine agency has added a momentary pleasure to most of them, as, for example, in the case of a sycophant, who 240b
is a terrible beast and very harmful, yet his nature nevertheless includes a certain pleasantness that is not entirely unrefined. Some would also condemn as harmful a prostitute and many other similar creatures and practices that are very pleasant at the time. A lover, however, besides being harmful to his darling, is also a most unpleasant thing to live with on a daily basis. There is an ancient saying to the effect that people who are one age enjoy those of the 240c
same age (I suppose the equality of age leads to similar tastes in pleasure and produces friendship through such similarity), yet even companions of this sort can grow tired of being together. Moreover, compulsiveness of every sort is said to be oppressive to everyone, and a lover, in addition to the dissimilarity of age, certainly has that in relation to his darling. An older man associating with a younger one will not be willingly left behind either by day or by night. He is driven by a tormenting compulsion that leads him on by giving him con- 240d
tinual pleasure from seeing, hearing, touching, and experiencing his beloved through all his senses, so that he delights in serving all his darling's needs.

Yet what consolation or pleasure can he give his beloved that could prevent the extended time they spend together being extremely unpleasant for the beloved? The beloved must look at a face that is old and past its prime, and other things that go along with that which it is unpleasant even to hear talked 240e
about, let alone to deal with when one is constantly compelled to confront them: being suspiciously guarded all the time against everybody; and hearing importunate and exaggerated compliments as well as criticisms that are intolerable when he is sober but when he is in his cups and indulges freely in coarse and uninhibited language, become not only intolerable but disgusting.

While a lover loves he is harmful and unpleasant, but when he ceases to love, he becomes dishonest regarding the future—for which he made many promises with frequent vows and pleadings. Thus, while he was barely managing to get his beloved to tolerate the onerous relationship at the time on the 241a
basis of a hope for the benefits to come, when the time comes to pay up, since the lover has switched to a different ruler and commander in himself, namely, intelligence and judiciousness instead of love and madness, he has become a different person. His darling does not realize this and asks for a return on his kindness in earlier times, reminding him of what was said and done, as though he were talking to the same person. However, the lover is ashamed to admit straightforwardly that he has become a different person, nor can he make good the vows and promises he made when he was ruled by his earlier folly, 241b
having now recovered his mind and become judicious, lest by doing what he did then he again become the same person he was then. As a result of this the former lover runs away, and acts like someone compelled to default. When the shell falls with the other side up, he changes directions and departs in a rush.[46] The other, angry and calling upon the gods, is forced to pursue. From the beginning he has not understood that he should never have gratified a lover, who is inevitably out of his mind, but rather one who is in possession of 241c
his mind and not in love. To do the opposite is inevitably to enslave oneself to someone who is untrustworthy, peevish, jealous, disagreeable, harmful to one's property, harmful to one's physical condition, and above all harmful to the education of one's soul, than which there neither is nor ever will be anything that is truly more valuable to human beings or to the gods.

So, dear boy, one must take these things into consideration and realize that the friendship of a lover does not come from goodwill, but from something like the desire for a satisfying meal. As wolves cherish lambs, so lovers befriend boys.

241d

That's it, Phaedrus! You won't hear another word from me! Let my speech for you end right there.

P: But I assumed that was its mid-point and you were about to make an equal number of points about the nonlover, mentioning his good qualities and why one ought to gratify him rather than the other. So, why are you stopping now, Socrates?

S: Didn't you notice, you lucky fellow, that I've gone beyond a dithyram- 241e
bic to an epic style,[47] and have done that while being critical? If I begin praising the other, what do you think I'll do? Do you see that I'll surely be possessed by the Nymphs to whom you deliberately threw me? So, I'll say it in a single sentence: whatever characteristics we condemned in the one, the opposite good characteristics are present in the other. Why make a long speech?
What's been said is enough for both. So, my tale[48] shall suffer whatever it 242a
deserves, and I shall cross this stream and depart before you force me to do anything else.

P: Not yet, Socrates, while it's still so hot. Don't you see that it's already nearly noon, which is called the standing-still time?[49] Let's wait and discuss what's been said and leave a little later, after it cools off.

S: Phaedrus, you are simply amazing and have a superhuman[50] enthusiasm for speeches! Of the speeches that have been made during your lifetime,
I suspect that no one's produced more than you, either by delivering them 242b
yourself or by compelling others to do so in one way or another. I except Simmias the Theban[51] from the account, but you easily surpass the others. Now once again you seem to me to have become the cause of my making a speech.

P: That's certainly not bad news! But how am I such a cause and what speech is this?

S: Just as I was about to cross the stream, my good man, my familiar daimonic sign came to me;[52] it always holds me back from something I am about 242c
to do. All at once I seemed to hear a voice forbidding me to leave before I purify myself, as I have committed an offense against the divine. Now, I am a prophet, not a very serious one, but, like people who are barely literate, good enough for my own purposes. So, I already clearly understand my offense. In fact, my friend, the soul really is prophetic in a way. Even while I was delivering my speech I was troubled by something, and was concerned, as Ibycus[53]
says, "that I might win honor among human beings by sinning against the 242d
gods." Now I perceive my offense.

P: What do you mean?

S: That terrible, terrible speech Phaedrus, both the one you brought and the one you forced me to deliver.

P: How is it so?

S: By being foolish and rather irreligious. What could be more terrible than that?

P: Nothing, if what you say is true.

S: Then what about this? Don't you believe that Love is the son of Aphrodite and is a god?[54]

P: So it's said.

S: Not by Lysias, nor by your speech that was uttered by my mouth after
it was bewitched by you. If Love is a god or something divine, as he surely is, 242e
he couldn't be evil, but both speeches just now spoke of him as though he were such. That was their offense in relation to Love. Yet their foolishness was very sophisticated; while saying what was neither sound nor true, they
puffed themselves up like something important in the hope that they might 243a
deceive some little humanoids into having a high opinion of them. So, my friend, I must purify myself, and there's an ancient purification for those who give offense in tale-telling. Though Homer didn't know about it, Stesichorus[55] did. When the latter was struck blind for speaking ill of Helen, he wasn't, like Homer, ignorant of the reason, but, as one adept in the arts of the Muses, he knew, and promptly composed these lines:

> That story was not true;
> Neither did you step into the well-oared ships,
> Nor did you come to the citadel of Troy. 243b

As soon as he had finished the entire so-called *Recantation*, he immediately recovered his sight. Now, I shall be wiser than they were in this matter. Before I suffer any punishment for my speaking ill of Love, I'll attempt to render my recantation to him, with my head bare and not hidden as before out of shame.

P: Nothing you could say would delight me more, Socrates.

S: That, good Phaedrus, is because you realize how shamelessly the two 243c
speeches were uttered, that last one and the one you read from the manuscript. If someone with a noble and gentle character, who loves or has ever loved another of the same sort, should hear us saying that lovers respond to small slights with great hostility and are jealous and harmful to their darlings, don't you think he'd believe he was listening to people brought up among sailors,
who've never seen love among free men? Wouldn't he disagree strongly with 243d
our criticism of Love?

P: By Zeus, perhaps he would, Socrates.

S: Then, because I'm ashamed before that person and afraid of Love himself, I want to wash out the unpleasant taste of what we've heard with a fresh speech. I also advise Lysias to write as quickly as possible that, other things being equal, one ought to gratify a lover rather than a nonlover.

P: Be assured that that will be done. After you speak in praise of the lover, I shall most certainly make Lysias in turn write a speech on the same subject. 243e

S: I'm sure of that, as long as you are who you are.

P: Then speak with confidence.

S: Where's that boy of mine I was talking to? He must hear this also, lest from not hearing it he go and gratify the one who doesn't love.

P: He's always here, right beside you, whenever you want him.

S: Now then, my handsome boy, bear in mind that while the previous
speech was by Phaedrus, the son of Pythocles, a man of Myrrinous, the one I 244a
am about to deliver is by Stesichorus, the son of Euphemus, of Himera.[56] And this is what must be said:

That speech is not true which says that when a lover is at hand one ought instead to gratify someone who does not love, on the grounds that the former is mad and the other is in command of his senses. If it were a simple fact that madness is evil, that would be good advice, but as it is, the greatest goods come to us through the madness that is given as a divine gift.

The prophetess at Delphi and the priestesses at Dodona[57] have done many
admirable things for Greece in public and private matters while they were 244b
mad, but little or nothing while in possession of their senses. If we should also speak of the Sibyl[58] and of others who through divinely inspired prophecy have foretold many things for many people and guided them into a better future, we would prolong a discussion of what is obvious to everyone. However, it is worth pointing out that the ancient people who gave things their names also believed that madness is neither shameful nor blameworthy; otherwise, they would not have connected the word itself with the noblest art,
that by which the future is judged, by calling it the *manikēs* [mad] art. They 244c
gave it that name because they believed it a fine thing when it comes as a divine gift. The present generation, however, awkwardly inserts a 't' and calls it the *mantikēs* [prophetic] art. Moreover, the ancients called the art by which people seek out the future while in possession of their senses, using birds and other signs, *oionoistikēs* [augury] since they provide *nous* [intelligence] and *historia* [information] for humanly inspired *oiēsis* [speculation] through their
dianoia [analysis], although modern people now call it *oiōnistikēs* [augury], 244d
making it sound more impressive by lengthening the second 'o.' Thus the ancients attest that as the prophetic art is more perfect and more valuable than the auguristic art, both in name and deed, so is the madness that comes from a god than the sanity that is of human origin.

In the second place, madness has appeared in certain families that have

been afflicted with the greatest diseases and problems because of ancient provocations and, through prophecy, has found relief for those needing it by 244e
recourse to prayers and services for the gods. Thus, through purifications and rituals it happens upon, it makes those who are mad safe, both for the present and for the future, obtaining deliverance from their present afflictions for those who are maddened and possessed in the right way.

A third kind of possession and madness comes from the Muses. It seizes 245a
a gentle, inexperienced soul and awakens within it a Bacchanalian enthusiasm for lyrical songs and other kinds of poetry, glorifying countless ancient deeds for the education of posterity. If anyone comes to the halls of poetry without the madness of the Muses, convinced that technique alone will make one a good poet, both the poetry of this man who is in possession of his senses and the man himself will fall short of perfection and be eclipsed by the poetry of those who are mad.

In addition to these, I could tell you about many other examples of the 245b
admirable effect of the madness that comes from the gods. So, let us not fear that, and let us not be upset by any speech that tries to startle us with the claim that a judicious friend should be preferred to a passionate one. Let it carry off the spoils of victory when it has shown this in addition: that love is not sent from the gods for the benefit of the lover and the beloved. We must prove the opposite, that this sort of madness is given by the gods for the greatest possi- 245c
ble good fortune. Our demonstration will not be believed by the clever, but it will be believed by the wise.

First, then, we must determine the truth about the nature of a soul, both divine and human, by observing its experiences and its actions, and this is the beginning of our demonstration.

Every soul is immortal, for that which is always changing is immortal.[59] In the case of what changes other things or is changed by other things, when that stops changing, it stops living. Only what changes itself, since it needs nothing beyond itself, never stops changing. It is the source and origin[60] of change for the other things that change, but an origin is not a thing which comes into being. Everything that comes into being necessarily comes into being from an origin, but the latter does not itself come from an origin. For if 245d
an origin came into being from something, it would not come into being from an origin.[61] Since it does not come into being, it also necessarily does not perish. If the origin were destroyed, it could never come into being from anything nor could anything else come into being from it, since everything must come into being from an origin. Therefore, the origin of change must be what changes itself, and it is not possible for this to be destroyed or to come into being. Otherwise, the entire universe and everything that comes into being would collapse into a static condition and that which is changed would never 245e
again come into being.[62] Now, since what is changed by itself has been shown to be immortal, one is not ashamed to say that this very characteristic consti-

tutes the essence and definition of the soul.[63] Every object that is changed from without lacks a soul, but every object in which change comes from within itself has a soul, as that is the nature of the soul. If this is so, then, and what changes itself is none other than the soul, a soul would by necessity be 246a
something that does not come into being and is immortal.

As for the immortality of the soul, then, that is enough, but as for its form, we must say the following. To specify what sort of thing it is would by all means be a task for a god and a lengthy exposition, but to say what it is like would be briefer and is something a human being could do. So, let us take the latter approach. Compare it to the combined capacities of a team of winged horses and their winged charioteer. Now, all the horses and charioteers of the gods are good and of good stock, but in other cases they are of mixed quality. In our case, the driver holds the reins of a pair of horses, one of which is noble 246b
and good and of similar stock, while the other is of the opposite stock and opposite in character. Thus, the driving in our case is inevitably difficult and troublesome.

Now, we must try to explain why we speak of mortal as well as immortal living beings.[64] Every soul travels around the entire heavens, appearing in different forms at different times, and cares for everything that lacks a soul. When a soul is perfect and has its wings, it travels through the sky and takes 246c
part in the governance of the entire cosmos, but if it loses its wings it drifts along until it can grasp onto something secure and settle down. There, it takes on an earthly body which then seems to move itself because of the soul's power. This united whole of a soul and a body fastened together is called a living being and has the name "mortal." We are unable to give a coherent account of an immortal being, but, although we have never seen and cannot adequately conceive of a god, we fashion an idea of a sort of immortal living 246d
being that has a soul and a body which are joined together eternally. But let that and the way it is spoken of be as suits the god.[65]

Let us consider instead the reason why a soul loses its wings, why they fall off. It is something like this. The natural function of a wing is to carry what is heavy upward and raise it to the region where the race of the gods dwells. In a way, they have more in common with the divine than any other bodily part, and since the divine is noble, wise, good, and everything else of 246e
that sort, such things are very nourishing to the wings of the soul and make them grow, while shame, evil, and other things of the opposite sort are detrimental and can even destroy them completely.

The mighty Zeus takes the lead in the journeys through the heavens, driving his winged chariot and arranging and managing everything. A host of gods and other divine beings follow him, arranged in eleven groups. Hestia stays behind alone in the dwelling-place of the gods, but the others who are 247a
ranked among the twelve as ruling gods lead the way, according to the position each has been assigned.[66] Many and blessed are the sights along the high-

ways on this side of the heavens, and the happy race of the gods ranges among
them, each performing its own task. Whoever is able and willing follows
them, since jealousy has no place in the company of the divine. Whenever
they go to a feast or banquet, they travel directly to the highest point, the sum- 247b
mit of the arch that supports the heavens. The evenly balanced chariots of the
gods, with their tractable teams, make the journey with ease, but the others
have difficulty. The horse with bad character is heavy and, if it was not well
trained by its charioteer, it sinks down and drags him toward the earth, where
hard toil and an arduous testing await the soul. When those that are called the
immortals reach the summit, they go outside and stand on the back of the
heavens.[67] While they stand there, the revolution of the heavens carries them 247c
round, and they study what lies beyond the heavens.

Of that place beyond the heavens none of this world's poets has yet sung
worthily, nor shall any ever do so. But it is like this—for one must dare to
speak the truth, and especially when the subject is the truth itself. That place is
occupied by the being that really is, which is intangible and without color or
shape. It is perceived only by the intellect, the pilot of the soul, and is the
object of the true kind of knowledge. The mind of a god, which draws its 247d
nourishment from intelligence and pure knowledge, and that of every soul
that cares about getting what is proper for it, cherishes the opportunity to
observe what is and is nourished and happy while it studies the truth during
the time it takes the circular revolution to carry it back to its starting point. On
its circular journey, it sees justice itself, it sees judiciousness, and it sees
knowledge, not the knowledge that is connected with becoming and varies 247e
with the varying things we now say are, but rather the knowledge that exists
in the realm of what really is and really is knowledge. When it has studied and
enjoyed the other things that really are, it returns to the region within the
heavens and goes home. When it arrives there, the charioteer stations his
horses at their feeding trough, puts ambrosia before them, and gives them nectar to drink. Such is the life of the gods. 248a

As for the other souls, the one that most closely follows and best resem-
bles its god lifts its charioteer's head into the outer region and is carried
around the circuit, although it has trouble with its horses and hardly sees the
things that are. Another soul at times rises and at times sinks because its
horses are unruly, and it sees some things but not others. All the rest follow
behind, trying to reach the upper region but unable to do so. They are carried
around together beneath it trampling and jostling one another as each tries to 248b
get ahead. So, there is great clamor and conflict, and much sweating, and
because they have bad charioteers, many are maimed and many break their
wing-feathers. Despite much effort, all these finish the journey without being
initiated into the vision of what is, and afterward they feed on mere opinion.

The reason for the great eagerness to see the plain of truth is that the
meadow there provides the pasturage that is appropriate for the best part of the 248c

soul and the nature of the wing that carries the soul aloft is nourished by this.

The decree of Adrasteia[68] is as follows. The soul that has seen some of the truth by joining a god on the journey will be free from suffering until the next revolution, and if it can continue to do this forever, it will always be free from harm. Whenever it is unable to follow so that it does not see and through some misfortune is burdened with forgetfulness and evil, and because of the heavy burden loses its wings and falls to the earth, then the rule is this: In its first birth this sort of soul is never implanted in a wild animal, but rather the 248d
one that has seen the most is implanted in a seed that will become a man who is a friend of wisdom[69] or of beauty or else someone devoted to the Muses and the affairs of love. The next in order is implanted in the seed of a law-abiding king or a military commander; the third in that of a politician, a manager, or a businessman; the fourth in that of an athlete who is a friend of exercise or else of someone who will cure the ills of the body; the fifth will lead a life involved with prophecy or the mysteries; for the sixth the life of a poet or of 248e
someone else involved with the imitative arts will be fitting; for the seventh that of an artisan or farmer; for the eighth that of a Sophist or a demagogue; for the ninth that of a tyrant. In every case, whoever lives justly receives a better fate, and whoever lives unjustly, a worse.

A soul does not return to the place from which it came for ten thousand years, because it takes that long for it to regain its wings—except for the one 249a
that has a pure friendship with wisdom or combines its love for young boys with a friendship with wisdom. If they choose this sort of life three times, then these souls will depart after the third revolution of a thousand years, having regained their wings in three thousand years. The others, however, when they have completed their first life, are brought to judgment, and after they are judged, some go to the places of punishment beneath the earth to serve their sentence, while others are borne aloft by Dike[70] to a certain region under the heavens where they pass their lives in the manner merited by the life they lived in human form. After a thousand years both come to the casting of lots 249b
for the choice of their second life, and each chooses as it wishes. Here a human soul may enter into the life of a wild animal and what was at one time a human being may return from a wild animal into a human being again. However, a soul that has never seen the truth cannot take on this latter form, because a human being must acquire understanding of what is said through principles drawn together by reasoning into a unity out of the multiplicity of 249c
perceptions. This is a recollection of what our soul saw when it was travelling with a god, looking down on the things we now say are and rising up into what really is. For this reason it is proper that only the thinking of the friend of wisdom will make the wings grow, because, through memory, it is always as close as possible to that which by its proximity makes a god divine. When a man deals correctly with remembrances of this sort, he is always initiated perfectly into perfect mysteries, and he alone really becomes perfect. Since he

stands apart from the busy antics of humankind and draws close to the divine,
he is rebuked by most people for being out of his wits. They do not realize that 249d
he is possessed.

So then, the whole speech up to this point has been about a fourth kind of
madness. Whenever someone sees beauty in this world he is reminded of true
beauty and his wing-feathers grow. When he has regained his wings he longs
to fly up, but he is unable to and gazes upward like a bird, not caring for the
things below, and for this reason is regarded as mad. Of all the kinds of pos- 249e
session this is the best and is from the best source, both for the one who has it
and for the one who shares in it, and it is because of his participating in this
kind of madness that the one who loves the beautiful is called a lover. For, as
has been said, every soul of a human being by virtue of its nature has seen the
things that are, otherwise it could not have entered into this kind of living 250a
being; but it is not easy for every soul to recall those things on the basis of the
things of this world. Some barely saw the things there at the time, and others
who fell to earth had the misfortune of being corrupted by some of their associations and have forgotten the sacred things they saw before. Few are left
who have much of a memory of them, and they, when they see some likeness
of those things, are astounded and delirious, although they do not understand
the experience because their perception is so unclear. Thus, there is no 250b
enlightenment in this world's images of justice, judiciousness, and all the
other things souls value. However, as they approach these resemblances with
their feeble organs, a few do with difficulty see the original through the
resemblance, although earlier, when we were following Zeus while others followed another of the gods, there was a brilliantly shining beauty to see. When
we saw those blessed visions with that happy company we were initiated into
the mysteries Themis[71] says are the most blessed, and we celebrated those
rites while we were whole in every way and unacquainted with the evils that 250c
awaited us in another time. Whole also, and simple, steadfast, and blessed
were those visions in the pure brilliant light when we were initiated and
admitted into the highest mysteries, and we ourselves were also pure and
unmarred by that which we call the body and now carry around, imprisoned
within it like an oyster in its shell.

Let that be our tribute to memory, then, for the sake of which, and
because of a longing for those earlier times, such a lengthy statement has been
made. Concerning beauty, as we said, it shone brightly along with those 250d
things, and, since coming here, we have grasped it shining most distinctly
through the most distinct of our senses. For sight is the keenest of the sensa-
tions coming to us through the body. Wisdom is not visible to it because the
sort of clear image of itself that would be required for sight would provoke
terrible, loving desires, as would be the case with any other of those objects of
love. It is beauty alone which has that fate, and thus is the most evident and
the loveliest. 250e

When the person who was not recently initiated, or who has been corrupted, sees the namesake of beauty in this world, he is not swiftly carried
from here to beauty itself in that other place; so he feels no awe when looking
at its namesake. Instead, he abandons himself to pleasure and tries to mount
others in the manner of a four-footed beast and to sow his seed. He takes
hubris as his companion and is neither afraid nor ashamed to pursue a plea- 251a
sure that is contrary to nature. However, when the recent initiate, who saw
many things in that early time, sees a godlike face or some form of body that
imitates beauty well, he at first gets goose bumps and something of the earlier
dread comes upon him. He is awestruck, as though he were gazing upon a
god, and, if he were not afraid that people would think he was a raving
maniac, he would offer sacrifice to his darling as to a sacred statue or a god.
As he looks at him, his goose bumps go away and an unusual warmth and
sweating seizes him. He is warmed by the effluence of beauty he receives 251b
through his eyes, which naturally moistens the wing-feathers. As he grows
warmer, the follicles, which had earlier hardened and closed so that the feathers could not sprout, are softened; and as the nourishing moisture flows over
them, the shafts of the feathers swell and begin to grow from their roots over
the entire form of the soul, which was feathered all over before.

At this point the entire soul is throbbing with excitement. It is like the 251c
experience of cutting teeth and the itching and irritation that occur around the
gums when the teeth are just coming through. The soul of the one who is
beginning to sprout feathers itches and is irritated and excited as it grows its
wings. Whenever it looks at the boy's beauty, it takes in a flood of particles
flowing from him (which is why longing is called a flood of passion) and is
nourished and warmed by it, and it obtains relief from its pain and rejoices.
When it is alone and dries out, however, the openings of the passages through 251d
which the feathers push their way out become quite dry and close up, shutting
the shoots of the feathers up inside. The shoots, which are imprisoned with the
flood of passion, pulsate like throbbing arteries, and each presses against the
outlet of its passage, so that the entire soul is driven to a frenzy by the pain of
the prickling all over it. Yet when it again remembers the beauty of the boy, it
rejoices, although it is perplexed and troubled by the oddness of an experience
that is a mixture of both these conditions. In its agony, it cannot sleep at night
nor stay in one place during the day. Filled with longing, it runs wherever it 251e
thinks it might see the one who possesses beauty. When it sees him and is
bathed with a flood of passion, the openings that had been tightly closed are
released; it gains release from the pressures and pangs, and at that moment
savors the sweetest of pleasures. It will not leave him willingly and values 252a
nothing more highly than the beauty of the boy. On the contrary, it forgets
mother, brothers, and all associates, and if its property is lost through neglect
thinks nothing of it. It now despises customary decency and taste, which it
used to take great pride in, and is ready to be a slave and sleep wherever it is

allowed to, as near as possible to the object of its longing. It not only is in awe of the one who possesses beauty; it finds in him the only healer of its greatest sufferings. 252b

Well, you beautiful boy, for whom my speech is given, human beings call this experience "love," but when you hear what the gods call it, because of your youth, you will probably laugh. I believe some of the Homericists quote two verses to Love from the secret epics, of which the second is quite hubristic and not very metrical. They sing as follows:

> Mortals do indeed call the winged one *Erōs* (Love),
> But immortals call him *Pterōs* (Feathered), because
> he necessarily develops wings.[72]

You may believe these verses or not, but the cause and the nature of lovers' 252c
experience are as I have stated.

Now, whoever is seized from among the attendants of Zeus is able to bear the burden of the one named Pteros in a more dignified manner, but when those who were the servants of Ares[73] and made the circuit with him are captured by Love and think they have been wronged in some way by the one they love, they become murderous and ready to sacrifice both themselves and their darlings. Thus, so long as he remains uncorrupted during his first life in this 252d
world, each person lives in accordance with the manner of the god whose procession he had been part of, honoring and imitating the god as far as possible, and he behaves this way in his relations with those he loves and with everyone else as well. Each person selects his love from the ranks of the beautiful according to his own style, and he fashions his own sacred statue, as it were, adorning it and holding ritual celebrations in its honor, as though the beloved were himself the god.

The followers of Zeus want the person they love to be a Zeus-like soul. 252e
So, they search for one who has the nature of a friend of wisdom and a leader, and when they find such a person they love him and do everything they can to encourage him along that path. If they have not done this before, they now set out to learn what they can from whatever source is available and to figure things out for themselves. They have ample resources within themselves for 253a
their search for one with the nature of their own god because they are compelled to keep their eyes fixed on their god. Holding onto their memory of him, they are inspired by him and derive their customs and practices from him, insofar as it is possible for a human being to be like a god, and since they take the beloved to be the cause of all this, they cherish him even more. They draw refreshing drink from Zeus and, like the devotees of Bacchus, pour it into the soul of their beloved, making him as similar as possible to their god. 253b

Those who followed Hera seek a regal person, and when they find one, they do all the same things for him. So also the followers of Apollo[74] and each of the other gods go out and seek their own boy whose nature accords with

that of their god, and when they have acquired one, by imitating the god themselves and through persuasion and training, they lead their darlings into the practice and style of the god, as far as each can do so. They are never jealous or spiteful in relation to their darlings, but rather expend all their effort in the attempt to guide him into being as similar as possible to themselves and the 253c
god they honor. Thus the desire of true lovers and the initiation of the one who is befriended by his friend who has been driven mad by love are beautiful things and lead to their happiness, if they accomplish what they desire in the way I describe—if he is captured, that is. And the one who is caught is captured in the following way.

Just as at the beginning of this tale we divided each soul into three parts, two in the form of horses and the third in the form of a charioteer, so now let 253d
us continue with these. Of the horses, we say that one is good and the other not, but we have not described the goodness of the good one nor the badness of the bad. Now we must do so. Well, then, the one has a more beautiful stance, with correct conformation and good development. It carries its neck high, is somewhat hook-nosed and light in color, and it has dark eyes. It is a lover of honor conjoined with judiciousness and a sense of what is respectable and is a companion of what is truly reputable. It needs no whip but is driven simply by a word of command. The other, however, is crooked 253e
in conformation, gross, and awkwardly constructed with a thick, short neck, a flat nose, dark skin, and grey, bloodshot eyes. A companion of *hubris* and insolence, it is shaggy-eared and deaf and barely responds to a combination of whip and goad.

So, when the charioteer sees the vision of his beloved, his entire soul is warmed by the perception and filled with longing's tickling and prickling. The horse that is obedient to the charioteer, constrained now as always by a 254a
sense of what is respectable, restrains itself, not leaping upon the beloved; but the other no longer heeds the charioteer's whip and goad. It leaps forward powerfully, giving its yoke-mate and the charioteer all kinds of trouble, and forces them to approach the darling and mention to him the delights of sexual activity. At first the two indignantly resist being compelled to do terrible, 254b
unlawful things, but they finally give in to the unending harassment and go where they are being led, agreeing to do what is demanded. Thus, they come close to the darling and see his radiant face.

When the charioteer sees him, he is reminded of the nature of beauty and sees it again, standing on its sacred pedestal beside judiciousness. Fearful and awestricken at the sight, he falls back, and this forces him to pull on the reins with sufficient violence to set both horses back on their haunches, the one 254c
willingly, because it does not resist, but the hubristic one very much against its will. As they move back a bit, the entire soul is drenched with sweat because of the shame and alarm of the one horse, but the other, barely having recovered its breath as the pain from the bit and its fall diminishes, angrily

rails against its charioteer and yoke-mate, heaping abuse upon them as unmanly cowards for backing out of the arrangement they had agreed upon. It again forces its unwilling partners forward and only reluctantly gives in when 254d
they beg it to postpone the project until later. Then, when the appointed time comes and they pretend not to remember, it forcefully reminds them, neighing and pulling them until it again forces them to approach the darling with the same propositions. When they get close to him, it takes the bit in its teeth, and with head down and tail stretched out it shamelessly drags them forward. But the charioteer has the same reaction as before, even more violently, and like a 254e
chariot-race driver recoiling from the barrier he jerks the bit back even more violently than before and forces it from between the teeth of the hubristic horse, bloodying its abusive tongue and jaws, forcing its legs and haunches firmly to the ground, and tormenting it with pain. After it experiences this same treatment many times, the wicked horse abandons its *hubris* and humbly obeys the intentions of the charioteer. Now when it sees the beautiful boy it is consumed with fear, and from then on the soul of the lover follows its darling in respectful awe.

Thus, a lover takes care of all his darling's needs and treats him like an 255a
equal of the gods, because he is not pretending but truly loves him, and the darling himself naturally becomes a friend to the one who cares for him. Even if he has rejected his lover in the past, deceived by schoolmates and others who said it is shameful to associate with a lover, yet, as time goes along, destiny and increasing maturity lead him to accept his lover into his company. For it is fated that bad is never to be a friend to bad nor good not to be a friend 255b
to good. When he has accepted the lover and enjoyed his conversation and his company, the goodwill of the lover that is revealed in their close relationship amazes the beloved, and he discovers that all his other friends and relatives offer no friendship at all in comparison with this friend who is divinely inspired. As the relationship continues and he comes close to his lover and touches him at the gymnasium and in other places where they associate, then the flow of that stream which Zeus as the lover of Ganymede[75] named "the 255c
flood of passion" surges in abundance upon his lover. Some of it enters into the lover, and when he is filled to the brim, some of it spills over; and as the wind or an echo rebounds from smooth, hard surfaces to the place from whence it originated, so the stream of beauty returns to the beautiful darling through his eyes, which is the natural route to the soul. Arriving there and setting him all aflutter, it moistens the passages of the feathers and causes the 255d
wings to grow and in turn fills the soul of the beloved with love.

So, he loves, yet he is at a loss as to what he loves. He neither knows what has happened to him nor can he explain it. He is like someone who has caught an eye infection from someone else and cannot account for it. He does not realize that he is seeing himself in his lover as in a mirror. When his lover is present, he feels the same cessation of pain that his lover does, and when his

lover is away he again shares his lover's longing and being longed for in the
same way. He possesses a love-response that is the reflection of love, but he 255e
supposes it to be friendship rather than love and calls it that. He feels a desire
like that of his lover, though less strong, to see, to touch, to kiss,[76] to lie beside
him; and, as is to be expected, soon afterwards he does just that.

When they are lying together, the lover's undisciplined horse tells the
charioteer that it thinks it deserves to enjoy a little pleasure in return for all its
suffering. The darling's undisciplined horse says nothing, and the darling, full 256a
to bursting and at a loss as to why, embraces his lover and kisses him, welcoming him as a person with the best intentions. While they are lying
together, the darling's undisciplined horse would not refuse its part in gratifying the lover, if the darling should ask, although its good yoke-mate in turn,
along with the charioteer, opposes this with modesty and reason. Now, if the
better aspects of the mind prevail by leading them into an orderly life and a
friendship with wisdom, they will lead a blessed and harmonious life here. By
binding that by which evil comes into the soul and setting free that by which 256b
goodness comes in, they become well-disciplined and orderly. When they
have accomplished this, they will have shed their burdens and will recover
their wings, and they will have won the first of the three rounds in that truly
Olympian struggle. Neither human judiciousness nor divine madness can provide a human being with any greater good than that.

If on the other hand, they engage in a coarser way of life, befriending not
wisdom but fame and honor, then perhaps sometime when they are drunk or at 256c
some other careless moment the undisciplined horses in the two of them may
catch their souls off guard, bring them together, take the choice most people
call a blessed thing, and carry through on the act. Having once done this, they
continue doing it in the future, though rarely, since what they are doing has not
been decided by their whole mind. These two are also friends, then, though
less so than the other pair, and remain together both while they are in love and 256d
after love has departed, for they believe they have each given and received the
strongest vows, which it would be unlawful to break by ever becoming enemies. In the end they lack their wings, but they emerge from the body with the
impulse to grow wings, so they carry away no small prize from their erotic
madness. The rule is that those who have already begun the journey up toward
the heavens shall not go down into the darkness of the journey under the earth,
but rather they shall continue their illustrious life, happily travelling together. 256e
When they gain their wings they shall do so together because of their love.

Things such as these, then, my boy, divine things, the friendship of a
lover will bring to you, but a relationship with one who does not love, diluted
with a mortal judiciousness and dispensing benefits that are both mortal and
miserly, produces in the soul of the befriended that servile condition most
people praise as a virtue that will cause it to wander mindlessly around the 257a
earth and beneath it for nine thousand years.

This recantation is offered and paid to you, Love my friend, as the best and most beautiful we are capable of. In language and in other ways it was forced to be somewhat poetical because of Phaedrus. Forgive what occurred earlier and be favorable toward this. Be merciful and gracious, and do not in anger take away or diminish the skill in the art of love that you have given me. Grant that I be even more highly esteemed than now by those who are beautiful. If Phaedrus and I said anything harsh about you in the earlier speech, 257b
blame Lysias as the father of that speech. Make him cease from such speeches and turn him toward friendship with wisdom, as his brother Polemarchus[77] has been turned, so that his lover here will no longer be ambivalent, as he is now, but rather will dedicate his life entirely to love through speeches that are characterized by friendship with wisdom.

P: I join with you in that prayer, Socrates, if in fact we will be better off should those things happen. But for some time now I've been amazed by 257c
how much finer an achievement this speech is than your earlier one. I'm afraid Lysias would seem inferior by comparison, if he should be willing to match another speech of his own against it. In fact, you amazing man, one of the politicians was recently criticizing him for this very thing, referring to him throughout his diatribe as a speech-writer. As a result, he may refrain from writing any more for us out of a concern for his friendship with fame and honor.[78]

S: That's ridiculous, young man! You're way off in your opinion of your associate if you think he'll be frightened by that sort of noise. However, 257d
you're probably assuming that his accuser meant what he said as a criticism.

P: He did give me that impression, Socrates, and you're well aware yourself that the people with the greatest power and dignity in our cities are ashamed to write speeches and to leave written works behind them because they're afraid they may be called Sophists by posterity.

S: It's like Pleasant Bend, Phaedrus. You've forgotten that it's the long bend in the Nile that's called that,[79] and besides the matter of the bend you've 257e
forgotten that those politicians who think most highly of themselves dearly love writing speeches and leaving written works behind them. In fact, whenever they write a speech they so cherish those who praise it that, on each occasion, they add at the beginning the names of those who commend them.

P: What do you mean? I don't understand.

S: You don't understand that at the beginning of a politician's composi- 258a
tion the name of its admirer is written first.

P: How so?

S: The writer says something like "it was resolved by the council" (or "by the people" or both) and "proposed by so-and-so," very solemnly stating his own name and eulogizing himself. Then, after that, he states what he has to say, showing off his own wisdom to his admirers and sometimes producing a very lengthy composition. Does it seem to you that this sort of thing is anything other than a written speech?

P: Not to me. 258b

S: When it holds up, the author leaves the stage rejoicing, but if it's knocked down, he loses his status as a speech writer and isn't considered good enough to be an author. Then he and his associates go into mourning.

P: Most certainly.

S: Clearly, not as people who despise the practice, but as people who admire it.

P: Definitely.

S: And what about this? When an orator or king succeeds in gaining the power of a Lycurgus, a Solon, or a Darius,[80] and acquires immortality in his 258c
city as a speech writer, doesn't he then think of himself as an equal of the gods even while he's still alive and doesn't posterity think about him the same way when they study his writings?

P: Most certainly.

S: Then, do you think that anyone of that sort, whoever he is and however much he dislikes Lysias, would criticize him on that basis, that he's a writer?

P: From what you're saying, it's not very likely, for it seems he'd be criticizing the object of his own desires.

S: This then, should be clear to everyone, that there's nothing shameful 258d
about the activity of writing speeches as such.

P: How could there be?

S: What is shameful, I take it, is speaking and writing, not well, but shamefully and badly.

P: Obviously so.

S: Then, how does one write well or badly? Do we need to consult Lysias about this question, Phaedrus, and anyone else who has written or will someday write something, whether a composition about public or private affairs, whether in verse as a poet or without it as an ordinary writer?

P: Are you asking whether we ought to do this? What would one live for, 258e

I would say, if not for the sake of such pleasures? Surely, one wouldn't live for the sake of those pleasures that can be enjoyed only after pain, which is the case for nearly all bodily pleasures and is why they are rightly called slavish.

S: Well, we seem to have some free time. Moreover, as the cicadas above our heads sing and converse with each other in the summer heat, they also seem to me to be watching us. If they should see us not conversing but 259a
drowsily dozing under their spell like most people at midday, they'd justly laugh at us, thinking we were a couple of slaves visiting their retreat by the spring for a noontime nap, like sheep. If, however, they see us conversing and sailing by them without falling under their Siren-like spell,[81] then in admiration they may grant us the gift they have from the gods to give to human beings. 259b

P: What's this gift they have? I don't think I've heard of it.

S: No? It's really inexcusable for a man who's a friend of the Muses not to have heard of such things. It's said that before the Muses existed, these cicadas were human beings, but after the Muses were born and singing made its appearance, some people in those days were so overwhelmed by the pleasure of it that they were caught up in singing and forgot to eat or drink and died 259c
before they realized what was happening. The race of the cicadas then developed from them, and they received from the Muses this gift of not needing any food from their birth, so that they sing continuously without eating or drinking until they die. Afterwards they go and report to the Muses who among those here honors each of them. They report to Terpsichore those who have honored her in the choral dance, disposing her to be more friendly to them, and they report to Erato those who have honored her in the affairs of love, and so on to the others, according to the form of honor belonging to each. To Calliope, the oldest, and to Ourania, who comes after her, they report those who spend their time in friendship with wisdom, honoring the arts connected with these two, who most among the Muses are concerned with the heavens and with speeches divine and human and whose song is the most beautiful. So, there are many reasons why we should talk and not take a midday nap.

P: We should talk, surely.

S: Then, we must examine the question we just now proposed for inves- 259e
tigation, namely, what constitutes speaking and writing well or badly.

P: Obviously.

S: Then, for things that are going to be said properly and well, mustn't there be knowledge of the truth in the mind of the speaker about the subject he intends to speak on?

P: In that regard, Socrates my friend, I've heard that it isn't necessary for one who intends to be an orator to understand what's really just, but only what 260a would seem so to the masses who'll be passing judgment, nor what's really good or beautiful but what will seem so. It's from the latter, and not from the truth, that persuasion derives.

S: Anything wise men say, Phaedrus, is definitely "not a word to be cast aside."[82] We must examine it, in case they're saying something worthwhile, and in particular we mustn't dismiss what's just been said.

P: What you're saying is right.

S: Then, let's examine it this way.

P: How?

S: If I were trying to persuade you to defend yourself in battles by 260b
acquiring a horse and neither of us knew what a horse was, but I did happen to know this much about you, that Phaedrus thinks a horse is the domestic animal with the longest ears...

P: That would be ridiculous, Socrates.

S: Not yet; but if I were seriously trying to persuade you by composing a speech in praise of the donkey, labelling it a horse and saying that the beast would be a highly valuable acquisition both for at home and in the army, useful as a mount in battle and able to carry your equipment, and beneficial for 260c
many other purposes...

P: That would indeed be utterly ridiculous.

S: Well, isn't it better to be ridiculous and friendly rather than clever and hostile?

P: That seems evident.

S: Then, when an orator who is ignorant about good and evil encounters a city in the same condition and tries to persuade it by offering praises, not of the specter of a donkey as though it were a horse, but of what is evil as though it were good, and by catering to the opinions of the masses, he persuades it to do evil rather than good, what sort of harvest do you suppose his rhetoric will reap from what it has sowed? 260d

P: Not a very satisfactory one.

S: Well now, my good man, have we abused the art of making speeches[83] more roughly than we should? Perhaps it might reply: "Why are you amazing fellows being so foolish? I force no one to remain ignorant of the truth while learning how to speak. On the contrary, if my advice is of value, it's to take me on after acquiring the truth. What I emphasize is this: Without me, the person who knows how things are will be of no account in the art of persuasion."

P: Well, if it says that, won't that be a just response? 260e

S: I'll say so, if the arguments advancing toward it testify that it is an art.[84] I seem, as it were, to hear certain arguments approaching and protesting that it's lying and isn't an art but an artless routine. As the Spartan says, there is not and never shall be a genuine art of speaking apart from a grasp of the truth.[85]

P: We need those arguments, Socrates. Lead them here and examine 261a
their meaning carefully.

S: Come forward, noble creatures, and persuade Phaedrus, who has such beautiful children,[86] that unless he develops a satisfactory friendship with wisdom, he will never speak satisfactorily about anything. Let Phaedrus answer.

P: Ask your questions.

S: Well then, isn't rhetoric as a whole a sort of art of leading souls by means of speeches, not only in the law courts and other such public assemblies, but also in private situations? Doesn't the same art deal with both major
and minor matters, so that using it correctly is no more important in connec- 261b
tion with significant matters than in connection with trivial ones? What've you heard about this?

P: Not that, by Zeus, not that at all! Certainly, one can speak and write artfully in connection with lawsuits, and also one can speak in an artful manner before public assemblies, but I've not heard of extending it beyond that.

S: Can it be that you've heard only of the treatises on the art of making speeches by Nestor and Odysseus, which they composed during their free time in Troy? Haven't you heard of those of Palamedes?[87]

P: No, by Zeus, nor have I heard of Nestor's unless you're casting Gor- 261c
gias as Nestor and Thrasymachus and Theodorus as Odysseus.[88]

S: Perhaps, but let's leave them aside. Tell me, what are the contending parties in the law courts doing? Aren't they just contradicting each other? What should we say?

P: Just that.

S: About what's just and unjust?

P: Yes.

S: Then, the person who does this artfully can make the same thing
appear to the same people as just at one time and unjust at another, as he 261d
wishes?

P: Of course.

S: In public assemblies he can make the same things seem good to the city at one time and the opposite at another time?

P: So he can.

S: Then, don't we know that the Eleatic Palamedes speaks artfully when he makes the same things appear to his hearers as both similar and dissimilar, one and many, and at rest and in motion?

P: Certainly.

S: So, the art of contradicting is not only connected with the law courts
and public assemblies. On the contrary, there seems to be this single art, if it is 261e
an art, that is connected with every kind of speaking. By means of it anyone whatsoever can make everything that is capable of it appear similar to everything else it is capable of resembling, and he can expose anyone else who makes one thing similar to another and tries to hide what he's doing.

P: What exactly do you mean?

S: I think the point can be made clear by searching in this direction. Does deception occur more often when there's a great difference between things or when there's little difference?

P: When there's little. 262a

S: So, if you move across to an opposite position by small steps, you're more likely to escape detection than if you make the transition by large steps.

P: Of course.

S: Then, the person who intends to deceive someone else, but not to be deceived himself, must have an accurate knowledge of the similarity and dissimilarity of things.

P: Necessarily.

S: Will such a person, if he is ignorant of the truth about each thing, be able to recognize the similarity to other things, whether small or great, of the thing he's ignorant about?

P: That would be impossible. 262b

S: When people are deceived and their opinions are contrary to the facts, it's clear that this condition slips in as a result of certain similarities.

P: Surely, that's how it happens.

S: If a person who possesses this art doesn't know what each thing is, is it possible for him to carry people along in small steps by means of similarities, leading them on each occasion away from what's so to the opposite, or to avoid this himself?

P: No, never.

S: Then, my friend, the person who doesn't know the truth and has gone chasing after opinions will provide a ridiculous and, so it seems, artless art of making speeches. 262c

P: That seems likely.

S: Well, do you want to look in Lysias' speech that you're carrying and in the speeches we've given for examples of what we're calling artless or artful?

P: By all means! At present we're talking rather abstractly, because we don't have appropriate examples.

S: Why, then it seems it's by a bit of luck that the two speeches that have been given contain an example of how someone who knows the truth can mis- 262d
lead his audience by playing around with words. I myself, Phaedrus, credit the gods of this place, and perhaps also those representatives of the Muses singing overhead who may have inspired us with this gift. I myself surely don't share in any art of speaking.

P: That may be as you say; only make clear what you mean.

S: Read me the beginning of Lysias' speech.

P: "You understand my situation, and you have heard how I think it 262e
would be to our advantage for this to happen. Because I am not your lover, I deserve not to be disappointed in what I request. When lovers' desires cease, they regret..."

S: Stop. We must say how Lysias misses the mark and produces something artless, mustn't we?

P: Yes. 263a

S: Well then, isn't the following obvious to everyone, namely, that about some things of this sort we are in agreement, but about others we take opposing positions?

P: I think I understand what you're saying, but clarify it further.

S: When someone says the word 'iron' or 'silver,' don't we all think of the same things?

P: Certainly.

S: What about 'just' or 'good'? Don't we go off in different directions and disagree with one another and even with ourselves?

P: Definitely.

S: So on some matters we agree, but on others we don't? 263b

P: That's so.

S: In which, then, are we more easily deceived, and in which is rhetoric more potent?

P: Obviously, in those on which we keep changing our position.

S: Then, the person who intends to pursue the rhetorical art must first make a thorough survey of these matters and find some distinguishing mark of each of the two kinds of issues, that is, the kind on which most people inevitably change their position and that on which they don't.

P: The person who grasps that, Socrates, will surely have learned a fine 263c
thing.

S: Next, I suppose, in each case he must pay attention and note precisely to which of the two kinds the subject he intends to speak about belongs.

P: Of course.

S: Well then, shall we say that love is one of the things people take opposing positions about, or not?

P: One of the things people take opposing positions about, surely. Otherwise how could you get away with saying what you did earlier about it, that it's harmful to both the beloved and the lover and then on the other hand that it's the greatest of good things?

S: You make an excellent point! But tell me this also, since because of 263d
my inspired state at the time I don't remember at all, did I define love at the beginning of my speech?

P: You did, by Zeus, quite emphatically.

S: Ah! So you claim that the Nymphs, who are the daughters of Achelous, and Pan, the son of Hermes,[89] are much more artful in making speeches than is Lysias, son of Cephalus. Or am I speaking nonsense? Did Lysias also at the beginning of his erotic speech compel us to take love as one definite
thing, which he had a conception of, and then proceed to finish his speech, 263e
arranging everything to fit in with this? Do you want us to read the beginning of his speech again?

P: If you think we should, but what you're looking for isn't in it.

S: Speak, please, so that I can hear the man himself.

P: "You understand my situation, and you have heard how I think it would be to our advantage for this to happen. Because I am not your lover, I

deserve not to be disappointed in what I request. When lovers' desires cease, 264a
they regret their earlier generosity,..."

S: Why, he seems to be a long way from doing what we're looking for. He's trying to swim through the speech on his back in reverse, starting from the end rather than from the beginning. He begins with what the lover should say to his darling at the conclusion. Or is what I'm saying not so, Phaedrus my chief friend?

P: Indeed, Socrates, he does begin his speech with the conclusion. 264b

S: What about other matters? Don't the sections of the speech seem to have been thrown together randomly? Does there appear to be any necessity for what comes second in his remarks being placed second, rather than one of the other things he says? It seemed to me, as one who knows nothing about it, that the writer just said whatever occurred to him, though in a not unrefined manner. Do you know of some necessity of speechwriting on the basis of which he placed these points beside one another in this order?

P: You're kind to believe that I am capable of making such a precise critique of his work. 264c

S: I suppose you could say this, that every speech ought to be organized like a living being with its own body, lacking neither head nor feet, but having both a middle and extremities, written so as to complement both each other and the whole.

P: Of course.

S: Then, examine whether or not your associate's speech has that characteristic. You'll find that it doesn't differ at all from the epitaph some say is inscribed on the tomb of Midas the Phrygian.

P: What epitaph is that, and what's the matter with it? 264d

S: It goes like this:

> A bronze maiden am I, placed on Midas' tomb,
> As long as water flows and trees grow tall,
> Remaining here on his much lamented grave,
> I tell all who pass that Midas is buried here.

I expect you notice that it makes no difference whether any line is spoken first 264e
or last.

P: You're making fun of our speech, Socrates.

S: Then, so you won't be upset, let's leave that speech alone—though it does seem to me to offer many examples that one could profit from examining, though certainly not things that anyone should try to imitate. Let's turn instead to the other speeches. I think there was something in them that should be investigated by those interested in examining speeches.

P: What're you referring to? 265a

S: The two were opposites in a way. One said that one ought to please the one who loves, the other the one who doesn't.

P: And quite manfully.

S: I thought you were going to state the truth and say "madly"—which is just what I was going to ask about. We said that love is a sort of madness, didn't we?

P: Yes.

S: And that there are two forms of madness, one caused by human sickness and the other by a divine disruption of customary behavior.

P: Certainly. 265b

S: We distinguished four parts of the divine type, associated with four
gods: Prophetic madness was ascribed to the inspiration of Apollo, the madness
connected with the mysteries to Dionysus, poetic madness in turn to the Muses,
and the fourth, the erotic madness that we said is the best, to Aphrodite and
Love. We described erotic passion in, I don't know, a sort of figurative manner,
perhaps touching on something of the truth but also probably being led astray at
other points. The mixture was a not altogether unconvincing speech, and we 265c
playfully sang, in properly worshipful tones, a sort of mythical hymn to Love,
who is my master and yours too, Phaedrus, and the guardian of beautiful boys.

P: For my part, it was certainly not unpleasant to listen to.

S: Let's take up the question now of how the speech managed to shift from censure to praise.

P: What do you mean?

S: It appears to me that while in other respects it was playfully done,
among those remarks two principles were mentioned by chance, and if someone could grasp their essence in an artful manner, it wouldn't be insignificant. 265d

P: What principles?

S: To bring together things that are scattered about and see them in terms of a single form, so that by defining it one can always make clear what one intends to expound. Just so, in the case of what was offered earlier as a definition of love, whether the definition was stated well or poorly, it did enable the speech to proceed in a manner that was at any rate clear and self-consistent.

P: What's the other principle you refer to, Socrates?

S: Being able to dissect a thing in accordance with its forms, following 265e
the natural joints and not trying to hack it apart like an incompetent butcher. Just so, the two earlier speeches both took the lack of good sense in one's
thinking as a single form. Then, just as the body, which is one thing, is natu- 266a
rally divided into pairs, with both parts of each pair called by the same names and labelled left and right, so also, the two speeches assumed that derangement is by its nature a single form in us, but divisible into two parts. One speech cut off the left-hand part and continued dividing this, not quitting until it found among the parts what we are calling a sort of left-hand love, which it very justly censured. The other speech led us into the sections of the right-hand part of madness, and finding a kind of love which has the same
name as the other but is divine, it held it up and praised it as the cause of our 266b
greatest goods.

P: What you say is very true.

S: I, myself, Phaedrus, am a lover of these dividings and collectings as what enable me to speak and to think, and when I believe that someone else is able to see the natural unity and plurality of things, I follow him, "walking behind him in his footsteps as in those of a god."[90] Moreover, up to now, I've called those who're able to do this dialecticians,[91] though whether I address them correctly or not only a god knows. However, tell me what those who
have learned from you and Lysias now call them. Is this that art of making 266c
speeches by means of which Thrasymachus and others have become skilled speakers themselves and make others such as well, if the latter are willing to bring them offerings fit for kings?

P: They may act like kingly men, but they lack knowledge of what you're talking about. You seem to me to name this form of art correctly when you call it dialectical, but I believe the rhetorical kind is still eluding us.

S: What're you saying? Could there be any fine and noble thing that is 266d
undertaken in an artful manner in separation from these principles? If so, you and I certainly shouldn't despise it, but should state what the remaining part of the rhetorical art is.

P: Well, Socrates, a great many things are written in the books on the art of making speeches.

S: You do well to remind me. First, I believe, an introduction must be given at the beginning of the speech. These are the things you mean, aren't they, the fine points of the art?

P: Yes. 266e

S: Second is a statement of the facts with any direct evidence to support it, third is indirect evidence, fourth is what seems probable, and I believe confirmation and supplementary confirmation are spoken of by that outstanding master-artist in words, the man from Byzantium.

P: Are you speaking of the good Theodorus?[92]

S: Who else? He also speaks of a refutation and supplementary refutation 267a
that must be made in both prosecution and defense. But shouldn't we bring the illustrious Evenus of Paros[93] into our circle? He first invented insinuation and indirect praises, and some say he also states indirect censures in verse as an aid to memory—a wise man. Shall we let Tisias[94] and Gorgias rest in peace, who say that what's probable is more important than what's true, who make trivial matters seem major and major matters trivial through the power of speech and present what's new as old and vice versa, and who discovered how to make 267b
speeches of concise or unlimited length on any and every subject? Prodicus[95] once laughed when he heard this latter point from me, and said that he alone had discovered what the art requires of speeches: What is required is that they be neither long nor short, but of the proper length.

P: Ah, most clever Prodicus!

S: Shouldn't we mention Hippias? I believe the visitor from Elis would agree with Prodicus.

P: Why not?

S: What shall we say about the sacred things of Polus'[96] speeches (such
as speaking repetitiously and speaking in maxims and speaking with similes) 267c
and the terms Licymnius[97] gave him to facilitate eloquence?

P: Weren't there some such things from Protagoras,[98] Socrates?

S: In particular, my boy, there were correctness of diction and many other fine things. Yet the mighty Chalcedonian[99] appears to me to be supreme in the art of making speeches that arouse pity for old age or poverty. He was also fiendishly clever at rousing a crowd to anger and then when they were angry, calming them down again with his incantations, as he said, and he was 267d
unbeatable at slandering as well as overcoming slander, regardless of its source. Everyone seems to be in general agreement about the conclusion of speeches, though some call it recapitulation while others give it other names.

P: Do you mean summarizing the points at the end to remind the audience of what's been said?

S: That's what I mean. Do you have anything further to say about the art of making speeches?

P: Only minor points not worth mentioning. 268a

S: Let's leave aside minor matters, and hold these other points up to a stronger light to see how and where the art functions.

P: It's a very powerful art, Socrates, especially in large meetings.

S: So it is, but, you divine[100] fellow, look and see whether you think, as I do, that their warp has gaps in it.

P: Just point them out.

S: Well, tell me, if someone came to your associate Eryximachus or his father Acumenus[101] and said, "I know how to apply certain sorts of things to people's bodies so as to induce warmth or coolness if I want to, and if I 268b
choose I can make them vomit or make their bowels move, and a great many other such things; and because I know these things I'm a competent physician and can make a physician out of anyone else to whom I transmit knowledge of these things." What do you think they'd say if they heard that?

P: What else but to ask whether he also knew to whom one should do these things and when, and to what extent?

S: What if he then said, "Not at all; rather, I expect the person who has 268c
learned from me to be able to work out what you refer to by himself"?

P: I think they'd say the fellow was mad, that after reading something in a book or chancing upon some medications he supposes himself to have become a physician, when he knows nothing of the art.

S: What if someone met Sophocles or Euripides and said that he knew how to compose long orations about a trivial matter and very short orations about an important matter, that he could compose those that would arouse pity, when he wanted to, or, on the other hand, frightening and threatening ones, and many other such, and that he believed that by teaching these things 268d
he gave people the ability to compose tragedies?

P: I expect they too would laugh at anyone, Socrates, who thought a tragedy was anything other than the proper arrangement of those elements so that they harmonize with one another and the whole.

S: Yet I don't think they would berate him in a rough, rude manner. They would act like the musician who meets a man who thinks he understands harmony because he knows how to produce the lowest and highest notes on the lyre. He wouldn't speak to him in a savage manner, saying, "You worth- 268e
less wretch, you make me sick!" As a devotee of the Muses, he would speak more gently, saying, "You excellent fellow, whoever intends to understand harmony must necessarily know that, but a person who has what you've

acquired may not understand harmony in the least. What you know must be learned as a prerequisite for understanding harmony, but is not harmony itself."

P: Absolutely right.

S: So Sophocles would say that the person showing off to them knew the 269a
prerequisites for tragedy but not tragedy itself, and Acumenus would say that the man in his case knew the prerequisites for medicine but not medicine itself.

P: Most certainly.

S: What do you think about honey-tongued Adrastus, or even Pericles?[102] What if they heard about these splendid artistic devices we were just referring to, conciseness of speech and speaking with similes and the many other things we were considering and said we were going to hold up to the
light for examination. Would they, like you and I, make some coarse, rude 269b
remark to those who've written about these things and teach them as the art of rhetoric? Or, since they're wiser than we are, would they rebuke us and say, "Phaedrus and Socrates, you mustn't be harsh but forgiving, if certain people who lack knowledge of dialectic[103] are unable to give a definition of what rhetoric is and because of being in this condition think they have discovered rhetoric when what they have learned are the necessary prerequisites to the
art. You must be forgiving if such people believe that when they teach these 269c
things to others they've provided a complete course in rhetoric and that since there's nothing to the task of using these devices in a persuasive manner and putting the whole thing together, their students must take care of that by themselves in their speeches."

P: Of course, Socrates. It does seem likely that it's something like this that makes up the art these men teach and write about as rhetoric. What you said seems true to me. But how and where can one acquire the art that belongs
to the real orator and to the person who is able to persuade? 269d

S: Acquiring the ability to become a perfect competitor, Phaedrus, is probably, and perhaps necessarily, in this as it is in everything else. If you are naturally a rhetorical person, you'll be a famous orator, provided you add on knowledge and practice. Should you lack any of these, in that respect you'll be imperfect. As far as the art itself is concerned, it seems apparent to me that the way to go is not the road travelled by Lysias and Thrasymachus.

P: What is the way, then?

S: It's really not surprising, you excellent fellow, that Pericles became 269e
the most perfect of all in rhetoric.

P: Why?

S: All the great arts require facility at conversation and lofty speculation about nature; these seem to be the sources of high-mindedness and the ability 270a
to be completely effective in every situation. That's what Pericles added to his natural talent. I believe he spent some time with Anaxagoras,[104] who was that sort of person, and by steeping himself in lofty speculation grasped the nature of intelligence and the lack of it (topics about which Anaxagoras regularly made long speeches) and drew from that what he could usefully apply to the art of making speeches.

P: What do you mean by that?

S: That the method of the medical art is the same as that of the rhetorical 270b
art.

P: How so?

S: In both cases the nature of something must be analyzed, in the one that of the body and in the other that of the soul, if you intend to proceed in an artful manner and not merely by means of practice and experience in providing in the one health and strength by prescribing medication and diet and in implanting in the other the conviction and excellence you want by means of speeches and refined rules of conduct.

P: That seems quite likely, Socrates.

S: Then, do you think it's possible to formulate a worthwhile analysis of 270c
the nature of a particular soul without an understanding of the nature of the soul in a general sense?

P: If we are to follow Hippocrates the Asclepiad,[105] one can't make a worthwhile analysis of a particular body, either, without taking that approach.

S: He gives good advice, my friend, yet even in the presence of Hippocrates we must review the analysis to see whether it's cogent.

P: I agree.

S: Then, consider how Hippocrates and the true account speak about the nature of something. Isn't this the way we should think about the nature of anything whatsoever? First, determine whether that, in regard to which we 270d
desire to be artful ourselves and to be able to make others such, is simple or complex. Then, if it's simple, inquire as to what natural capacities it has, what it can do to what, and in what ways it can be affected and by what. If it has more than one form, enumerate these and consider each of them as in the case where there was a single form: on the one hand, what it is its nature to do by itself and on the other hand in what ways it can be affected and by what.

P: That seems likely, Socrates.

S: At any rate, an approach that lacked these steps would seem like the stumbling of a blind man. Surely we mustn't compare the person who pursues 270e
any subject whatsoever in an artful manner to someone who's blind or deaf. On the contrary, it's obvious that anyone who teaches someone about speeches in an artful manner will show precisely what the essential nature of that thing is toward which one will direct one's speeches, and that, I assume, is the soul.

P: Of course.

S: Then, every effort is aimed at that, for it's in the soul that one tries to 271a
produce conviction. Isn't that so?

P: Yes.

S: It's obvious, then, that both Thrasymachus and anyone else who teaches the art of rhetoric seriously will first write very accurately about the soul and will make us see whether it's simple and uniform in nature or complex like the form of the body. That's what we mean by showing what its nature is.

P: Certainly.

S: Secondly, he'll describe what it is its nature to do with what, or to have done to it by what.

P: Of course.

S: Thirdly, he'll classify the various kinds of speeches and kinds of soul, 271b
fitting each kind of one to a kind of the other, and he'll also classify the ways in which souls can be affected, giving explanations of every case and showing by what sort of speeches one soul will inevitably be persuaded and another not.

P: At any rate, that would be the best way, I think.

S: So it is, my friend. There will never be any other way than this of speaking or writing in an artful manner in a demonstration or an actual oration, neither on this topic nor on any other. However, current writers about the 271c
arts of making speeches to whom you've listened are crafty and keep their thorough knowledge of the soul hidden. So, until they speak and write in this way, we won't believe that they write in an artful manner.

P: What way is that?

S: It's not easy to provide the actual words, but I'm willing to state the manner in which one must write if one intends to be as artful as possible.

P: Speak then.

S: Since the power of speech consists in the leading of souls, the person
who intends to be an orator must know what kinds of souls there are. Now, 271d
there are a certain number of them, of various types, so that some people are of one sort and others of another. Moreover, after these have been distinguished in this way, there are a certain number of kinds of speeches, and each speech is a particular type. Thus, people of a certain sort are easily persuaded by speeches of a particular type to do certain sorts of things for a certain reason, while people of a different sort will not be persuaded for other reasons. After one has an adequate understanding of these matters, one must be able to
perceive and distinguish these types accurately when one observes them actu- 271e
ally occurring in practice; otherwise, one won't yet have any advantage from what one heard when one was attending lectures before. When one is qualified to say which sort of person will be persuaded by which sorts of speeches and one has the ability to determine for oneself regarding a person one
encounters that this is the person and the very nature that the lectures before 272a
were about, now actually present, to whom one must apply speeches of this particular sort in this manner in order to persuade him of these kinds of things, when one has acquired all this, understands when one should speak and when one should keep silent, and can distinguish when it is appropriate and when inappropriate to use concise speech, speech that arouses pity, exaggeration, and each of the other kinds of speeches one has learned about, then and not until then, will the art be properly and completely mastered. If someone falls short in these matters in his speaking, teaching, or writing, while he may
claim to speak in an artful manner, the one who doesn't believe him is in the 272b
stronger position. "Well now," the writer on this topic will perhaps say, "does this seem correct, Phaedrus and Socrates, or should we describe the art of making speeches in some other way?"

P: It's impossible to accept any other account, Socrates, yet it seems no small task.

S: What you say is true. That's why all our statements must be examined backwards and forwards to see whether there's a quicker and easier way along
the road to this art so that one won't waste effort on a long and rough road 272c
when there's a short and smooth one. If you've heard anything that would be helpful from Lysias or anyone else, try to remember and say what it was.

P: I could try, but at the moment I've nothing like that to offer.

S: Then, would you like for me to recount a speech I've heard from some of those concerned with these matters?

P: Of course.

S: It's said, Phaedrus, that it's legitimate to speak on behalf of the wolf.[106]

P: Then, do so. 272d

S: Well, then, they say there's no need to be so pompous or to make a long uphill struggle of coming to grips with these matters. As we said at the beginning of this discussion, the person who intends to be competent at rhetoric has no need at all to be concerned about the truth regarding which actions are just or good or which human beings are such by nature or by training. In court, no one cares at all about the truth of these matters, but only about what's persuasive, and that is what is probable. It's to this that the per- 272e
son who intends to speak artfully must attend. Sometimes one mustn't tell what was actually done, if what was done isn't probable; instead one should say what is probable, in both prosecution and defense. Every time one speaks, one must pursue the probable, often bidding truth farewell. When this hap- 273a
pens throughout one's speech, it supplies the entire art.

P: Socrates, you've stated just what those who claim to be artful in making speeches say. I remember that we touched briefly on this sort of thing earlier, and it seems to be a point of great importance to those concerned with these matters.

S: Well, you've thumbed through Tisias carefully; let's allow Tisias to speak about this also. Does he say that the probable is nothing more than what seems to most people to be the case? 273b

P: What else could he say?

S: Apparently, after he discovered that wise and artful point, he wrote that if someone who is weak but brave beats up a strong coward and steals his cloak or something and is brought to trial for it, then neither of them ought to tell the truth. The coward should deny that the brave man was acting alone when he beat him up, and the other should contend that there were only the two of them, making effective use of the claim, "How could someone like me assault someone like him?" The coward, of course, won't mention his cow- 273c
ardice, but will quickly try to produce another lie, which will supply his opponent with a basis for further refutation. And in other cases speaking artfully will be similar, won't it, Phaedrus?

P: Of course.

S: My, what a cleverly hidden art he has discovered—Tisias or whoever it may happen to be and whatever he enjoys being named after.[107] But my friend, should we or shouldn't we say to him...

P: What? 273d

S: This: "Tisias, for some time now before you came along, we've been saying that this probability comes about for the general public because of a

similarity to the truth, and we just explained how the person who's seen the truth always knows best how to find these similarities. If you have anything other than that to say about the art of making speeches, we'll listen, but if not, we'll accept what we just went over, namely, that unless a person can distin- 273e
guish the natures of those who are listening and can divide the things that exist in accordance with their forms and comprehend each individual thing in terms of a single form, one will never be as artful in one's speeches as a person can be. One will not acquire this ability without a great deal of effort, which the sensible person ought not to expend for the sake of speaking and acting before human beings, but so as to be able both to say what's pleasing to the gods and to do everything in a manner that pleases them to the best of one's ability. Those who're wiser than we, Tisias, say that the intelligent person mustn't practice doing what will please one's fellow slaves, except coincidentally, but rather what will please one's good and noble masters. So don't 274a
be surprised if the way round is long; one must make the circuit for the sake of great purposes, not for the sort you have in mind. Yet these latter purposes also, if someone is interested in them, will be achieved best by this means, as our discussion shows."

P: That seems very good advice to me, Socrates, if only one could follow it.

S: It's a noble thing to attempt noble deeds and then suffer the consequences. 274b

P: Certainly.

S: Then, let that be enough about the art and the lack of art in making speeches.

P: Of course.

S: But the question remains, doesn't it, as to what's appropriate and inappropriate regarding writing, that is, when it's done properly and when improperly?

P: Yes.

S: Then, do you know how best to please the god[108] in connection with speeches, whether making them or discussing them?

P: Not at all. Do you?

S: I can tell you what I have heard from our predecessors, but only they 274c
themselves know the truth. If we could discover that ourselves, would mere human opinions continue to concern us?

P: A ridiculous question. But tell what you say you've heard.

S: Well, then, I heard that at Naucratis in Egypt there lived one of the ancient gods of that region, the one whose sacred bird they called Ibis. The name of the divine being himself is Theuth.[109] He was the first to invent mathematics, geometry, and astronomy, as well as backgammon and dice, and, 274d
moreover, written letters.[110] At that time Thamus was the king of all of Egypt around the great city of the upper region that the Greeks call Egyptian Thebes. They call the god Ammon. Theuth came to Thamus and demonstrated his arts, saying that they ought to be passed on to the rest of the Egyptians. Thamus asked about the usefulness of each and, as Theuth went through them, condemned some and praised others, depending on whether Theuth's claims 274e
seemed well-taken or not. It's said that Thamus presented many points both for and against each art, which would take a long speech to report, but when it came to letters, Theuth said, "This branch of learning, your majesty, will make the Egyptians wiser and improve their memories, for I've discovered a magic potion[111] for memory and wisdom." But Thamus replied, "Most artful Theuth, while one person is able to create the products of art, another is able to judge what harm or benefit they hold for those who intend to use them. Now you, the father of letters, as a result of your affection for them, are stat- 275a
ing just the opposite of what their effect will be. If people learn them it will make their souls forgetful through lack of exercising their memory. They'll put their trust in the external marks of writing instead of using their own internal capacity for remembering on their own. You've discovered a magic potion not for memory, but for reminding, and you offer your pupils apparent, not true, wisdom. After they have heard many things from you, but without instruction, they will seem to be very knowledgeable when they are for the most part ignorant, and they will be hard to get along with, since they will 275b
have only the appearance of wisdom instead of being really wise."

P: Socrates, you easily make up stories about the Egyptians or anyone else you want to.

S: My friend, those at the temple of Zeus at Dodona said that the first prophetic speeches were those of an oak tree. Back then, since they weren't wise the way you young people are today, people were content in their simplicity to listen to an oak tree or a rock, if it spoke the truth. For you, perhaps it makes a difference who the speaker is and where he comes from. You don't 275c
just consider whether what's said is so or not.

P: You rightly rebuke me. I think the situation regarding letters is just as the Theban says.

S: So, the person who thinks he is leaving behind an art in written form, and in turn the person who receives it, on the assumption that anything clear and reliable will be available from something in written form, would be exceedingly simple-minded as well as really ignorant of the prophecy of

Ammon, if he thinks that written works are anything more than reminders for the person who knows the subject of the written material. 275d

P: Quite right.

S: In a way, Phaedrus, writing has a strange character, which is similar to that of painting, actually. Painting's creations stand there as though they were alive, but if you ask them anything, they maintain a quite solemn silence. Speeches are the same way. You might expect them to speak like intelligent beings, but if you question them with the intention of learning something about what they're saying, they always just continue saying the same thing.
Every speech, once it's in writing, is bandied about everywhere equally 275e
among those who understand and those who've no business having it. It doesn't know to whom it ought to speak and to whom not. When it's ill-treated and unfairly abused, it always needs its father to help it, since it isn't able to help or defend itself by itself.

P: You're quite right about that also.

S: What about this? Can we see another kind of speech that's a legiti- 276a
mate brother of that one and see how it comes into being and how it is from its birth much better and more powerful than that one?

P: What kind of speech is this, and how do you mean it comes into being?

S: That which is written along with knowledge in the soul of the learner, that's able to defend itself by itself and knows to whom it ought to speak and before whom it ought to keep silent.

P: You mean the living and ensouled[112] speech of the person who knows, of which a written speech may justly be called a kind of image.

S: Precisely. Now, tell me this. Would a sensible farmer who had some 276b
seeds he cared about and who wanted to produce a crop plant them with serious intent in the heat of summer in gardens for Adonis[113] and enjoy seeing them bloom beautifully in eight days? If he did such things at all, wouldn't he do them for the sake of amusement and at festivals? In those cases where he was serious, wouldn't he use the farmer's art and plant in suitable ground and prefer having what he has sown reach maturity in the eighth month?

P: Probably, Socrates, as you say, he'd do the one seriously and the other 276c
otherwise.

S: Shall we say that the person who has a knowledge of what's just, beautiful, and good is less sensible about his seeds than the farmer?

P: Not in the least.

S: Then, when he's serious he won't write them in ink, using a pen to sow speeches that are unable to defend themselves in discussion and unable to teach the truth effectively.

P: That's not likely.

S: No, it isn't. He'll sow his gardens of letters for amusement, it seems, 276d
and will write, when he does write, to store up reminders for himself, and for all who follow the same track, against the forgetfulness that may come with old age, and he'll enjoy watching their tender shoots grow. While others resort to other kinds of play, refreshing themselves with drinking parties and whatever is related to these, this person, it seems, instead of indulging in these kinds of play, will engage in those I'm speaking of.

P: You refer to a very noble kind of play, Socrates, in contrast to a 276e
worthless kind, that of the person who is able to play with speeches, telling tales about justice and the other things you mention.[114]

S: So it is, Phaedrus my friend, but far more noble, I think, is the serious treatment of these subjects when someone uses the dialectical art and, selecting an appropriate soul, plants and sows in it speeches that are accompanied by knowledge, speeches that can defend both themselves and the one who planted
them and that are not barren but contain a seed from which others grow up in 277a
other abodes, so that this process is rendered eternal and immortal.[115] Such speeches make the person who possesses them as happy as a human being can be.

P: What you speak of is nobler by far.

S: Now that we've agreed about these matters, Phaedrus, we can decide about those others.

P: What are they?

S: We've gotten to this point because we wanted to know about the following: what we were going to make of the criticism of Lysias as a writer of
speeches, and, with regard to speeches themselves, which were written in an 277b
artful manner and which not. It seems to me that what is artful and what is not has been made abundantly clear.

P: I thought so, but remind me again how it went.

S: Until one knows the truth about each of the topics one speaks or writes about and is able to define each in its own terms; and until after defining them, one knows how to cut them up again in accordance with their forms until one reaches what's indivisible; and until one comes to an understanding of the nature of the soul in the same way, discovering the form that fits each
nature, and arranges and organizes one's speech accordingly, offering to a 277c
complex soul complex speeches that cover all the musical modes and simple

speeches to a simple soul; only then will one be able, insofar as it's in accord with its nature, to deal with the race of speeches in an artful manner, either in connection with teaching or in connection with persuading—as the entire preceding discussion has reminded us.

P: Certainly, that is just about how it appeared to us.

S: Then, what about the question as to whether it's a noble or shameful 277d
thing to make and write speeches and under what circumstances doing so can justly be made a basis for criticism or not? Didn't what was said a little while ago make clear...

P: What?

S: That if Lysias or anyone else, whether for private use or in public when writing something political as a legislator, ever wrote or shall write anything in the belief that it would possess great clarity and permanence, then such action would make the writer subject to criticism, whether or not anyone says so. Being ignorant, when awake as well as when asleep, of what's just
and unjust and of what's good and bad truly cannot escape being subjected to 277e
criticism, even if the entire populace praises it.

P: So it cannot.

S: Well, then, Phaedrus, the sort of person whom it is likely that you and I would pray that we both become is the person who believes that there's necessarily a lot that's playful in a written speech on any topic, and that no speech whether in verse or in prose has ever been written that is worthy of much serious consideration, nor any recited in the rhapsodes' manner, that is, for the sake of persuasion without questioning or instruction. He will be the
sort of person who believes on the contrary that the best of them in fact have 278a
been reminders for those who know, and who believes that the only speeches that are clear, complete, and worthy of serious consideration are those about what's just and beautiful and good that are taught and spoken for the sake of learning and actually written in the soul. He will be the person who believes that his speeches of this sort ought to be spoken of as his legitimate sons, including primarily the one inside himself, if any can be found there, but also
any descendants and brothers of that one that have developed along with it in 278b
a worthy manner in the souls of others, and he will bid farewell to other sorts of speeches.

P: What you're saying is certainly what I myself wish and pray.

S: Then, we've amused ourselves enough with these issues about making speeches. You go and tell Lysias that we two went down to the spring of the Nymphs and the shrine of the Muses and listened to speeches that commanded us to say the following to Lysias and to anyone else who composes 278c

speeches, and also to Homer and anyone else who's composed poetry, whether without musical accompaniment or to be sung, and thirdly to Solon and whoever else has written political statements that he calls laws. They commanded us to say that if one has composed these things with knowledge of what the truth is, can defend them by talking about what one has written, and by one's own speaking is able to show the inferiority of what's been written, then such a person ought not to be referred to as having a title connected with these latter things, but rather a title connected with those things one is 278d
serious about.

P: What titles would you give them, then?

S: To call them "wise" seems excessive to me, Phaedrus, that's appropriate only for a god, but to call them a "friend of wisdom"[116] or something of that sort would be both more fitting for them and more harmonious.

P: And not at all inappropriate.

S: On the other hand, the person who has nothing more valuable than what he's composed or written, who spends a lot of time changing his works this way and that, pasting them together and pulling them apart, him, perhaps, 278e
you will justly call a poet or a writer of speeches or laws?

P: Of course.

S: Then, tell that to your associate.

P: But what about you? What're you going to do? Isn't it the case that your associate ought not to be neglected?

S: Who's that?

P: The handsome Isocrates.[117] What message will you take to him, Socrates? What shall we say he is?

S: Isocrates is still young, Phaedrus, but I'm willing to say what I proph- 279a
esy for him.

P: What?

S: What lies in his nature seems to me to be superior to what is in Lysias' speeches, and to be combined with a nobler character. It wouldn't be at all surprising, given the kinds of speeches he's now engaged with, if as he grows older he succeeds in making the speeches of his predecessors look like the work of children. Nor would it be a surprise if that doesn't satisfy him and a more divine impulse leads him on to greater things. By virtue of his nature, my friend, a certain friendship with wisdom is present in the thinking of the man. That's the message I'm taking from the gods here to my darling, 279b
Isocrates, and you take the other to your darling, Lysias.

P: It shall be done. But let's go, since the heat's become less severe.

S: Shouldn't we offer a prayer to those here as we depart?

P: Of course.

S: Pan,[118] my friend, and the other gods of this place, grant that I may develop inward beauty and that my external possessions be in friendly accord
with what is within. May I consider the wise rich, and may I have no more 279c
gold than a sensible person can carry and manage.

Do we need more than that, Phaedrus? The prayer's sufficient for me.

P: Let me join in that prayer. Friends' things are held in common.

S: Let's go.

5
Commentary on the Phaedrus

As in the case of the commentary on the *Symposium*, this commentary presupposes a basic familiarity with the text of the dialogue and with the topics discussed in the general introduction. My intention is to encourage the reader to focus on the entirety of the text and to open up the reader's reflection on the dialogue by commenting on various issues and interpretations. I am particularly concerned to bring out the possible significance of dramatic and literary aspects of the dialogue and to suggest how a consideration of such factors can impact on the interpretation of the philosophical content of the dialogue. I try to initiate the task of working out the implications of and adjudicating between rival interpretations, but the fulfillment of that task belongs to the conversation with the dialogue that this commentary is designed to stimulate. Thus, the commentary is not designed to fulfill or complete the dialogue, but to return the reader to the dialogue with a renewed enthusiasm and appreciation for the richness and complexity of Plato's text.

THE THEME OF THE DIALOGUE AS A WHOLE

In dealing with the *Phaedrus*, the reader encounters an unexpected perplexity as to whether the dialogue has a unifying, overall theme. This question, which was discussed even in ancient times, results from the apparently disjointed character of the dialogue: its first half contains three speeches about the advantages and disadvantages of erotic relationships, while its latter half is devoted to a detailed discussion of the art of making speeches. Thus, a reader may at first think the dialogue is to be seen as another examination of the nature of ἔρως (*erōs*), but this issue seems to be completely abandoned in the latter part of the dialogue so that the reader begins to think of the dialogue as an analysis of the requirements for excellence in speaking. Under this latter reading, the early analyses of *erōs* seem to be merely incidental exercises, perhaps illustrating rhetorical techniques, while under the reading that focuses on the analysis of *erōs*, the discussion of speechmaking seems oddly anticlimactic, if not irrelevant.

It is tempting, especially for one who has just been reading the *Symposium*, to focus on the lofty depiction of *erōs* in Socrates' second speech and its grand myth. This was the approach of many ancient readers and is still common among contemporary readers of the dialogue.[1] However, this approach has the result of making the two parts of the dialogue seem largely irrelevant to each other, which, as C. J. Rowe points out, is "intolerable in a work in which Socrates specifically complains about an author (Lysias) for failing to put together an *organic* composition (264b–c)."[2] Hence, commentators attempt to develop an interpretation that will unify the dialogue, and this generally involves giving primary emphasis to the discussion of the art of making speeches. From this point of view, the speeches in the early part of the dialogue are seen as illustrations of rhetoric, but there is some controversy as to whether their content can also be seen as directly related to this theme.

James Arieti makes the radical claim that the speeches all serve merely to illustrate the techniques of rhetoric and that there is no reason to assume that Plato intends the reader to take anything that is said about *erōs* in any of the speeches seriously. Arieti even argues that the second speech of Socrates should be seen an illustration of how a clever rhetorician can make bad ideas seem plausible. He sees the emphasis on the connection between *erōs* and madness as indicating that *erōs* is antithetical to reason, and he argues that Socrates cannot plausibly be seen as genuinely in favor of irrationality.[3] Thus, for Arieti, the only significance of the speeches is in their illustrating the dangers of rhetoric. However, most commentators take a more positive view of the philosophical significance of the content of the speeches, especially that of Socrates' second speech.

The key issue is how to understand the connection between *erōs* and rhetoric. Walter Hamilton suggests that the *Phaedrus* shows that there is a good kind of rhetoric, namely, one that is based on a knowledge of the truth. The point of Socrates' second speech, he argues, is to show that such knowledge can only be attained through the inspiration of *erōs*. Thus, Socrates' speech describes the experience that is the basis for true rhetoric.[4] This approach requires some careful explication of just what is meant by "the inspiration of *erōs*," of course. In a somewhat similar vein, A. W. Price argues that the unity of the *Phaedrus* is found in the recognition that "the best love will achieve its goal through the best rhetoric."[5]

Hackforth argues that the primary purpose of the *Phaedrus* is to defend philosophy and to propose a reformed type of rhetoric to serve the ends of philosophy. The key to the latter is presented, he claims, as the method of collection and division, and this is illustrated in the speeches—positively in those of Socrates and negatively in that of Lysias. However, this does not mean that the topic of *erōs* is incidental to the discussion of rhetoric. Hackforth argues that philosophy is seen here as a kind of love and that the relation between teacher and disciple in the quest for philosophical understanding is that of two lovers whose love for each other is grounded in their common love of truth.[6] This view of the dialogue points toward a topic that deserves more explicit attention in the interpretation of the *Phaedrus*, namely, the treatment of friendship (φιλία, *philia*).

C. J. Rowe offers a view on this question about the theme of the dialogue that is similar to that of Hackforth. He claims that the relationship between the lover and the beloved that is depicted in Socrates' second speech is a metaphor for that of the philosophical teacher and pupil, and moreover, Socrates as the ideal philosopher is shown to be both a dialectician, that is, the good kind of rhetorician, and a lover.[7]

A quite different approach is taken by Charles Griswold. He argues that the unifying theme of the dialogue is the quest for self-knowledge. In his interpretation, Phaedrus is depicted as peculiarly lacking in such self-awareness and understanding; thus, the speeches about *erōs* and the discussion of rhetoric illuminate the nature of such self-knowledge and inform us about how to obtain it.[8]

We can see, then, that while most commentators find some positive connection between the analysis of *erōs* in the speeches in the first part of the dialogue and the critique of rhetoric in the later section, just how to understand that connection remains controversial. Everyone agrees that the speeches illustrate some of the principles of rhetoric discussed in the dialogue, and most agree that the analysis of *erōs*, especially in Socrates' second speech, should be seen as involving points about the nature of *erōs* that Plato intends for the reader to take positively. However, just what those points are, whether they are consistent with the views Socrates presents in the *Symposium*, and how they are related to the discussion of rhetoric are topics of continuing debate.

SETTING THE SCENE:227A–230E

Socrates' opening statement introduces two important motifs in the dialogue: friendship (φιλία, *philia*) and travelling. Both motifs are illustrated in the actions and interactions of Socrates and Phaedrus in the dialogue and appear in various forms in their conversation. Both are explicitly mentioned at the very end of the dialogue as well. We could read the dialogue as a reflection on how one should undertake the journey of life and the role of relationships and conversations with others in that journey. The question with which Socrates opens the dialogue can lead us to ask where we are and where we are heading, and after examining, in company with Socrates and Phaedrus, where we should go and how we should get on, the dialogue concludes with an emphasis on the importance of friendship and an exhortation to take the next step. These two motifs shape the dramatic structure of the dialogue that provides the framework for reflecting on the topics introduced by Socrates and Phaedrus in their conversation.

It is immediately clear that λόγος (*logos*, speech), in various forms, is going to be a major theme in the dialogue. Lysias is known as a speechwriter (228a), and Socrates indicates his enthusiasm for hearing Lysias' speech (227b) and identifies himself as a "lover[9] of speeches" (228c) who is "obsessive about listening to speeches" (228b).

A further important motif in the dialogue is introduced by Phaedrus' characterization of Lysias' speech as "an attempted seduction" (227c). Both of Socrates' speeches maintain this format, and the seductive character of rhetoric is an important theme in the later discussion of the art of making speeches.

Phaedrus is characterized as youthfully exuberant in this first section of the dialogue. Socrates, whom Plato presents as knowing Phaedrus well (228a), is at first gently mocking of Phaedrus, though he does not dismiss him as a mindless chatterbox. Their relationship takes on a playfully erotic tone at several points.[10] Phaedrus' enthusiasm for Lysias' speech is later revealed to have a superficial basis, and an interesting question about the dialogue is to what extent Phaedrus overcomes his initial superficiality.

Readers who are attracted to allegorical interpretations will find it hard to resist speculating about the significance of the act of wading in the pure, sparkling waters of the Ilissus and of the presence of the tall plane-tree (229a), which appears "in the midst of" their *logoi* (plural of *logos*) (230a).[11] Some readers interpret the plane-tree as representing discourse and the chaste tree, mentioned at 230b in Socrates' description of the place they decide to stop along the Ilissus, as symbolizing true Socratic love.[12]

Plato uses the beginning of the walk down the Ilissus as the moment to introduce the first of the myths that are such a striking part of the *Phaedrus* (the dialogue also contains an unusual number of references to specific divine beings). Phaedrus mentions the story of the abduction and seduction of Oreithuia by Boreas and asks Socrates whether he believes it to be true (229c). Socrates' response is important for the interpretation of the entire dialogue. Saying that he would not be odd if he disbelieved such stories (229c), Socrates surprises us by asserting that he *does* believe these traditional myths (230a). We know that in other dialogues Socrates emphatically denies many stories about the gods because they portray the gods as engaging in immoral activities, but at the same time, he often affirms his belief in the gods.[13] The important question is what it means to believe that such stories are true, and this passage in the *Phaedrus* gives an indication of the answer to that question.

Socrates begins by rejecting a way of understanding such stories that he ironically attributes to the "wise" (229c). This type of interpretation tries to give a literal reading to the myth, in this case claiming that the child was blown off the rocks to her death by the wind (229c). Socrates points out that this sort of approach to the myths will result in a great deal of tedious analysis that he suggests will largely be a waste of time (229d–e). He says that he himself has no time for such activities, but turns his energies toward fulfilling the Delphic oracle's exhortation to know himself (229e).

Does this mean that Socrates "believes" these myths, but thinks they have no real significance for the philosopher, that is, for the person who is serious about understanding the journey of life? The answer to this question is immediately revealed by the way Socrates presents his effort to know himself. He says that he asks himself whether he is "a beast more complex and agitated than Typhon" (230a).[14] By this use of the image of the mythical character Typhon to raise a question about the character of his own soul, Socrates shows us that myths can be used as metaphors to illuminate issues about life in this world. In fact, Socrates does this explicitly and repeatedly in the dialogue. What is striking is that he calls this believing that the myth is true.

Truth in the myth, then, does not require some sort of literal description of the content of this or any other world. Socrates can acknowledge that these stories are human creations (275b–c) and that their significance lies in what they can show us about our world and our lives without seeing this as undermining their truth.[15] The fact that this way of understanding mythical *logos*[16] is made explicit in the *Phaedrus* is one of its most interesting features. It opens the question of Plato's understanding of the mythopoetic function of *logos* in a context where elaborate poetic metaphors play a central role in the text.[17]

With this in mind, it is not difficult to see how the story about Oreithuia fits into the dialogue. It effectively raises the issue of how *erōs* is related to activities that seem irrational, or at least drastic (or "hubristic"), by ordinary standards. The literal-minded reading, which sees at best a garbled reference to the death of a child, fails to see the truth of the myth.

The significance of the suggestion that Oreithuia was playing with Pharmaceia is brought out by Socrates' use of the term φάρμακον, *pharmakon*, at 230d, which is related to Pharmaceia (Φαρμακεία). The term refers to a potion used in medicine or magic for good or ill, and thus has a striking ambiguity. At 230d Socrates uses it to refer to Lysias' speech (*logos*) that Phaedrus is using to seduce him into going out into the countryside. To use such a metaphor for *logos* is quite provocative (on a par with William Burroughs' metaphor in *Naked Lunch*: Language is a virus from outer space).[18] By hinting that Oreithuia was playing with *logos* when she became involved with the god, Socrates implies that *logos* is a power, even a magical power, that can work good or ill and also points toward themes that become more explicit later on in the dialogue about the power and significance of *logos*.

After Socrates' grandiloquent, and surely somewhat ironic, praise of the spot they have chosen to stop along the Ilissus (230b–c), Phaedrus reiterates how out of place Socrates seems (230c–d). He accuses Socrates of pretending to be a visiting stranger, a ξένος (*xenos*). This passage is commonly translated so that what Phaedrus says next is clearly false, that is, translators make him assert that Socrates has never gone out of Attica or even outside the walls of Athens.[19]

That this is not so is shown in the immediate context by Socrates' remark about the location of the place where Boreas abducted Oreithuia (229c). He is obviously familiar with the area and even knows that there is an altar at the spot. Moreover, we know that he went on several military campaigns. The syntax of the Greek is a bit ambiguous, but the context makes clear what is meant.

Socrates' explanation of why he seems somewhat out of place in this setting, fits the usual image of him as a lover of *logos*: "The countryside and the trees don't want to teach me anything, but the people in town do" (230d). However, this remark contrasts oddly with his later rebuke of Phaedrus at 275b–c in which he says that the oak tree at the temple of Zeus at Dodona does speak the truth, in a prophetic voice, to those who are able to hear it. Perhaps at 230d the problem is not that the trees *cannot* teach Socrates anything, but that they do not *want* to, as he says. Kenneth Dorter suggests that the problem is that when they first reach the spot by the plane-tree on the Ilissus, Socrates is not yet adequately attuned to the mythical side of *logos*.[20]

LYSIAS' SPEECH: 230E–234C

All scholars agree that this speech is in the style of Lysias, which we know from extant speeches that are undoubtedly authentic. Whether or not it is actually from his hand or a Platonic invention cannot be determined.[21] Aside from its paradoxical theme (that you should prefer to have an affair with someone who does not love you rather than with someone who does), what most strikes the reader about this speech is its beginning *in media res*, which foreshadows its generally haphazard organization. Socrates points this out later at 264a–b as one of its major flaws. The speech is stitched together by repeated connectives, rather than logical order—or organic form (264c).

It is probably unfair to Lysias (or to the way he is being portrayed by Plato) to take the content of this speech too seriously. It seems more reasonable to take it as the sort of display piece represented by Gorgias' famous defense of Helen's virtue. Nevertheless, Phaedrus seems to take the speech seriously, and Socrates responds to the content of the speech as well as its style. The view of *erōs* in Lysias' speech, and in Socrates' first speech, seems similar to the "common" *Erōs* of Pausanias in the *Symposium*.

The remark at 231e, "if prevailing convention (νόμος, *nomos*) makes you fear that you will be criticized if people find out," suggests a complexity in Athenian attitudes towards homosexual liaisons. A similar suggestion is contained in Pausanias' speech in the *Symposium* at 182d ff.

TRANSITION TO SOCRATES' FIRST SPEECH: 234C–237A

In a remark that seems ironic and is similar to the one he made at 228B, Socrates again associates Phaedrus' enthusiasm for Lysias' speech with the divinely inspired madness of religious devotees (234d). Phaedrus' "madness" turns out to be particularly uncritical, like the "irrational desire"[22] that Socrates describes as *erōs* at 238b, but this seems to anticipate Socrates' discussion of madness in his second speech.

Another interesting motif in the dialogue is also made explicit here (234d), namely, the relation between the playful and the serious. Phaedrus accuses Socrates of treating Lysias' speech as a "joking" (παίζειν, *paizein*) matter, clearly intending this as a criticism. Socrates replies by asking if Phaedrus thinks he is not being "serious" (ἐσπουδακέναι, *espoudakenai*) but "playful" (*paizein* again) instead. Phaedrus replies "Not at all," implying that Socrates could not be both at the same time, and, by invoking Zeus under his title "the god of friendship," emphasizing their friendship as a context where seriousness is appropriate. Socrates offers a broader view of friendship, as well as of the relation between being playful and being serious. Even Phaedrus becomes playful in his relation to Socrates when he sees the possibility of getting him to offer a speech in rivalry with that of Lysias (236c–e).

The verb *paizein* first appears in the dialogue at 229b when Phaedrus suggests that the waters of the Ilissus seem suitable for young girls to play beside. Socrates then uses it in describing the activity of Oreithuia and Pharmaceia at 229c. At 265c Socrates says that his second speech to some extent was "playfully" done, and at 276c–d he speaks of written speeches (perhaps Platonic dialogues?) as a kind of "play," a kind of play that Phaedrus suggests is of noble quality. Finally, at the conclusion of their discussion of the art of making speeches, Socrates says, "Then we've amused ourselves enough with these issues about making speeches" (278b). "Amused" here translates a form of *paizein*; the text could be read as: "we've played around enough...." Thus, the suggestion that being playful may be part of being serious, at least in some contexts, is quite explicitly present in the dialogue, and is especially connected with written speeches. It is hard not to see a reference to Plato's own work here and a message to the reader about the character of the dialogues as both playful and serious. The relationship depicted between Socrates and Phaedrus is also notable for its playful character.

Perhaps, in Socrates' claim at 235c that he may have heard something better than Lysias' speech from the poets, there is a hint that Plato does not have an unambiguously negative attitude toward the poets. The *Phaedrus* could be seen as undermining that traditional view of Plato. After all, Socrates explicitly ascribes his second speech to the poet Stesichorus (244a) and says himself that his speech is "somewhat poetical" (257a). It is also noteworthy that in this passage at 235c Socrates' famous insistence on his own ignorance occurs in a context that is clearly ironic, since he does in fact invent his speech himself.

SOCRATES' FIRST SPEECH: 237A–242A

Nothing in the dialogue is so out of character for Socrates as this first speech. He makes clear by word and deed that he does not agree with the thesis he is defending, repeatedly blaming Phaedrus for forcing him to make the speech (236e, 238d, 242d). He also points out that giving a polished speech of this sort is not characteristic of his engagement with *logos*, blaming his "unusual fluency" (238c) on his being possessed by the Nymphs of the place (238d, 241e).[23] Nevertheless, the speech possesses rhetorical characteristics that he later praises, especially its organic structure[24] and its beginning with the establishment of a "mutually agreed upon definition" (237c) of the main topic, namely, a definition of *erōs* (237d). Thus, it seems reasonable to say that, in this first speech at least, Plato intends the reader to take Socrates' effort as an example of good rhetoric with a bad content.[25]

This seems to suggest that the definition of *erōs* that is given here is not presented as philosophically satisfactory. This may be overlooked by readers who are inclined to be sympathetic to the reason/passion dichotomy that it involves.[26] Socrates here offers a view of action that is not consistent with his usual rejection of the claim that desire can overcome understanding. He characterizes *erōs* as an "irrational (without *logos*) desire" that "overpowers the judgment that directs us toward what is right" (238c). Since Socrates argues in detail elsewhere that one *cannot* do what one judges to be wrong[27] and says at 242e that what is said about *erōs* in this speech is "neither sound nor true," it seems plausible to assume that he understands this speech to be flawed in its definition of love as well as in its description of the effects of love. Like Aristotle, Socrates, as he is usually presented by Plato, assumes that a desire for something is based on a (possibly mistaken) judgment that the thing is good. Desire cannot overpower judgment; it is the servant of judgment.[28]

An important question is whether this definition of *erōs* is also used in Socrates' second speech. At 265e ff. Socrates says that his two speeches are based on the same definition of love, with the first analyzing one aspect of it (the "left-hand part") and the second analyzing the other. If this is the case, it seems to lend support to James Arieti's claim that the view of *erōs* in this dialogue cannot be taken as seriously intended by Plato because it promotes irrationality.[29] At 265b Socrates himself expresses some reservations about the definition of erotic passion in his speeches.

The necessity of starting with definitions (see 263c-d) so as to have mutually agreed upon assumptions is a common theme in the dialogues.[30] Without such agreement, conversations cannot make useful progress, but this still leaves open the question of the status of such agreed upon principles or definitions. Socrates sometimes seems to suggest that all conversations presuppose some such agreements. This seems to imply that no conversations will have absolute foundations, since the examination of one assumption will require the making of others—which raises an epistemological issue that goes beyond the content of the *Phaedrus*, though I say more about it below.

This first speech also contains two playful etymologies that are another dimension of the playfulness in the use of language in the dialogue (that of "clear-voiced" at 237a and the elaborate one of "*erōs*" at 238c, which are explained in the notes on the translation). This sort of playing with etymology can have the serious function of drawing our attention to aspects of a concept that may have been overlooked.[31]

SOCRATES CHANGES COURSE: 242A–243E:

Socrates' attempt to abandon the field after his "terrible" speech is quickly thwarted by his famous daimonic sign (242b–c) and Phaedrus' plea to stay until the heat of the day passes (in which even Phaedrus indulges in a little linguistic play (242a). This passage in which Socrates announces that he will give a second speech in order to expiate his sin contains some interesting elements.

Socrates casually asserts that Love is a god (242d), which contrasts sharply with the argument he attributes to Diotima and claims to firmly believe himself in the *Symposium* (202b–203a), namely, that Love is not a god at all, but a daimon, which is a kind of being in between gods and human beings. Even though he qualifies this assertion at 242e by saying, "If Love is a god or something divine (a θεός, *theos*, or something θεῖον, *theion*)," he does not use the term 'daimon' or 'daimonic' of Love.[32] Perhaps we should assume that this conversation with Phaedrus occurs before Socrates' encounter with Diotima. It is generally agreed that the *Phaedrus* was composed by Plato after the *Symposium*[33] and Socrates' remark at 242b about Phaedrus being the cause of many speeches seems designed to recall the *Symposium*, so this raises a question about Plato's concern for presenting Socrates in a consistent manner. If we assume that the view Socrates attributes to Diotima in the *Symposium* represents Plato's own best effort at an analysis of *erōs*, this "slip" by Socrates could be seen as further support for the claim that Plato does not intend for the reader to accept any of the views of *erōs* that Socrates offers in this dialogue, although it must be noted at the same time that the Greeks generally (and Socrates in particular in this dialogue) deal with stories about the divine realm in a flexible manner.[34] Alternatively, we could assume that this sort of cross-referencing between the dialogues is a mistake and restrict ourselves to an assessment of the conversation's philosophical dimensions in its own context.

Other elements in this transition passage relate to this issue of fundamental interpretive approach. Socrates is very ironic and playful in his approach to his second speech, raising a question about just how serious he is prepared to be. His flattery of Phaedrus at 242b seems a bit hyperbolic. He claims that he is a prophet at 242c, which, even if the claim is ironic, contrasts with his attitude of humility before the prophetess Diotima in the *Symposium* (206b). Moreover, such irony seems a bit cavalier on the part of one who is already in serious trouble with an important god, if we are to believe that his claims about needing to expiate his sin are sincere. Moreover, he attributes his second speech to the seventh-century poet Stesichorus (244a), although he has just put Stesichorus down by saying that he intends to be wiser about the danger he is in than Stesichorus was (243b), and he asserts at the end that the speech was "somewhat poetical" (257a), again raising a question of just how serious the reader is to assume Socrates is here. A final light-hearted touch is the playful way Socrates implies that his speech is really directed at (seducing) Phaedrus and Phaedrus accepts the role (243e). The situation reminds us of Alcibiades' story in the *Symposium.* Certainly the reader should adopt a careful, critical approach to the question of what Plato is trying to do in Socrates' second speech as well as to the philosophical assessment of the content of the speech.

Socrates' remark at 243c to the effect that anyone who heard the view of love just presented in his first speech would assume they were hearing the views of sailors rather than those of free men, suggests that the understanding of the nature of *erōs* in his first speech is faulty. This again raises the question of whether his second speech is based on the same fundamental definition of love as the first.

SOCRATES' SECOND SPEECH: 243E–257B:

The structure of Socrates' second speech is as follows. He is concerned to show that although the lover is mad, madness is not always a bad thing—and particularly not in this case. In doing this, he briefly discusses three types of nonerotic, beneficial madness (244a–245b), and then gives a lengthy defense of *erōs* as a good kind of madness (245c–257b). In this defense of erotic madness, he first argues for the immortality of the soul on the basis of its being self-changing (245c–e), then develops an elaborate myth of the experiences of the soul using as an image of it a charioteer and his team of horses (246a–256e), and concludes with a prayer to *Erōs* (257a–b).

A. *In Defense of Madness: 244a–245b*

Socrates begins by pointing out that the previous speeches warning against associating with a lover because lovers are mad (μαίνεσθαι, *mainesthai*, which has the same root as μανία, *mania*, madness) and not in command of their senses (σωφρονεῖν, *sōphronein*) are based on the assumption that madness is always a bad thing (244a). He will argue that madness is sometimes a good thing, particularly when it has a divine source. This refutation does not strictly require that love be shown to be a good kind of madness, but Socrates does go on to say this. The question is what we are to make of this claim that love is a kind of madness. In particular, does this mean that it is in some important sense ir- or non-rational? Many commentators argue that the eloquent defense of the lofty significance of *erōs* in Socrates' second speech involves an endorsement of a basis of action and belief that goes beyond the reach of reason so that the ultimate truth is held to be ineffable, that is, beyond the grasp of *logos*.[35] However, this view assumes that the second speech is based on the same definition of *erōs* that is used in Socrates' first speech.

The three examples Socrates gives are again a curious mixture of the apparently serious and the playful. In discussing the positive benefits that have come from prophetic madness,[36] he combines a general reference to the guidance of seers with a pair of fanciful etymologies (244b–d). (Elsewhere Socrates speaks quite disparagingly of prophets,[37] and he puts the life of the prophet fairly low in the hierarchical order at 248d.) The second kind of madness is not clearly distinct from the first, since it is still a matter of the benefits of prophetic madness, though involving recommendations for sacrifices and rituals to expiate past sins rather than guidance about future events (244d–e). (Socrates' reference to his own prophetic abilities at 242c, which seems ironic, includes both these functions.) The third example is the madness of poets (245a), a commendation that sits uneasily in the mouth of Socrates, given what he says about the poets in the *Republic*, his critique of poetic inspiration in the *Ion*, and his even lower ranking of the life of the poet in the hierarchical order at 248e. He concludes with a claim that many other examples could be given "of the admirable effect of the madness that comes from the gods" and asserts that he will prove that erotic madness "is given by the gods for the greatest possible good fortune" (245b–c).

In what follows the reader must consider in what sense Socrates takes love to be a kind of madness. Is it a form of irrationality in the sense that it involves behavior that is contrary to, or at least not a function of one's (rational) understanding of what is good, or is it madness only in the sense that it involves unconventional, i.e., hubristic, behavior, which, as in the case of Socrates in the *Symposium*, may be based on superior understanding of what is good? That it is this latter sort of madness that is intended is suggested by the distinction Socrates makes at 265a between "two forms of madness" as "one caused by human sickness and the other by a divine disruption of customary behavior."[38] Using the term in a pejorative sense, one could speak of love as a condition that is irrational in that it leads the lover to engage in bad behavior, that is, behavior that is not based on an accurate understanding of what is truly good. However, in his first speech, where Socrates presents a picture of a person acting contrary to their best judgment and in these examples of madness at the beginning of the second speech, the idea is different; in these instances we are dealing with behavior that is presumed to be based on something other than the actor's understanding, at least, that understanding that can be rationally articulated. The question, then, is that of in what sense the erotic passion that Socrates praises in his second speech is a kind of madness.

One could argue that the only connection between love and the three kinds of madness introduced here is that love is also god-given.[39] This would be quite compatible with claiming that it is not madness in the sense of a condition that violates or transcends the limits of rationality. It is also possible that Plato is having Socrates engage in a discussion that is based on common opinions as the mutually agree upon assumptions, so that the issue of whether the view of *erōs* here is consistent with views about love and the rational basis of action defended in other dialogues is irrelevant. The question of how to interpret the discussion of love in Socrates' second speech remains surprisingly difficult.

B. An Argument for the Immortality of the Soul: 245c–e

Socrates' effort to show that love is a good kind of divinely given madness begins with an argument for the immortality of the soul. This argument is different from the final argument in the *Phaedo* at 102a–107b, which has as its key premise that the soul is the bearer of life and hence cannot admit death, and from the argument in the *Republic* at 608d–611a, which is based on the principle that something can only be destroyed by its own specific evil, yet the specific evil of the soul, namely, injustice, does not destroy it. If we assume that in the *Symposium* Socrates solemnly denies the possibility of immortality, there is an obvious conflict with this effort to prove the immortality of the soul. This is not the place to critique the arguments in other dialogues, nor is it the place to consider the general question of whether Plato takes the possibility of immortality seriously. It is generally assumed that Plato does believe in immortality, and it is generally believed that he takes these arguments to be sound. Nevertheless, the argument in the *Phaedrus* is quite curious.

In the first place, it seems oddly out of place. Just as Socrates begins a great mythical and poetic discourse, we find a dry, highly abstract argument on an issue that seems tangential at best. The claim that the soul is immortal is not required for what is said about the nature and importance of love, except as an element in the mythical stories, nor does Socrates place any emphasis on it in his expression of the practical implications of the mythical stories he tells. Moreover, a demonstration of the literal truth of the claim is not needed to include it as an element in the myths; there are many fantastic elements in the stories for which no proof is offered or expected. Later on, at 270b ff., Socrates does emphasize the importance of understanding the nature of the souls of one's hearers so that one can speak effectively to them, and perhaps that is the justification for having Socrates introduce this argument, though his discussion of the form of the soul in terms of the metaphor of winged charioteers and their teams of horses in various conditions seems to fit that task more adequately. Finally, like the argument in the *Phaedo*, this argument is odd because, if it effectively establishes its conclusion, it proves the immortality of the souls of all living things—including plants, a conclusion it is difficult to take seriously. This probably does not occur to the contemporary reader (nor, apparently, to contemporary commentators—I have not found anyone who takes note of this), but the ancient Greek reader would recognize that ψυχή, *psuchē*, "soul," is being spoken of here in the general sense of the principle of life, which is not unique to humans, nor even to animals. Plato could surely not have been unaware of this. He seems to go out of his way in the argument to emphasize that the soul Socrates is talking about is found in "every object in which change comes from within itself" (245e), which clearly includes all animals and plants.

The argument is based on an analysis of what is needed to account for the phenomenon of change.[40] It asserts that change is occurring and argues that an infinite regress of external causes of change is impossible. There must be something that changes itself, that is, causes changes in itself, therefore, as well as causing changes in other things. The next step is to argue that these self-changers do not come into being or perish, and here the argument is somewhat obscure. One possible reading is that the claim is that self-changers cannot be produced (brought into being) by other self-changers. This possibility is rejected, perhaps (the text is difficult) because it would require what is self-causing to be caused by something that is not itself, which could, perhaps, be seen as contradictory.[41] Hence, there is no coming into being of things that change themselves. Moreover, these things cannot perish, for then the entire process of change would no longer exist, but it does exist. The argument concludes: "Now, since what is changed by itself has been shown to be immortal, one is not ashamed to say that this very characteristic constitutes the essence and definition of the soul" (245e).[42]

C. The Metaphor of a Charioteer with a Team of Horses: 246a–256e

The rest of Socrates' second speech is devoted to the development and explication of the figure of the charioteer and his team as a metaphor for the soul.

1. The Form of the Soul: 246a–246e. Socrates begins with a surprising caveat regarding the specification of the form of the soul. He says that only a god could state what it is; all a human being can do is say what the form of the soul is like, that is, give a metaphor for it. This is odd since he has just made a statement at 245e that he says states "the essence and definition (*logos*) of the soul." Moreover, he had no such qualms regarding the definition of the form of love, and he offers no reason for this apparent restriction on the human capacity for understanding in this case. He simply adopts a more poetic approach, introducing a metaphor and inventing a story to go with it, and exploring how it illuminates the subject, while giving only a pro forma excuse for doing so. The Socrates of the *Phaedrus* is increasingly odd. Given his later emphasis on the importance of knowing the nature of the soul in order to engage properly in *logos*—and knowing its nature in rather precise detail (271a–c), it is hard to take seriously this rather cavalier dismissal of the possibility of doing so. It does not seem plausible to attribute to Plato the modern notion that knowledge is fundamentally composed of metaphors because language is fundamentally metaphorical. Perhaps Plato simply wanted to explore a more poetic approach.[43]

The metaphor and the mythical world constructed around it are Plato's distinctive creation, but they involve elements drawn from familiar traditional sources, especially Pythagorean and Orphic teachings. The whole is quite fantastic, and there is nothing in the text that requires us to assume that anything is intended literally; some elements, such as the claims about the role of sprouting wing-feathers in erotic experience, *cannot* be taken as anything other than marvelous, poetic fiction. One could argue that the stories of transmigration, reincarnation, the transcendent location of the forms, etc., fall into the same category. Socrates' consistent attitude seems to be one of using these myths to illuminate the human situation in the everyday world.[44]

This picture of the soul fits well with the tripartite psychology of the *Republic*.[45] However, the functions of the two horses do not precisely correlate to those assigned to the appetitive and spirited parts of the soul in the *Republic*. For example, there is no suggestion that the good horse, which corresponds to the appetitive part in the *Republic*'s model, would ever oppose the charioteer, that is, reason—a view that fits the Socratic denial of *akrasia* better than the *Republic*'s image. Moreover, it should be noticed that insofar as the soul is said to be immortal in the *Phaedrus*, it is the entire soul, including the appetitive and spirited parts, that is immortal, and not only the rational part that corresponds to the charioteer. However, this sort of analysis is probably inappropriate as a way of dealing with such a poetic depiction.[46]

2. The Heavenly Journey: 246e–249e. Again using the motif of the journey, Socrates paints a marvelous picture of the realm where souls properly dwell. This passage contains a famous description of the transcendent realm of the forms that is so far removed from the realm of ordinary existence that it is *outside* the heavens themselves, even beyond the normal realm of the gods.[47] Whether any of the details of this mythical picture are to be taken literally is difficult to determine. Since many of the details are clearly fantastic, it is not easy to defend the claim that some of them are to be taken literally. Nevertheless, the traditional interpretation of Plato's views assumes that he does believe that the forms are not part of the world of ordinary existence and that only in that realm beyond the heavens do things really exist. This creates epistemological and metaphysical problems that require equally mythical stories to resolve, such as the theory/story of recollection, mentioned in the *Phaedrus* (249c), and also in the *Meno* (81a–d) and the *Phaedo* (72e–77a).

Socrates' discussion of reincarnation includes at 248d–e a hierarchical list of vocations that is reminiscent of the caste system of ancient India. There are several other parallels between these stories that Plato includes in the dialogues and traditions we know as Eastern. Whether this is the result of a common early source or a sign of cross-cultural communication cannot be determined from the available evidence.

At the end of this section, Socrates refers to the philosopher as one who has been "initiated perfectly into perfect mysteries" (249c), reminding the reader again of the Diotima section of the *Symposium*, and suggests that the common notion that philosophers are "out of their wits" (παρακινῶν, *parakinōn*, disturbed) is based on a failure to realize that they are "possessed"(249d), that is, "enthused" (the term is ἐνθουσιάζων, *enthousiazōn*, having a god inside). This again raises the question of whether the philosopher ultimately transcends the reach of reason (*logos*).[48] Is this simply a statement appropriate to the mythical context, or an affirmation of an epistemological view according to which truth is ultimately ineffable? In dealing with this question the reader should pay close attention to Socrates' explications of the practical implications of these stories.

3. Recollecting the Heavenly Visions: 249d–250c. At the beginning of this section, Socrates notes that he will be speaking of the benefits of *erōs* with regard to both the lover and the beloved, not only from the point of view of the beloved as was the case in his earlier speech and that of Lysias (249e, cf. 253c).

Socrates now begins to connect this fourth kind of madness, *erōs*, with beauty, creating interesting parallels with the Diotima passage in the *Symposium*, although the notion of recollection is missing from the *Symposium*. Acknowledging both the common human response to beauty and the fact that some people have more adequate understandings of beauty, justice, etc., he introduces a story of how people recollect the things they saw, more or less clearly, on their heavenly journeys with the gods. This notion of recollection is argued for, rather than simply asserted, in the *Meno* (81a–d) and the *Phaedo* (72e–77a); the presentation in the *Phaedo* is more similar to this passage.[49]

4. The Erotic Response to Beauty: 250d–252b. Socrates begins (250d) with an explanation of why the recovery of our heavenly visions is prompted by the sight of visible beauty that is about on a par with his explanation of why he will only offer a metaphor of the soul. This explanation fits too well the context of his making a speech to a young boy about the benefits of love for it to carry much weight as a serious philosophical defense of the priority of the experience of beauty in the discovery of truth and the acquisition of virtue.

The reference to homosexual activity at 250e is surprisingly harsh, both in terms of the metaphor[50] and in terms of the mention of "a pleasure that is contrary to nature."[51] Perhaps Socrates is being ironic (as one might kid an audience of college professors by claiming that higher education has a pernicious effect on students), or perhaps this can be accounted for by the fact that Socrates is referring to a man who has no recollection of the heavenly beauty and hence "feels no awe when looking at its namesake." Nevertheless, he later cautions against actually engaging in homosexual intercourse (254a ff.), and comes close to suggesting that it is inherently demeaning or worse. This is surprising after reading the *Symposium* and in the context of the homosexually loaded playfulness in Socrates' second speech and between Socrates and Phaedrus in the *Phaedrus* itself, as well as the kidding of Socrates about his enthusiasm for handsome young men in other dialogues.[52] This raises a question as to whether or not Socrates is being presented by Plato as one who approves of homosexual relationships. Nevertheless, as Socrates goes on to describe the experience of the man who does recall his heavenly vision of beauty when he is confronted with a handsome young man, he speaks of the experience in terms that are both positive in tone and blatantly sexual, referring to erection, ejaculation, and the entire experience of sexual arousal (251d ff.).

This section concludes with another bit of playful etymology (252b). The tongue in cheek character of these obviously contrived etymologies is a striking motif in the *Phaedrus*. It is another way of drawing our attention to *logos*.

5. The Search for God-like Darlings: 252c–253c. This section provides a characterization of the loving relationship, always represented as the standard homosexual pair of an older lover and a younger beloved, in terms that draw on the story of the heavenly journeys in the trains of the gods. The motif of friendship (*philia*) reappears explicitly at 253c. Socrates makes clear that the relationship he is characterizing as based on the madness of *erōs* is an example of *philia*.

6. The Charioteer's Horses: 253c–254e. Socrates exploits the possibilities of the image of the pair of horses to illuminate the experience of internal conflict. The details of such poetic imagery should not be pressed too closely. We should not try to derive a detailed theory of the psychology of action from this story. It is interesting that one of the horses, the good one, always cooperates with the charioteer, and on the basis of judgment, not force (254a). Also, the charioteer is never over-ruled by the bad horse, though it takes some effort for the charioteer to resist the pull of the bad horse's attraction to "the delights of sexual activity" and "terrible, unlawful things" (254a). Here again, the activity of sexual intercourse is spoken of in negative tones, though the context may suggest that the intercourse aimed at was "hubristic" (254e). Hackforth argues that the intent here is the sublimation of "sheer lust."[53]

At 253c Socrates refers to his *logos* as a *mythos* ("tale").

7. The Benefits and Confusions of Love: 255a–e. The connection between love and friendship again comes out in this section. Socrates asserts that the friendship that occurs between true lovers is far superior to any other, and particularly mentions the conversations (*logos*) they engage in (255b). Socrates also claims that the beloved begins to partake of erotic desire, so that the traditional one-sidedness of this sort of erotic relationship is overcome, though the beloved does not at first understand the nature of this experience (255d–e). It is not clear whether the beloved's love is stimulated by seeing his own beauty, indirectly perceived via the reflection in his lover's eyes, or by partaking of the lover's passion that has developed as a result of the stimulus of the beloved's beauty (255c–d). The text seems to suggest both. At any rate, the erotic response is always to the perception of an earthly beauty that is connected in principle with the beauty beyond the heavens, a connection that is developed more fully in Diotima's analysis in the *Symposium*.

8. Two Kinds of Loving Friendship: 255e–256e. The issue of actual intercourse between the lovers again arises, and Socrates again treats it as something to be avoided. Those in whom "the better aspects of the mind (that is, their thinking, διάνοια, *dianoia*) prevail" refrain from intercourse and instead engage in philosophy (friendship with wisdom) (256a).[54] They achieve this, the best possible life, "by binding that by which evil comes into the soul and setting free that by which goodness comes in" (256b). This statement seems to make a surprisingly strong and rather hyperbolic condemnation of homosexual intercourse, though it is perhaps somewhat mitigated by Socrates' description of the second-best relationship between lovers. It also seems to make the even more startling suggestion that one achieves goodness (the Greek term translated as "goodness" is ἀρετή, *aretē*, often rendered as "virtue") by sublimation or suppression of the desire for sexual intercourse. This sort of hyperbole makes the interpretation of this passage difficult.

In the second type of loving friendship, the lovers do engage in intercourse, "though rarely, since what they are doing has not been decided by their whole mind (*dianoia*)" (256c). This pair is also established on the upward path.

The condemnation of homosexual intercourse in the *Phaedrus* (but *not* homosexual erotic desire, which is treated as a positive motivator since it "causes the wings to grow," 255d) seems to be in conflict with the tone of Socrates' remarks in the *Symposium*, although one can reconcile the two presentations by claiming that Socrates does not in fact approve of actual homosexual *intercourse* in the *Symposium*. One could claim that his refusal of Alcibiades' advances was not based simply on the fact that agreement would not have been in Alcibiades' own best interest, but also reflected Socrates' personal rejection of such activity. This would also require that the life of the true lover depicted in terms of Diotima's staircase does not involve returning to the first step, at least not in the sense of engaging in intercourse. This is the traditional reading of Plato's views as represented by these passages, and it is assumed that the ribbing of Socrates for his obvious enthusiasm for handsome young men does not imply that he engaged in intercourse with them.[55]

9. A Concluding Prayer to Love: 257a–b. The two major divisions of the dialogue both conclude with a prayer, here to Love and at the end of the dialogue to Pan. This structural feature again highlights the remarkable presence of the gods in this dialogue and the religious tone of these speeches. No other dialogue is so filled with the gods. As in the *Euthyphro*, Socrates connects the divine with what is highest and best in the realm of human possibilities. However, it seems unlikely that he means to undermine the ultimacy of one's responsibility for the condition of one's soul or the supremacy of reason and speech (*logos*) in the achievement of virtue. It does not seem appropriate to interpret this prayer as suggesting that our fate is in the hands of the gods or that what we need lies beyond the grasp or power of *logos*.[56] That would not fit well with the hope for Phaedrus that Socrates expresses at the end of his prayer (257b) and at the end of the dialogue (277e ff.).

Socrates' comment that his speech was "somewhat poetical" (257a) surely refers to the highly metaphorical and mythical character of his language. It also seems to suggest that the reader is expected to exercise some judgment in interpreting the speech.

His reference to his expertise in the activities of love (the phrase in the Greek text is literally "the art connected with the activities of love" or "the erotic art") (257a) reminds the reader of Socrates' similar claim in the *Symposium* (177d, 212b).

Socrates seems to sum up the point of his speech in his hope that Phaedrus "will dedicate his life entirely to love through speeches that are characterized by friendship with wisdom (φιλοσοφία, *philosophia*)" (257b). The "speeches" (*logoi*, the plural of *logos*) Socrates refers to surely include conversations and not only the sort of monologues that dominate the first half of the dialogue. The dialogue itself may be taken as a model of the sort of life that Socrates has in mind. That Phaedrus responds to the prayer by saying he will join Socrates in making it "if in fact we will be better off should those things happen" (257b–c) raises a question about how much progress he is making toward fulfilling Socrates' hope for him. At least he recognizes that Socrates' second speech is much better than either of the previous two (257c).

THE ART OF MAKING SPEECHES: 257B–278B

A. *Is It Degrading to Write Speeches?: 257b–258d*

At this point the character of the dialogue changes dramatically. Phaedrus prompts the switch to a discussion of the art of making speeches by noting that Lysias may not want to compete with Socrates' speech because he may be concerned about being called a "speech-writer" (257c). Socrates points out that in fact those who write speeches behave in a manner that makes it clear that they would love to have the reputation of being effective writers of speeches (257d ff.). He concludes that it is the universal opinion that "there's nothing shameful about the activity of writing speeches as such" (258d). What is shameful is doing it badly (258d).

There is a certain shifting of focus throughout the coming discussion with regard to just what activity is being discussed. The initial reference is to writing speeches, but at 258d Socrates once mentions "speaking and writing" (258d), only to return to discussing writing alone. Then, Phaedrus' response at 258e clearly assumes that the topic includes listening to speeches, not just writing them. At 259e Socrates again refers to "speaking and writing," but then immediately focuses on speaking and (except for a passing mention at 261b, 264b–c, and 272a) says nothing more about writing until 274b, where Socrates raises a question about the activity of writing in contrast to that of speaking. Up to 274b, then, the issue is really the making of speeches, including delivering them. In fact, it is clear that Socrates is sometimes thinking of engaging in discourse where one will be responding to other speakers and not just reading or reciting a manuscript or delivering a formal address. Accordingly, he begins to refer in a more general way to "the art of making speeches" and "the art of rhetoric," and at 274b says that he has concluded his discussion of "the art and the lack of art in making speeches," and turns to a discussion of writing as such.

The general discussion is not really limited to the sort of formal, prepared displays that are illustrated in the three speeches in the first half of the dialogue, therefore. In this regard, the English term 'speeches' may be misleading; Socrates is talking about the activity of speaking in general, including conversation or dialogue, as he points out explicitly at 261a–b. What he says about this art of making speeches applies to written speeches as well, though there is something special about writing as such that he will discuss after 274b.

Socrates concludes this section by asking whether they should inquire about how to write well, referring to writing of every sort, but only to writing (258d). However, he and Phaedrus immediately abandon this restriction on the subject. Phaedrus responds somewhat vaguely that the pleasures of such activity are the best possible, and he seems to mean the activity of inquiry and not that of reading/writing/listening to formal speeches (which might have been expected on the basis of the earlier characterization of him at 242a–b). It seems unlikely that he has in mind the sort of self-examination that such inquiry always is for Socrates. The importance of knowledge of the self, which surely includes one's own self, in mastering the art of speech is a major point in the ensuing discussion.

B. The Myth of the Cicadas: 258e–259d

Phaedrus' ignorance of this story about the cicadas (259b) suggests that Socrates is making it up for the occasion, as Phaedrus explicitly accuses him of doing with the story about the invention of writing (275b). Thus, this seems to be another example of Socrates' playfully serious, flexible approach to stories about the gods. The point of this story is to extol the importance of engaging in conversation.

As for the names of the Muses, "Terpsichore" means "delights in dance," "Erato" is connected with *erōs*, "Calliope" means "beautiful voice," and "Ourania" means "heavenly." The last two are thus particularly appropriate for association with philosophical conversation in this context.

It is not clear just what gift Socrates has in mind when he says the cicadas have received a gift "from the gods to give to human beings" (259b). The cicadas' gift is that of "not needing any food from their birth, so that they sing continuously without eating or drinking until they die" (259c). He then suggests that what the cicadas do for human beings is to report their behavior to the appropriate Muses. Perhaps he is suggesting that the best life for a human being would consist of continual conversation—as Socrates seems to suggest at *Apology* 40e–41c in his description of what he expects the next life to be like, if there is one. At 262d Socrates again refers to the gift of the cicadas and apparently identifies it as the art of speaking. In the context, however, he implies that it is at best only the technical aspects of rhetoric, since he is referring to the ability of someone who knows the truth to intentionally deceive an audience. Moreover, he seems to be saying that Lysias as well as himself in the persona of the giver of his first speech have been inspired with this gift. Thus, the point of the story remains somewhat vague, beyond its general commendation of speaking as a worthy activity.

C. A Good Speaker Must Know the Truth: 259e–260d

Socrates reiterates that the question to be examined is: What constitutes speaking and writing well or badly? (259e). He and Phaedrus discuss this question for the rest of the dialogue in a somewhat rambling way that is appropriately conversational.

Socrates begins by asking whether it is necessary in order to speak properly and well for the speaker to know the truth about the subject (259e). Phaedrus responds that some say that what is important is to know, not the truth, but what the audience believes; a persuasive speaker is one who can cater to the prejudices of the audience (259e–260a). Socrates points out this means that it would be proper for a speaker who does not know what is just to encourage an audience who is also ignorant of the truth to engage in what are in fact unjust actions, and that could not be proper speaking (260b–c). Though Phaedrus agrees (a bit vaguely, 260d), Socrates shifts the focus, and this issue is dealt with more clearly and emphatically later (272b–274a).

D. An Initial Definition of the Art of Making Speeches: 260d–262c

What Socrates does is to focus on the implication of Phaedrus' remark at 259e–260a to the effect that the art of speaking is only the art of persuasion, an art that is independent of a concern for truth. This was an explicit topic of controversy in Plato's day and is also discussed in the *Gorgias*, where Socrates objects to the rhetorician's indifference toward truth. Is the art of making speeches simply a set of techniques for manipulating audiences, or is knowledge of the truth an essential part of it? Socrates will argue for the latter view, but he begins by looking seriously at the former claim, that there is no "art" of speaking,[57] only an "artless routine" (260e). His point will be that one cannot effectively manipulate an audience without knowledge of both the topic and the audience. It is this knowledge that constitutes the art of making speeches.

In his analysis Socrates presents arguments that show why the art of making speeches is an art. He calls upon the arguments to convince Phaedrus that unless he develops a proper friendship with wisdom he will never speak well and properly (261a).

Socrates calls rhetoric the "art of leading souls by means of speeches" (261a), a statement that is consistent with the claim that the art of making speeches is the art of persuasion (though Socrates will show that this is not an alternative to the view that the art requires knowledge of the truth, contrary to what Phaedrus assumed at 259e–260a). Socrates begins by arguing that there is only a single art of speaking that applies to all occasions involving speech, public and private (261b–e). He points out that effective speakers can make opposite positions seem equally plausible (261d) and concludes that this single art is that of making things appear similar to each other, whether they are or not, along with the ability to detect this practice in others (261e). He focuses on cases where the intent is to make what is false appear true, which one must do in order to argue for both sides of a case.

Socrates will later question whether a speaker who argues for opposite positions can truly possess the art of making speeches, since that would involve defending as true what one knows to be false, but at this point he directs Phaedrus to examine what must be the case for one to engage in this practice of establishing similarities between things (261e–262c). Leading an audience to a new place involves bringing them little by little from where they started to where the speaker wants them to end up, convincing them that each step of the argument involves a similar position to its predecessor. Socrates uses as his example a speaker who is intentionally deceiving an audience, persuading them to believe something the speaker knows to be false, by presenting as essentially similar things that are significantly different. He points out that this obviously cannot be done without a knowledge of the nature of the things being talked about (262b–c). Otherwise the speaker would not be able to construct the chain of (misleading) similarities and, what is more, would also be vulnerable to a similar manipulation. (This last point again adds the art of listening to that of speaking.) Thus, Socrates shows that those who claim to practice the "art" of speaking as only a way of manipulating an audience, cannot in fact hope to function effectively without a knowledge of the truth. He now turns to the speeches given earlier in the dialogue for examples of this knowledge.

E. Artfulness in the Earlier Speeches: 262c–264e

Socrates' reference at 262c to "the two speeches that have been given" is ambiguous. Some readers see this as a reference to Lysias' speech and to both of Socrates' as a unit, while others see it as referring only to Socrates' two speeches. Nothing of importance seems to ride on this issue, and both views can be plausibly defended.[58]

Socrates begins his search for signs of artfulness in the earlier speeches by making a somewhat surprising assertion: He says that they "contain an example of how someone who knows the truth can mislead his audience by playing around with words" (262d). Since this obviously applies to his speeches and not that of Lysias, it is an uncharacteristically bold claim of competence on the part of Socrates, and also raises again the question of whether Socrates' first speech is based on a definition of love that Plato means for the reader to accept, as well as the question of whether Socrates' two speeches are based on the same definition of love. Perhaps the remark is ironic.[59] Socrates goes on to assert the crucial importance of beginning with a definition of what is being talked about, when the topic is controversial (263a–d), and does not again claim that the definition he gave in his first speech was correct. Instead he merely says that he did the right thing in giving a definition (263d). Indeed, Socrates later implies that the definition may not have been correct, saying, "whether the definition was stated well or poorly, it did enable the speech to proceed in a manner that was at any rate clear and self-consistent" (265d). The method for establishing correct definitions is brought up in the next section (264e–266d).

In the course of discussing this point Phaedrus makes a remark that suggests that he is beginning to gain a better understanding. He shows that he grasps Socrates' point about the controversial character of the definition of love by saying that it is that lack of a generally agreed upon assumption about the nature of love that enabled Socrates to take opposite positions on the question of whether love is a good or bad thing (263c). This may be a sign that Phaedrus is overcoming his initial naïveté.

In this section Socrates also asserts that a speech should have an organic structure, with a definite beginning, middle, and ending (264c–d). He doesn't explain this point beyond using the metaphor of a living body, which he uses again at 265e and 266a, and reciting a poem that lacks such structure. The fact that Socrates connects this metaphor with understanding the forms suggests that the presence of proper, orderly development in a speech is a sign of the speaker's understanding of the topic.

F. A Comparison of Socrates' Two Speeches: 264e–266d

Socrates now compares his two speeches and draws two important points from them. His first point is that though the speeches were "opposites in a way" (265a), they defined love as a kind of madness, distinguishing two forms of madness (one the result of human sickness and the other of divine origin), and further distinguished four parts of the divine type (265a). How to understand this and whether it means the two speeches were based on the same definition of love is not answered by this passage because no attention is given to the question of in what sense madness is one or two. That is, is the term 'madness' being equivocated on? As noted earlier, madness can be something that is incompatible with rationality or something that involves unusual or uncommon behavior that is nevertheless thoroughly grounded in reason. At any rate the disclaimer Socrates offers at 265b–c should cause considerable pause to anyone trying to find a view of love or madness here that Plato intends to present as philosophically satisfactory:

> We described erotic passion in, I don't know, a sort of figurative manner, perhaps touching on something of the truth but also probably being led astray at other points. The mixture was a not altogether unconvincing speech [the reference is to his second speech], and we playfully sang, in properly worshipful tones, a sort of mythical hymn to Love.

The second point Socrates derives from his earlier speeches is affirmed much less ambiguously. This is the specification of the principles of collection and division and the affirmation of their value.[60] He begins by suggesting that the use of these principles was not part of what was playful about his speeches (265c), and he concludes his discussion of them with a remarkable affirmation: "I, myself, Phaedrus, am a lover of these dividings and collectings as what enable me to speak and think, and when I believe that someone else is able to see the natural unity and plurality of things, I follow him, 'walking behind him in his footsteps as in those of a god'" (266b). Moreover, he says that he calls people who have this ability "dialecticians," and Phaedrus agrees that the art he has just described is correctly called that, though (in a comment that perhaps raises a question about his philosophical development) he says it is not clear to him that this is the rhetorical art they have been seeking (266c). Socrates, however, is sceptical that any art could be independent of these principles of dialectic and suggests that they consider whether there could be an art of rhetoric that was distinct from this sort of dialectic (266d).[61]

Insofar as the reader is looking for seriously intended philosophical claims to carry away from the *Phaedrus*, nothing is a less ambiguous candidate than this notion of the principles of dialectic. Nothing is more clearly affirmed and illustrated in the dialogue.[62] Socrates' speeches and his entire conversation with Phaedrus illustrate the power of collection and division. Love and friendship find their highest fulfillment, as well as their ultimate basis, in dialectic, the art of conversation.

The uses of the principles of division and collection in the *Phaedrus* show that they are not rigid, mechanical procedures with a single unvarying form (such as division into dichotomies and the use of nonoverlapping hierarchies), but general practices of looking for both unity and diversity in the search for understanding.[63] Hackforth's complaint that the divisions in

Socrates' speeches do not in fact follow "a formal divisional procedure" is based on an inappropriately rigid interpretation of the principle.[64]

G. The Techniques of Rhetoric: 266d–269c

Phaedrus initiates a search for aspects of the rhetorical art that are separate from the dialectical art of collection and division (266d). Socrates lists the various techniques that are the focus of the teachers of rhetoric (266d–267e) and gives a devastating critique of the significance of such things for the art of rhetoric by using analogies with medicine and the art of writing tragedies (as well as an appeal to what the great orators of the past would say) to show that, at best, they only teach things that are useful to a speaker who has a knowledge of dialectic (268a–269c). Lacking that essential knowledge themselves, they fail to provide it to their students. So far from being teachers of the art of rhetoric, they do not even possess the art themselves and are mere teachers of "an artless routine" (268e, 269b–c). Socrates then goes on to say a bit more about the knowledge that is the basis of the art of making speeches.

This negative critique of the famous teachers of rhetoric who were so important in Athens reads like an appeal to prospective students of rhetoric to avoid cheap imitations and enroll in the one school that teaches the true art.[65] It seems to give the dialogue a practical tone that suggests that Plato is being in earnest in this section of the text, whatever we conclude about the content of the great mythical hymn that is Socrates' second speech. Perhaps the three speeches in the dialogue are all intended to illustrate, with increasing effectiveness, the dangers of a rhetoric that is not grounded in dialectical knowledge. Certainly, many of the techniques Socrates lists in this section are illustrated in his second speech.

H. Rhetoric Requires Knowledge of the Nature of the Soul: 269c–272c

Phaedrus asks how one acquires the true art of rhetoric (269c), and Socrates replies that the crucial thing is knowledge and practice (269d). The mention of practice adds an interesting dimension, but Socrates says nothing else about it. He now brings out some additional characteristics of the knowledge that is essential to the art of making speeches, besides the dialectical principles of collection and division discussed above.

Socrates first makes a curious comment in connection with high (ironic?) praise of Pericles as a master of rhetoric (269e–270a). He seems to be making a very important claim about the most profound matters, but some of the terms he uses are difficult to interpret and his reference to the philosopher Anaxagoras, whose views Socrates finds inadequate in the *Phaedo*,[66] further complicates matters. Socrates says that what is required for "all the great arts" is "facility in conversation and lofty speculation about nature" (269e–270a). The Greek terms translated as "facility in conversation" and "lofty speculation" are ἀδολεσχίας, *adoleschias* (often used in a pejorative sense and read as "idle talk" or "babbling") and μετεωρολογίας, *meteōrologias* (literally, "talk about things in the sky"). Plato uses the first term in a pejorative sense at *Theaetetus* 195b–c, *Statesman* 299b, and *Republic* 489a. However, he does have Parmenides make a positive recommendation of the usefulness of *adoleschias* at *Parmenides* 135d. Parmenides describes it as preliminary training for serious philosophical thinking, which could also be the intent here. The term *meteōrologias* is used literally at *Cratylus* 404c and *Timaeus* 91d and metaphorically in a positive sense at *Cratylus* 396c and 401b. However, it is used in a pejorative sense, and in combination with *adoleschia*, at *Statesman* 299b. As a result of these ambiguities, the question of how to interpret Socrates' remark here is quite controversial. The issue is further complicated by the fact that Socrates is quite critical of Pericles at *Gorgias* 515b ff. We can read the passage as ironic praise of Pericles (assuming the two terms are used pejoratively), who is "the most perfect of all in rhetoric" (269e) in the sense that he perfectly mastered the "artless routines" of popular rhetoric.[67] At any rate, Socrates seems to settle down immediately to a serious explication of one kind of knowledge that is essential for the true rhetorician.

Drawing an analogy with the medical art's need for knowledge of the body, Socrates argues that the rhetorical art needs a knowledge of the soul, both in the general sense and with reference to particular audiences (270b–c). At 270d Socrates gives a more detailed statement of what is involved in understanding anything whatsoever. In effect, this is a filling out of what is involved in using the principles of collection and division. One must focus on a single genus, separating a complex group into its simple parts first, and then inquiring as to what it is capable of doing and experiencing.[68] Thus, since the aim of speech is to produce conviction in the soul, the speaker must know the essential nature of soul (270e–271a). Once again, Socrates shows that by admitting that speech is the art of persuasion, the popular rhetoricians are committed to its being based on knowledge of the truth, and not merely on an awareness of what people believe. Moreover, Socrates argues that rhetoric will also require a knowledge of which kinds of speeches to use with different audiences (271b). He concludes with an emphatic assertion that there is no other way of being artful in speaking and writing than by means of this knowledge (271b), and points out that, if they possess this knowledge, current writers about rhetoric are keeping it well hidden (271c). Socrates then gives a complex summation of what the true rhetorician must know about souls in order to make proper use of the routines and techniques on which the popular teachers of rhetoric focus (271c–272a). We wonder what role the metaphor of the charioteer and team of horses, travelling in the trains of various gods, plays in the acquisition of this knowledge. Socrates does emphasize at the beginning of his second speech that it is crucial to understand the nature of the soul (245c), and implies that this is the focus of the bulk of his speech (246a).

Socrates then offers an exhortation to examine what has been said as closely as possible (272c). In such passages Plato seems to speak directly to the reader. Perhaps he is again encouraging readers to sign up for his Academic program, rather than the Sophists' short courses, as well as reminding us of the importance of critical reflection on what is being said.

I. Conclusion of the Analysis of the Art of Making Speeches: 272c–274b

Socrates concludes his general discussion of the art of making speeches by reiterating his point that rhetoric requires a knowledge of the truth. He reminds Phaedrus that the popular view is that what the effective orator should express is not what is true, but what is probable, that is, what people are most likely to believe, even if the speaker knows this is false (272d–273a). Socrates again insists that one can only hope to do this effectively if one knows the truth, since what seems likely to the general public does so "because of a similarity to the truth" (273d). He insists that this includes a knowledge of both the nature of the audience and of the topic of one's speech (273e). Acquiring this knowledge will require substantial effort, but it is clearly worth the effort when one notes that one speaks, not just before human beings, but before the gods—as is made explicitly clear in this dialogue. Making speeches should be seen as a matter of pleasing the gods and not just ones "fellow slaves" (273e); it is an activity in which intentional deception does not play a legitimate role. No human activity is more important than the activation of one's capacity for *logos*. It is not only Aristotle who sees the possession of *logos* as the distinguishing characteristic of human being.[69] Socrates' reference to "the way round" and "the circuit" at 274a again reminds us of the myth in his second speech.

Socrates concludes their examination of the art of making speeches with the poignant remark, "It's a noble thing to attempt noble deeds and then suffer the consequences" (274a–b). A reminder to the reader that the proper use of *logos* may not lead to popularity and affluence.

J. The Nature of Writing: 274b–277a

Although it is not made entirely clear in Socrates' remarks in the transition passage 274b–c,[70] the topic he now turns to is a comparison of the activity of writing and written documents to conversation, or perhaps to oral presentations that are followed by discussion. In effect, Socrates finally returns to the question he raised at 258d: "How does one write well or badly?"

Socrates tells a story that he claims to have heard from "our predecessors" (274c), although Phaedrus accuses him of having made it up (275b). The moral of the story is that writing serves to remind people of things, but cannot provide them with the understanding that constitutes true wisdom. If anything, it hampers the acquisition of wisdom by weakening people's memory[71] (274c–275a).

Before Socrates expands on this theme, there is an interesting exchange with Phaedrus over the value of such mythical tales. Phaedrus complains that Socrates is making up "stories [the Greek term is the plural of *logos*] about the Egyptians or anyone else you want to" (275b), apparently meaning to include at least Socrates' story about the cicadas at 258e–259d. Socrates takes this as a suggestion that such made-up tales cannot be taken seriously as expressions of truth and rebukes Phaedrus by pointing out that in an earlier day people were willing to take seriously even statements attributed to oak trees and rocks, if the statements contained the truth. The issue is not who the speaker is (nor, we may perhaps add, whether the outer form of the story is literally true), but whether what is said is true (275b–c). Phaedrus accepts the rebuke, and they engage in an examination of the implications of Socrates' story for the significance of writing and written documents (275c–277a).

It is tempting to make a general application of this passage to the use of myths in the entire dialogue, and in other dialogues. Socrates can take the gods and their heavenly realm seriously without insisting that these images are literally true in themselves. The story of recollection can be a dramatic way of affirming the capacity of human beings to derive an insight into universal principles from their particular experiences. The depiction of the forms as otherworldly objects can be a dramatic way of emphasizing their importance and their role as standards for judging individual opinions. The story of reincarnation can be a dramatic way of defending the importance of being reconciled to the contingencies of one's life without giving up hope for improvement in the future. The story of Oreithuia warns us about the dangers of erotic passion. All these stories are true, therefore, and to be taken seriously as (playful) stories that remind us of important truths. Such stories, like written documents, only yield their truths under examination.

Socrates begins by stating the general theme of his discussion: One cannot hope to communicate the truth in a clear and reliable way by means of the written word alone (275c). The problem with written speeches is explained by comparing them to paintings, which speeches resemble in that like paintings they cannot clarify or defend themselves. Moreover, like paintings they can be handled by people who lack the training to understand them (275d–e).

It is immediately clear that Plato could not have written this section of the dialogue without being aware of its application to his own works and to this dialogue in particular. Thus, it seems plausible to assume that this section will contain some indication of how Plato thinks the dialogues (and the stories in them) should be read. We are not disappointed. He implies that the dialogues (and especially the *Phaedrus*?) are above all playful, though this does not mean they lack serious purpose. One should read them for enjoyment, but also to remind one of important truths and to stimulate the conversation that will produce true understanding.[72]

Socrates contrasts the written speech with one that "is written along with knowledge in the soul of the learner" (276a). By adding the qualification "with knowledge," Socrates makes it clear that he does not mean what has simply been memorized, as Phaedrus was apparently trying to memorize Lysias' speech without understanding the significance of its content at the beginning of the dialogue. What is "written on the soul" (inscribed in our hearts and minds) is an understanding that involves the ability to explain and defend what is understood, what Phaedrus calls "the living and ensouled speech of the person who knows, of which a written speech may justly be called a kind of image" (276a).

The depiction of written language as the dead image of living speech brings to mind the complaint of Jacques Derrida that this imagery encourages a false understanding of the nature and significance of language. Derrida argues that, while this way of thinking recognizes that the meaning of a written text is open to interpretation and hence does not straightforwardly contain a fixed meaning, it is connected with the assumption that language is nevertheless capable of capturing the truth in a final, absolute, and ultimate way. We would be better off, Derrida argues, if we reverse the imagery and treat the written word, which we recognize contains no finality or context-independent meaning, as prior and think of spoken language as an image of written speech. Derrida calls the view that language can express truth in a final, context-independent way, the logos theory of language. Whether or not Plato actually held such a view is open to controversy. Certainly what he says about living speech here does not suggest that it contains any final, context-independent statements that do not require continuing explanation and interpretation. It is just this need for interpretation for the hearer that leads to Plato's complaint about the value of written documents.

Using an analogy with the comparison between serious farming and the forcing of blooms for a festival (276b), Socrates suggests that written speeches are prepared only as a sort of amusement. When someone who understands things like justice and goodness is serious, he doesn't write about them, except "to store up reminders for himself, and for all who follow the same track" (276d). (The last phrase reminds us of the heavenly trains of the gods in Socrates' great myth.) We know from earlier passages that one must not assume that the serious and the playful are diametrically opposed, though Phaedrus' response to the analogy with farming and forcing blooms suggests that he may still not have understood this (276c).[73]

In summation Socrates reiterates the fact that written documents have limited value, but conversation based on the dialectical art is of profound importance (276e–277a). The implanting of speeches in souls, accompanied by the understanding that enables the hearer to explain and defend them, initiates a process of continual fertilization that is unending. To possess such speeches, that is, to thus activate one's capacity for *logos*, is to be as happy as possible. This passage recalls Diotima's views in the *Symposium* about the role of conversation in the good life and the kind of immortality that is possible for humans.

It is often pointed out that Plato achieves a marvelous sort of compromise between the written and the living forms of speech with his written documents that are in the form of conversations. What makes this a successful compromise is that Plato's written conversations require the reader to participate in them in order to read/hear them effectively. Their open-ended character and their many-sidedness stimulate the sort of reflexive give-and-take that makes for effective fertilization in living conversation.[74]

K. A Final Summation of the Art of Making Speeches: 277a–278b

Socrates provides a very thorough summary of the true art of making speeches as he has presented it in his discussion with Phaedrus. He begins by emphasizing that the proper use of speech requires that the speaker have a dialectical understanding of both the subject of the speech and the nature of the audience (277b–c). In this description of the methods of collection and division he mentions for the first time the idea that the process of division ultimately reaches indivisible ends. This notion of the so-called "atomic" (the word is based on the Greek term for "uncuttable" ἄτομος, *atomos*) forms suggests that the process of dialectical analysis is finite and reaches ultimate terminations. It is usually assumed that this also suggests that the realm of the forms has a single, fixed hierarchical structure. Such a view is defended more explicitly by Aristotle and is usually attributed to Plato also. This view would seem to imply that final statements of the natures of the forms would also be unchanging and not relative to conversational contexts. Whether Socrates means to affirm such a view here cannot be determined from this passage. It could be argued that Socrates' claim that a speech must conform to the natures of the souls of the audience implies that no such context-independent statements are expected, even if they are possible. What counts as the "indivisible" termination of a process of division may also depend on the (dialectical) context.

Socrates then reiterates his view of written documents (277d–278b). He asserts that it is foolish to think that written documents "possess great clarity and permanence"—even if everybody else thinks otherwise. We again cannot avoid seeing this as a reference to Plato's own writing, as well as all others. If we take it seriously, a great deal of the scholarship on Plato seems to be undermined. However, the "if" here is significant. After all, this reference is in a dialogue that is clearly very playful in style and content, and that applies to this comment as much as to the rest of the dialogue. Socrates' rather harsh statement to the effect that no written document "is worthy of much serious consideration" may perhaps be somewhat ironic (seen as a comment written by Plato), and we may be falling prey to the fallacy of not noticing the playfulness of this claim about the playfulness of written documents.[75] At any rate, it would seem precipitous to reject as inappropriate the careful, philosophical analysis of the arguments and texts of Plato's dialogues on the basis of the discussion of writing in this dialogue. Caution seems warranted here if for no other reason than that careful, serious reading of Plato's dialogues seems to be such an effective stimulus for just that sort of examination that Socrates suggests leads to dialectical knowledge.

Socrates concludes his summation of his view of rhetoric by reaffirming the preeminence of oral conversation as the only form of *logos* "worthy of serious consideration," and even if we see this as also a bit hyperbolic, the supremacy of dialogical conversation is obviously a major theme of the Platonic Socrates. One may also see in this passage at 278a–b a suggestion that Plato sees the living conversations he has inspired (and may inspire through his written works?[76]) as a much more significant legacy than his written "children."

Phaedrus agrees wholeheartedly with Socrates' view at 278b. Perhaps this indicates that he has been edified and persuaded by Socrates' conversation and has at last achieved some degree of philosophical sophistication where *logos* is concerned. If so, he will also have become a friend of wisdom, as well as of Socrates—and, potentially, of Lysias. The fertile development and spread of the *logos* that is written in the soul along with knowledge, that Socrates refers to in the conclusion of his summary, can and will continue as a natural part of friendship, a theme that becomes a major focus in the final pages of the dialogue.

L. A Proper Title for a Master of Logos: 278b–e

Socrates argues that anyone who speaks with a knowledge of truth and understands the true relation between the spoken and written word should not be referred to as a "writer" of speeches. A proper title for one who has mastered the rhetorical art should relate to what such a person is serious about, and that is not written documents. He suggests that it would be too much to call such a person "wise," *sophos*, since that is only appropriate for gods, but such a person could be called a "friend of wisdom," that is, a "philosopher," *philosophos*.

There is a lot going on in this little wordplay.[77] Surely Socrates is taking another slap at the Sophists, whose lack of wisdom he has been ridiculing above but who are referred to by a title (σοφιστής, *sophistēs*) that is based on the term wise and means "one who is a practitioner of wisdom." Socrates also brings out the root meaning of the term *philosophos*, that is usually translated as "philosopher," but literally means "friend of wisdom."[78] The implication is that such a person does not "possess" wisdom, but has a relationship with it that is analogous to that of friends—a relationship that is open-ended, developing, grounded in *logos* (and perhaps *erōs* in some sense), and involves a mutuality that is constitutive of their being. The last point receives special emphasis at the end of the dialogue. The passage reminds us of the view of Diotima in the *Symposium*, according to which a philosopher would be more accurately characterized as one who is engaged in the search for wisdom, in some sense lacking it, rather than as one who is in possession of it, since such a person could not love it. Philosophy is the activity of friendly conversation.

At 278d–e Socrates describes the person who is rightly called a "writer of speeches," or a poet.[79] It is tempting to see the description of one "who spends a lot of time changing his works this way and that, pasting them together and pulling them apart" (278d) as another ironic self-reference by Plato. Socrates directs Phaedrus to communicate this recommendation about titles to his associate Lysias (278e). When the term translated as "associate" (ἑταῖρος, *hetairos*) is applied to a woman it means "concubine" or "mistress." Thus, there may be an element of the playful sexual innuendo that pervades the *Phaedrus* here also. The innuendo is explicit in Socrates' ironic reference to Lysias and Isocrates as the respective darlings of Phaedrus and himself at 279b. The term 'darling' (παιδικά, *paidika*, an emphatic plural of the adjective meaning "childlike") is the standard term for the younger beloved in a homosexual relationship.

M. Socrates Makes a Prediction about Isocrates: 278e–279b

Isocrates (436–338 B.C.E.) is a prominent teacher of rhetoric and contemporary of Plato. Several of his written speeches are extant. Perhaps largely on the basis of this passage, ancient scholars assumed the two were friends who had a high regard for each other. However, many modern scholars find highly negative critiques of the views and practices of Isocrates in Plato's *Gorgias* and the *Euthydemus*, although Isocrates is not mentioned by name, and negative critiques of Plato in Isocrates' writings. Hence the interpretation of this passage in the *Phaedrus* has become controversial. It was written when Isocrates was a well-known figure and rival of Plato. Isocrates' school of rhetoric was very successful, and his written speeches were highly regarded in the ancient world. He insisted that he was a philosopher and spoke of people like Plato and Socrates as practitioners of eristic, that is, in W. H. Thompson's phrase, Lords of Disputation. Perhaps Plato is here saying that Isocrates has failed to fulfill an early potential. Hackforth rejects this interpretation, suggesting that Plato still hopes for the fulfillment of Isocrates' potential for greater things and may be trying to influence Isocrates with the praise in this passage.[80] Rowe, on the other hand, takes the praise of Isocrates to be entirely ironic.[81] At any rate, it is clear that in general the *Phaedrus* is profoundly critical of the views and practices of contemporary teachers of rhetoric.

N. The Final Prayer to Pan: 279b–c

The choice of Pan as the god to whom Socrates' final prayer is directed points to the importance of the theme of *logos* in the dialogue. Pan is not only associated with rural places, goat-herding, and *erōs*, he is also, at least by Plato, identified with *logos* itself. In the *Cratylus*, Plato has Socrates say that Pan, who is the son of Hermes, "is *logos* or the brother of *logos*" and as such he, like *logos*, signifies and articulates all things.[82]

The simple prayer that Socrates offers to Pan makes a charming conclusion to the dialogue.[83] It provides Phaedrus an opportunity to show that he has been persuaded by Socrates' discussion and, perhaps, has now achieved a proper understanding of and love for *logos*, as well as a true friendship with Socrates. More importantly, the prayer plays a special role in connection with the motif of friendship in the dialogue. Socrates makes use of the metaphor of friendship in a conspicuous way that supports the claim that Plato is emphasizing the metaphor in the term *philosophia*, which I discussed above.

The importance of this motif of friendship is also indicated by the occurrence of the traditional proverb "friends' things are held in common"[84] in Phaedrus' final comment, after which Socrates says only "Let's go" as he and Phaedrus continue their journey. The meaning of the proverb is important for the dialogue, and is also illuminated by the dialogue. It emphasizes the fact that insofar as one has a friend one has things that are not one's own. That is, in a friendship there are possessions that are the possessions of both partners; rather than mine and/or yours, they are ours. Indeed, the implication is that at least some of the possessions we have in such a case are not independent of the friendship, but a product of it. This seems especially to be the case where conversation and the products of conversation are concerned, for true conversation cannot occur without the mutuality and commonality of friendship. And since nothing is more important than conversation and its effects in Socrates' view, this means friendship is a very important phenomenon. The depiction of that phenomenon is an important motif of the *Phaedrus*.

Appendix: References to Love (Erōs) in Other Dialogues

Although no other dialogues treat *erōs* as a major theme (the *Lysis* does focus on friendship, *philia*), there are a number of references to *erōs* in other dialogues. They need to be studied within their own contexts, of course, but the reader may find it interesting to see some of the things Plato has his characters say in other dialogues about *erōs*. Throughout these passages, "love" is used only for *erōs* and Greek words related to *erōs*, and "friendship" always translates *philia*.

1. CHARMIDES *154B–C*

[Socrates reports that he said to Critias] "Now, my friend, I am not much at measuring, for in front of beautiful young men I am simply an unmarked ruler—virtually all young men appear beautiful to me! So, when this one appeared I was astounded by his beauty and stature, and everybody else seemed to be in love with him, too."

2. CHARMIDES *167E*

[Socrates reports that he said to Critias] "And would you say that there is a sort of love that is not a love of beauty, but a love of itself and of other loves?" [He reports that Critias said no.]

3. LYSIS *204B–C*

[Socrates reports that he said] "Hippothales, you need say no more regarding whether or not you are in love. Not only do I know that you are in love, but I also know that you are already deeply in love. In other regards I am useless and of no account, but somehow a god has given me the gift of being able to instantly recognize both a lover and one who is loved."

4. LYSIS *221D–E*

[Socrates is reporting a conversation] "Then, is desire, as we were saying earlier, the cause of friendship, and the one who desires is a friend to what he desires at the time when he desires it?..."

"That seems likely," he said.

"But the one who desires," I said, "lacks that which he desires, doesn't he?"

"Yes."

. . .

"What he lacks is that which has been taken from him?"

"How could it not be?"

"So, Menexenus and Lysis, it seems that love, friendship, and desire are apparently of what belongs to one."

They agreed.

"Then, if you are friends with each other, you will in some way belong to each other by nature."

"Definitely," they said.

"If someone desires, or loves, someone else, then, my boys," I said, "he would never desire, love, or befriend him unless he happened to belong in some way to the one he loved, either in his soul, or in some quality, habit, or form of his soul."

5. REPUBLIC *402D-403B*

[Socrates reports a conversation] "Well, then," I said, "when there is a harmonious combination by joining together a soul that has a beautiful character and a body of a matching form, both parts sharing the same imprint, would that be a most beautiful sight for anyone able to see it?"

"By all means."

"And what is most beautiful is most lovable?"

"How could it not be?"

"A cultured person would love people of that sort most of all, but if someone were disharmonious, he would not love that person."

"Not if that person had a defect in his soul," he said, "although if it was a defect in his body, he would endure it and still want to embrace him."

"I understand," I said. "You have, or have had, such a darling. I concede your point, but tell me this. Is there any commonality between excessive pleasure and judiciousness?"

"How could there be?" he said. "Such pleasure drives one out of one's mind no less than pain does."

"And between it and the rest of virtue?"

"Not at all."

"But what about this? Is there any commonality between excessive pleasure and being outrageous or undisciplined?"

"Most certainly."

"Can you think of any pleasure greater or more intense than that connected with sexual passion (ἀφροδίσια, *aphrodisia*)?"

"I cannot," he said, "nor one that is more maddening."

"But the correct sort of love is loving a well-behaved and beautiful person in a sensible and cultured manner?"

"Certainly," he said.

"Then, anything mad (μανικόν, *manikon*) or related to being undisciplined must not be made a part of the correct love?"

"It must not be."

"Then, this sort of pleasure must not be made a part of correct love, and the lover and his darling who love and are loved correctly must have nothing to do with it."

"No, by Zeus, Socrates," he said, "one must have no part in it."

"So, then, it seems you will decree that, in the city we are establishing, a lover may befriend his darling, spend time with him, and touch him like a son, if he can persuade him to allow it for the sake of beautiful things, and may do other things in consorting with anyone in whom he is seriously interested so long as he never seems to go beyond that limit."

6. REPUBLIC *439D*

[Socrates is reporting a conversation] "So, it is not unreasonable," I said, "for us to consider these to be two parts [of the soul] that are different from each other, pronouncing the part with which one reasons to be the rational part of the soul, and the part with which one loves and is hungry and thirsty and is aflutter with all the other desires, the nonrational and appetitive part, the companion of various replenishments and pleasures."

7. REPUBLIC *485B*

[Socrates is reporting a conversation] "So, let's agree on this about the philosophical nature, that it is always in love with the understanding that makes clear to it the being that is eternal and does not shift about through generation and decay."

8. REPUBLIC *499B–C*

[Socrates is reporting a conversation] "...we were forced by truth to say that no city or regime, nor any man, will ever be perfect until these philosophers...are put forward by some chance necessity, whether they want it or not, to take charge of a city...or else by some divine inspiration a true love for true philosophy is thrust upon the sons of the present rulers or kings or the rulers themselves."

9. REPUBLIC *555D–E*

[Socrates is reporting a conversation] "...they hate and conspire against those who have acquired their property and against others, because they love revolution."

10. REPUBLIC *574D–575A*

[Socrates is reporting a conversation] "In all this [evil-doing] those ancient beliefs about what is beautiful and what shameful that he had held from childhood and which kept him just are overwhelmed by beliefs newly released from confinement that are the bodyguards of Love and share its power. While he was still subject to the laws and his father and was a democratic man, they were set free only in dreams, but now, under the tyranny of Love he has become all of the time the sort of person he was before only occasionally in his dreams, neither refraining from terrible murder nor from any food or deed. Love lives within him, a tyrant in a state of total anarchy and lawlessness..."

11. REPUBLIC *587A–B*

[Socrates is reporting a conversation] "Does not what is most removed from reason (*logos*) also stand over against law and order?"

"Obviously."

"And does not that which is most removed appear to be the erotic (ἐρωτικαί, *erōtikai*) and tyrannical appetites?"

"By all means."

12. THEAETETUS *169B–C*

SOCRATES: Thousands of times I have encountered a Heracles or a Theseus who is a champion at speaking and been well and soundly thrashed, but such a terrible love for this kind of exercise has gripped me that I have not retired from the sport.

13. PHILEBUS *47E-48A*

SOCRATES: Anger, fear, longing, grief, love, admiration, envy, and so forth—don't you count these as pains of the soul itself?

PROTARCHUS: I do.

SOCRATES: Won't we find them full of extraordinary pleasures as well?...Don't you think there is a mixture of pain and pleasure in them?

14. LAWS *645D*

THE ATHENIAN: The drinking of wine makes pleasure, pain, passion, and love more intense, doesn't it?

15. LAWS *688A–B*

THE ATHENIAN: My instruction is that, in establishing the laws, the legislator must focus on one of the four virtues. He must keep all of them in view, but most especially and primarily that virtue which draws all the rest together.

This is practical wisdom (φρόνησις, *phronēsis*), along with intelligence and opinions that are accompanied by love and desire.

16. LAWS *711D*

THE ATHENIAN: When a divine love for the practices of good sense and justice is implanted in some mighty rulers...

17. LAWS *823D–E*

THE ATHENIAN: My friends, may you never have a desire or a love for hunting the beasts in the sea or for fishing for any of the animals that live in the water...

18. LAWS *836E–837D*

THE ATHENIAN: It is necessary to look at the nature of friendship and desire and of the things that are called love, if one intends to think about this matter correctly.

CLINIAS: How's that?

THE ATHENIAN: We speak of a friendship between people who are alike in virtue and between people who are equals, and further, of a friendship between people who are opposite types, such as between the needy and the wealthy. Whenever either of these becomes intense, we call it love.

CLINIAS: That's correct.

THE ATHENIAN: Now, this friendship between opposites is terrible and brutal and does not often involve our sharing anything in common, but that between people who are alike is civilized and involves a lifelong commonality. When there is a mixture of these two kinds of friendship, it is not easy to understand what the person who has this third type of love wants to happen to him. He is at a loss because he is afflicted by opposing inclinations, one directing him to embrace what is attractive and the other forbidding it. The person who loves the body, and hungers after youthful good looks as one hungers after ripe fruit, tells himself to have his fill, assigning no value to the state of the soul of the one he loves. However, the person who treats desire for the body as secondary, ranks viewing above loving, and really has a desire for the soul in his soul, considers stuffing the body with the body to be outrageous and also respects and even worships good sense, courage, greatness, and wisdom. He wants to live always in a chaste manner with a chaste beloved. The love that is a mixture of both is the one we have detailed as the third kind of love.

Notes

CHAPTER 1. GENERAL INTRODUCTION

1. The Greek term is ἔρως, *erōs*, which I discuss below.

2. For a useful, brief discussion of these issues, see W. K. C. Guthrie, *A History of Greek Philosophy*, vol. IV (Cambridge: Cambridge University Press, 1975), 41–56. For a recent challenge to this traditional way of grouping the dialogues, see Holger Thesleff, "Platonic Chronology," *Phronesis* 34 (1989): 1–26. Compare also Jacob Howland, "Re-reading Plato: The Problem of Platonic Chronology," *Phoenix* 45 (1991): 189–214.

3. Martha C. Nussbaum; *The Fragility of Goodness* (Cambridge: Cambridge University Press, 1986), 165–99.

4. Nussbaum, *Fragility*, 200–33.

5. For general discussions of this issue see Kenneth Dover, *Greek Homosexuality* (London: Duckworth, 1978); David M. Halperin, John J. Winkler, and Froma I. Zeitlin, eds., *Before Sexuality: The Construction of Erotic Experience in the Ancient Greek World* (Princeton: Princeton University Press, 1990); and David M. Halperin, *One Hundred Years of Homosexuality and Other Essays on Greek Love* (New York: Routledge, 1990).

6. Actually, it is not homosexuality that is being spoken of here, but bisexuality. There is no assumption that the normal male has sexual relationships only with other men, and there is at least the suggestion that lesbian relationships were also acceptable. Sexual desire is not assumed to be gender specific.

7. For a thorough and very helpful discussion of Plato's view of *logos*, see David Roochnik, *The Tragedy of Reason: Toward a Platonic Conception of Logos* (New York: Routledge, 1990).

8. An interesting, though controversial, discussion of this issue can be found in Martin Heidegger, *Early Greek Thinking* (New York: Harper & Row, 1975), 59–78.

9. Alcibiades places special emphasis on Socrates' involvement with λόγος in his characterization of him in the *Symposium*, and this is also a major element in the characterization of Socrates in the *Phaedrus*.

10. The well-known Aristotelian definition of a human being is usually translated as "the rational animal," but the Greek is just as accurately translated as "the animal that has speech" (ζῷον λόγον ἔχον, *zōon logon echon*).

11. Gerasimos Santas gives a succinct statement of the meaning of ἔρως, and of φιλία (*philia*), in *Plato and Freud: Two Theories of Love* (Oxford: Basil Blackwell, 1988), 8. David M. Halperin provides a very thorough discussion of the meanings of these terms in "Platonic *Erōs* and What Men Call Love," *Ancient Philosophy* 5 (1985): 161–204. He offers an appropriate warning:

> Although we often choose to employ a certain delicate periphrasis in speaking of sexual desire and call it, accordingly, "love," we must realize that by *erōs* Plato refers not to love in the global sense in which we often intend that word but to one kind or aspect of love—or, rather, to the intense *desire* which often goes by the name of love. That there does not exist in English a totally satisfactory way of expressing the exact meaning of *erōs* (we cannot, after all, substitute for "lover" some other word such as "desirer") only increases our obligation to be conceptually clear in our efforts to elucidate Plato's erotic theory. (p. 164)

12. Several examples of speaking of *erōs* where the object is something other than sex are included in the passages in the appendix. An English term that has a rather similar use is 'lust.' The Greek term ἀφροδίσια, *aphrodisia*, which refers to sexual passion (the term is based on the name of the goddess Aphrodite) is used more strictly.

13. In the *Symposium* I translate φιλοσοφία as "philosophy" or "the search for wisdom."

14. For a very helpful discussion of the early history of this issue, see Jacob Klein, *A Commentary on Plato's Meno* (Chapel Hill: University of North Carolina Press, 1965), 3–31. For a collection of recent essays confronting this issue and a thorough bibliography of recent work, see Charles L. Griswold, Jr., ed., *Platonic Writings: Platonic Readings* (New York: Routledge, 1988). There is also an annotated bibliography on this topic in Charles L. Griswold, Jr., *Self-Knowledge in Plato's Phaedrus* (New Haven: Yale University Press, 1986), 244–46, nn. 7 and 8.

15. For an excellent discussion of this issue and a perceptive defense of a holistic approach to interpreting Plato's dialogues, see Griswold, *Self-Knowledge in Plato's Phaedrus*, 9–16.

16. Some of the studies of individual dialogues in the Clarendon Press series do come close to completely ignoring literary and dramatic elements, however. See, for example, David Gallop, trans., *Plato: Phaedo*, Clarendon Plato Series (Oxford: Clarendon Press, 1975); and John McDowell, trans., *Plato: Theaetetus*, Clarendon Plato Series (Oxford: Clarendon Press, 1973).

17. James A. Arieti, *Interpreting Plato: The Dialogues As Drama* (Savage, Md.: Rowman & Littlefield, 1990).

18. See Arieti's chapter on the *Symposium* in his *Interpreting Plato*.

19. For a recent expression of this sort of approach, see Arthur A. Krentz, "Dramatic Form and Philosophical Context in Plato's Dialogues," *Philosophy and Literature* 7 (1983): 32–47.

20. Abraham Anderson gives a helpful analysis of this approach in his review of Thomas Pangle's *The Roots of Political Philosophy: Ten Forgotten Socratic Dialogues*; "Some Views of Socrates," *Ancient Philosophy* 11 (1991): 351–59.

21. Gerald A. Press makes this point about Arieti's view in his review of Arieti's book in *The Journal of the History of Philosophy* 30 (1992): 291–92.

22. Nussbaum, *Fragility*, 165–99.

CHAPTER 2. THE SYMPOSIUM

1. For a discussion of the internal and external evidence of the date of composition of the dialogue, see R. G. Bury, ed., *The Symposium of Plato* (Cambridge: W. Heffer and Sons, Ltd., 1973), lxvi–lxviii; and Kenneth Dover, ed., *Plato: Symposium* (Cambridge: Cambridge University Press, 1980), 10–11.

2. Some of Aristophanes' best-known plays are *The Clouds* (a caricature of Socrates), *The Birds* (a fantastic, utopian fantasy), and *Lysistrata* (about a supposed effort by the women of Athens to stop the long Peloponnesian War by withholding sex from their husbands).

3. [172A] Phalerum is a port town just east of Pireaus. Apollodorus was on his way to Athens.

4. [172A] The joke, apparently, is the use of a form of address that would normally be used only in a formal context, such as in court. A similar usage in our context is the practice in debates in Congress where one speaker addresses another as "the gentleman from New York."

5. [172b] This character is unknown beyond the reference here.

6. [172c] A Glaucon plays a prominent role in the *Republic*; and a Glaucon is mentioned at *Charmides* 154a and at 222b below. Whether any of these are intended to be the same person is not clear.

7. [173a] This was in 416 B.C.E.

8. [174b] Socrates is making a pun on Agathon's name, which means "good." The proverb is that good men do not need an invitation to go to the feasts of inferior men.

9. [174b] See *Iliad* XVII.587f.

10. [174c] See *Iliad* II.408.

11. [174d] See *Iliad* X.222ff.

12. [174e] The Greeks ate while reclining on couches, usually with two people on each couch.

13. [175c] This would be the last on the right, the traditional place of the host.

14. [175e] Here and throughout the *Symposium* I use the term "outrageous" to translate various forms of the term ὕβρις, *hubris*. The term refers to behavior that willfully violates customary practice, good sense, or the law. The claim that Socrates is "hubristic" is an important theme in the dialogue. The term occurs at 174b, 181c, 188a, 190c–d, 215b, 219c, 221e, and 222a.

15. [175e] The god of wine. Such a dinner would normally be followed by drinking contests.

16. [176c] Hermes is the god of luck. We might use the expression "a godsend" here.

17. [177a] A lost play. The phrase "the story is not mine" is apparently a quote from it.

18. [177a] The term 'love' is capitalized here to distinguish its use as a proper name, but this device does not exist in the Greek. Hence, there are times when the context leaves it unclear as to whether the reference is to the deity whose name is Love or to the concept or phenomenon of love. This ambiguity is particularly acute in Socrates' remarks about love, beginning with his dialogue with Agathon at 199c–201d. The reader may not always agree with my decisions about capitalization of this term.

19. [177b] Prodicus was a prominent Sophist, see *Protagorus* 315c–d.

20. [177c] Defending unexpected or even absurd conclusions was a common means of showing off one's rhetorical prowess. A defense of Helen of Troy was a popular theme for such displays.

21. [177c] The verb translated as "to gratify" (χαρίζεσθαι, *charizesthai*) is commonly used as a euphemism for giving in to the sexual demands of a lover. It is frequently used in the *Symposium* in contexts where there is no explicit reference to sexual activity, but the euphemistic sense would not be lost on the Greek reader in this sort of passage. Thus, this is one of the many ways in which the conversation in this dialogue is permeated with sexual innuendo.

22. [177d] Pausanias and Agathon were apparently lovers; see 193b and *Protagoras* 315e.

23. [177e] Aphrodite is the goddess of sexual passion.

24. [178b] *Theognis* 116f., 120. The works of the poet Hesiod contain the earliest extant Greek cosmological myths.

25. [178b] Acusilaus was reputedly a collector of myths. None of his work is extant.

26. [178b] An important Presocratic philosopher-poet of the early fifth century.

27. [179b] *Iliad* X.482; XV.262. *Odyssey* IX.381.

28. [179d] Plato's version of this story differs somewhat from that of others. See Aeschylus, *Bassarai*; Virgil, *Georgics* IV.453–527; Ovid, *Metamorphoses* X.1ff. In the most common version Orpheus fails to retrieve his wife because he breaks his promise not to turn and look back at her during their ascent from Hades. Orpheus is also famous for the power of his singing.

29. [180a] See *Iliad* IX.410–16; XVIII.88–96.

30. [180a] The issue is who is the suitor and who the object of pursuit. The "lover" is the dominant, usually older male. The "beloved" or the "darling" is not usually spoken of as "loving" his lover; he feels friendly affection for him. See 182c. Thus, since Patroclus was older and the younger darling is not expected to "love" his lover, Achilles' behavior was seen as extraordinary.

31. [180a] *Iliad* XI.786f.

32. [180b] This again assumes that the darling who is the object of love does not himself "love" his lover. He only "cherishes" (ἀγαπᾷ, *agapa*, the verb related to *agapē*) him.

33. [180d] That is, sexual passion.

34. [180d] The name means "sky" or "heavens." He is both the child and the husband of Gaia (earth).

35. [180d] A relatively obscure goddess, perhaps an early consort of Zeus. She is associated with the worship of Zeus at Dodona.

36. [181d] The term νόμος, *nomos*, can mean a customary rule or practice as well as an officially legislated law. It is unclear which sense is being used in Pausanias' speech.

37. [182c] The Greek practice of exercising and engaging in athletic contests in the nude was seen as quite scandalous by other cultures.

38. [182c] The story is that Aristogeiton was in love with Harmodius, but so was Hipparchus, the brother of the tyrant Hippias. Aristogeiton and Harmodius tried to kill both brothers, but only succeeded with Hipparchus. Nevertheless, in the popular memory, they were credited with ending the tyranny. See Thucydides VI.54–59.

39. [183e] *Iliad* II.71.

40. [185c] This is an occasion when a pun in the Greek can be directly reflected in English.

41. [186e] The legendary founder of medicine.

42. [187a] Heraclitus was an important philosopher who lived in Ephesus in the early fifth century. This saying proposes a way of understanding the principle of unity as a balance of opposing forces.

43. [187e] Another of the traditional Muses. Her name means "many hymns." Perhaps Plato has Eryximachus choose her because her name is closest to that of the "common" (πάνδημος, *pandēmos*) Aphrodite distinguished by Pausanias.

44. [188b] For the Greeks, meteorology was included in the study of the heavenly bodies.

45. [188d] "Judiciousness" translates σωφροσύνη, *sōphrosunē*, one of the cardinal virtues in Greek thought and the most difficult to translate. (The other three are wisdom, justice, and courage, to which piety or religiousness is sometimes added as a fifth.) *Sōphrosunē* is often translated as "moderation," "temperance," or "self-control." It has to do with proper behavior and proper desires in regard to things involving pleasure and pain. The judicious person likes and dislikes the proper things in the proper way and accordingly makes good judgments and adopts correct behavior, especially in areas that are thought of as involving pleasure and pain. It is not really "self" control, since the virtuous self does not have to be controlled because it desires the proper things. "Temperance" is too closely associated in contemporary language with abstinence from alcoholic beverages, and "moderation" involves a suggestion of mild-manneredness that can be misleading—Socrates is judicious, but I don't know that we would think of him as a moderate person.

46. [189b] That is, the Muse of comedy.

47. [189e] "Androgynous" translates ἀνδρόγυνον, *androgynon*, which is based on the Greek words for man (ἀνήρ, *anēr*) and woman (γυνή, *gynē*).

48. [190b] See *Odyssey* XI.305ff.; *Iliad* V.385ff.

49. [190d] The Greek text refers to a game in which one tries to balance on one foot atop a greased wineskin. Hopscotch is an appropriate modern substitute for the metaphor.

50. [192d] The god of blacksmithing.

51. [193a] The Spartans conquered the city of Mantinea in Arcadia and dispersed the population into four separate settlements in 385 B.C.E.

52. [195b] Cronos (time) is the father of Zeus, and Iapetus is one of the Titans, who lived at the same time.

53. [195d] Ate, whose name means "recklessness" or "mischief," is a daughter of Zeus. See *Iliad* XIX.91–94.

54. [196c] Aristotle attributes this epithet to the fourth-century rhetorician Alcidamas. *Rhetoric* 1406a. 17–23.

55. [196d] In the fragment from one of Sophocles' lost plays that is being used here, it is Necessity rather than Love that Ares (war) cannot resist.

56. [196d] The story in the *Odyssey* (VIII.266–366) is that Ares fell in love with Aphrodite, who was at the time married to Hephaestus. The latter made a trap of fine

chains and caught the two in bed together. When he called the other gods to witness their crime, he was chagrined to discover that all the gods envied Ares, despite his embarrassing situation.

57. [196d] Plato has Agathon carefully include all four cardinal virtues.

58. [196e] A quotation from a lost play by Euripides.

59. [198c] A famous fifth-century orator and teacher of rhetoric. He plays a major role in Plato's dialogue named for him and is referred to in several other dialogues; see *Phaedrus* 261c, 267a. Agathon's speech reflects and even parodies his style.

60. [198c] The punning reference to Gorgias as a Gorgon refers to the story about Odysseus' fear that Persephone would send up a Gorgon's head, which has snakes for hair, from Hades if he did not depart. The sight of such a head turns one to stone. See *Odyssey* XI.633–35.

61. [199a] An adaptation of Euripides' *Hippolytus* 612: "The tongue has sworn, but the heart is unsworn."

62. [201d] The name Diotima means "honored of Zeus." The name Mantinea is related to the word for prophet. There is no clear evidence of Diotima's being based on an actual person (although the matter is controversial), but there was a town of this name on the mainland.

63. [202a] The Greek term ἀμαθία, *amathia*, which, in accordance with standard practice, I translate as "ignorance," refers to the lack of understanding or learning, but it is closer to our notion of "misunderstanding." That is, *amathia* is the condition of believing false claims, not the condition of having no opinions at all. We do use "ignorance" in this sense, of course, but not always.

64. [202d] The distinction Plato has Socrates draw here between a daimon (δαίμων, *daimōn*, a spirit or demon) and a god (θεός, *theos*) is somewhat unusual. The *daimōn* is usually not treated as a significantly different kind of being from a *theos* in other dialogues and by other writers, and the term is often translated as "god."

65. [203d] That is, in "philosophizing," (φιλοσοφῶν, *philosophōn*). In this context it is important to bring out that the term refers to the search for, rather than the possession of wisdom.

66. [204b] That is, a "philosopher" (φιλόσοφος, *philosophos*).

67. [205b] The Greek term translated as "creativity" is ποίησις, *poiēsis*. Although it can be used to mean any kind of productive activity, it is often used in the restricted sense of "poetic" productivity, i.e., the writing of poetry and song. Our use of the term 'creativity' is somewhat similar.

68. [205d] This phrase is apparently a poetic quotation, but from an unknown source.

69. [205d] This is more true in Greek than in English because the English term 'love' is much broader than the Greek term *erōs*.

70. [207b] "On the basis of reason" translates ἐκ λογισμοῦ (*ek logismou*). The preposition *ek* means "out of" or "from," and the noun *logismou* (in the genitive case here because of the preposition) refers to the activity or process of exercising *logos*, which is "speech" or "reason," the gathering of the world that lays bare its meaning. *Logismos* is often translated as "reasoning" or "calculating."

71. [208c] Plato seems to be implying that this expression is characteristic of the Sophists. See *Euthydemus* 274a and *Hippias Major* 287c. The phrase, εὖ ἴσθι, *eu isthi*, which I translate here as "You know it," could also be translated as "Know it well!" or "You know perfectly well."

72. [208c] This is a poetic line of unknown origin.

73. [208d] See 179b–d in Phaedrus' speech.

74. [208d] See 179e–180a in Phaedrus' speech.

75. [208d] Codrus is a mythical king of Attica who went out of his way to be the first person killed by an invading enemy because an oracle had proclaimed that the Athenians would be conquered only if the invaders avoided killing the Athenian king.

76. [209a] "Good sense" translates φρόνησις (*phronēsis*), which is often translated as "prudence" or "practical wisdom." The term usually refers to practical virtues in general, rather than to a specific virtue, such as justice or courage.

77. [209a] "Judiciousness" translates σωφροσύνη (*sōphronsunē*), one of the cardinal virtues. The term was traditionally translated as "temperance" and is now sometimes read as "moderation" or, although this is misleading, "self-control." (The self of a virtuous person does not need to be "controlled"; it willingly does what is right.) It refers to a thoughtful, attentive, balanced approach that avoids becoming one-sided.

78. [209d] Lycurgus was reputed to be the creator of the constitution and laws of Sparta and is often mentioned together with Solon, who held a similar position with regard to the laws of Athens.

79. [212d] Talented and attractive, Alcibiades had been close to Socrates as a youth and is a rising power in Athens at the time of this story. His later sins against Athens led many to see him as a terrible traitor and to criticize Socrates for having been his guide. See Xenophon, *Memorabilia* I.2, 12–48.

80. [212d] Plato surely intends a pun here on Agathon's name, which means "good," as he does at 174b.

81. [214b] *Iliad* XI.514.

82. [214d] Poseidon, a brother of Zeus, is god of the sea.

83. [215a] Silenus was the father of the Satyrs, who are sometimes called Sileni. Satyrs had wild manners and ferocious sexual appetites. They were portrayed with some animal parts, such as goats' legs or donkeys' ears.

84. [215b] The Greek term translated as "statue-makers' shops" is literally "Herm carvers" and would have recalled to Plato's Greek readers the notorious incident of the destruction of the Herms the night before the sailing of the ill-fated Sicilian expedition, whose failure was the fatal blow for Athens in the long Peloponnesian War with Sparta. Alcibiades, who had been elected commander-in-chief of the expedition, was blamed for the destruction of the Herms (representations of Hermes, the god of good fortune and also the messenger of the gods, that were commonly placed before homes) and an order was sent for him to return from the expedition to be executed. This prompted Alcibiades' defection to Sparta.

85. [215b] Although the standard translation of αὐλός, *aulos*, is "flute," it was actually a double-reeded instrument similar to a modern oboe.

86. [215b] Marsyas competed successfully against Apollo in playing the flute and was flayed by the angry god as a result.

87. [215b] Plato depicts Socrates as having a snub nose and protruding eyes, typical features of a Satyr. See *Theatetus* 143e; see also Xenophon, *Symposium* IV.19.

88. [215c] Olympus, of whom we know little, is credited with composing certain tunes and is associated with mythical figures. His music was also reputed to have a powerful effect on listeners. See *Ion* 533b; *Laws* 677d; and *Minos* 318b.

89. [215e] The Corybantes worshipped the goddess Cybele. Their rites were characterized by extreme frenzy. See *Ion* 533e, 536c; *Phaedrus* 228b; and *Laws* 790e.

90. [215e] Pericles, the great leader in early fifth-century Athens, had no peer in his reputation as an orator.

91. [216a] The irresistible songs of the Sirens tempted men to their doom. See Homer, *Odyssey* XII.37–54, 154–200.

92. [217c] Such exercising was done in the nude. See 182b.

93. [218d] One would expect such offers to come from the lover rather than the beloved. See 217c and 222b.

94. [218e] The proverbial reference is to Glaucus' exchanging his golden armor for the bronze armor of Diomede. *Iliad* VI. 232–36.

95. [219e] The Homeric hero Ajax was highly invulnerable because of his immense, thick shield.

96. [219e] The city of Potidaea was under Athenian control but revolted in 432 B.C.E. It was again subdued after two years of warfare. This campaign is also alluded to in *Apology* 28e and *Charmides* 153a.

97. [220c] From *Odyssey* IV.242, 271.

98. [220d] The Athenian forces at Potidaea included contingents from their allies in Ionia.

99. [220e] The Athenians were defeated by the Thebans near Delios a little north of Attica in 424, and their retreat degenerated into a chaotic flight. See Thucydides IV.76ff.

100. [221a] Laches was an Athenian general who was killed at Mantinea in 418. He plays a major role in the discussion of courage in the *Laches* and there refers to Socrates' courage at Delios; *Laches* 181b.

101. [221b] The quoted phrase is derived from Aristophanes' *Clouds* 362.

102. [221c] Brasidas was a famous Spartan general. He was killed at Amphipolis in 422. See Thucydides II.25, 85ff.; IV.102–16; V.6.

103. [221c] Both the Greek Nestor and the Trojan Antenor are described in the *Iliad* as outstanding orators. See *Iliad* I.247ff.; VII.347ff.

104. [222b] Charmides is described as quite beautiful in the dialogue named for him; see *Charmides* 154a–155e. Euthydemus is also said by Xenophon to be beautiful; see *Memorabilia* IV.2, 40. (This is not the Sophist Euthydemus for whom the Platonic dialogue is named.)

105. [222b] Compare *Iliad* XVII.33; and Hesiod, *Works and Days* 218.

106. [222b] "Infant" translates νήπιον, *nēpion*, which is literally "one who does not yet speak." (This is also the root meaning of the term "infant.") Alcibiades is telling Agathon to learn from what he is being told about someone else's experience.

107. [222e] The original order on the couch was Agathon, Alcibiades, Socrates. Agathon, supported by Socrates, proposes Alcibiades, Socrates, Agathon. Alcibiades will propose Alcibiades, Agathon, Socrates.

108. [223d] The Lyceum was a place for exercise and conversation in a sanctuary of Apollo Lyceios (Apollo, the wolflike). It was outside the city walls on the east and was a favorite hangout of Socrates'; see *Euthyphro* 2a and *Lysis* 203a.

CHAPTER 3. THE COMMENTARY ON THE SYMPOSIUM

1. Bury suggests this. R. G. Bury, ed., *The Symposium of Plato* (Cambridge: W. Heffer and Sons, Ltd., 1973), xvi.

2. See Helen Bacon, "Socrates Crowned," *The Virginia Quarterly Review* 5 (1959): 415–30.

3. John Brentlinger argues for this interpretation in "The Cycle of Becoming in the *Symposium*," in *The Symposium of Plato*, translated by Suzy Q Groden (Amherst: University of Massachusetts Press, 1970), 6.

4. Bury's alteration of the text to make Apollodorus' nickname "maniac" (by replacing μαλακός, *malakos*, with μανικός, *manikos*) seems to be a result of failing to appreciate this point. Bury, *Symposium*, 6. Most translators follow Bury here. See Gro-

den, *Symposium*, 39; William Hamilton, trans., *The Symposium: Plato* (Baltimore, Md.: Penguin Books, 1951), 35; Alexander Nehamas and Paul Woodruff, trans., *Plato: Symposium* (Indianapolis: Hackett Publishing Company, 1989), 2.

5. However, A. E. Taylor (*Plato: The Man and His Work*, 7th ed. [London: Methuen & Co. Ltd., 1960], 211–12, 233–34) makes much of this passage and the similar one at 220c–d as proving that the historical Socrates was a "mystic." This issue is related to the question of what it is like to see the beautiful itself; see discussion of 210a ff.

6. See Martha Nussbaum, *The Fragility of Goodness* (Cambridge: Cambridge University Press, 1986), 165–99.

7. However, poetic works praising Love did exist. For example, there are poetic songs to Love by the chorus in Sophocles' *Antigone* and in the *Hippolytus*, both of which predate the occasion of the party in the *Symposium*.

8. The verb is ἐπίστασθαι (*epistasthai*) which refers to knowing in a strong sense.

9. See the chapter on the *Symposium* in James A. Arieti, *Interpreting Plato: The Dialogues As Drama* (Savage, Md.: Rowman & Littlefield, 1990).

10. Lysias' speech in the *Phaedrus* should probably be interpreted as an example of this sort of thing.

11. Xenophanes was born in Colophon in Ionia around 570 B.C.E. and may have traveled as far as Sicily. He reportedly lived to be a hundred. A fragment of his writings that has been preserved reads: "Mortals think that the gods were born, and that they have clothes, voices, and bodies like their own. The Ethiopians claim that their gods are snub-nosed and black, while the Thracians say that theirs have blue eyes and red hair. However, if cows, horses, or lions had hands and could draw and do the things that men can, horses would draw the forms of the gods like horses, and cows like cows, and would make them have bodies like their own." Gerasimos Santas provides useful summaries of all the speeches and agrees that the speakers are "star-examples...of the views they express" (p. 15). *Plato and Freud: Two Theories of Love* (Oxford: Basil Blackwell, 1988), 14–57.

12. Friedländer provides an excellent example of reading the earlier speeches as a series of preparations for the ultimate analysis of love in Socrates' speech. He finds in each speech various points that are built on and completed by Socrates: "Thus, the worth of all the previous speeches may be measured by the degree to which they approximate the goal set here by Socrates-Diotima" (p. 26). Paul Friedländer, *Plato*, vol. 3, Bollingen Series LIX (Princeton: Princeton University Press, 1969), 11–27. Santas argues that the first five speeches represent various current views of the nature of *erōs* that Plato is contrasting with his own view, which is given in Socrates' speech. *Plato and Freud: Two Theories of Love*, 15.

13. Nussbaum, *Fragility*, 165–99.

14. Gregory Vlastos, *Socrates, Ironist and Moral Philosopher* (Ithaca, N.Y.: Cornell University Press, 1991), 33. For Vlastos, the historical Socrates, unlike the Plato of the middle dialogues, does not have a doctrine of transcendent forms and is able to love concrete individuals. More on this below.

15. In his Introduction to his and Paul Woodruff's translation of the *Symposium,* Alexander Nehamas suggests that "there is something self-serving and self-righteous in Pausanias' rather prim attitude" (p. xvi).

16. Bury lists various defenders of each view and reports some of their justifications (*Symposium,* xxii–xxiii).

17. George Kimball Plochmann, "Hiccups and Hangovers in the Symposium," *Bucknell Review* 11 (1963): 1–18.

18. Bury discusses the possibility that it may be a parody of the views of Hippocrates; *Symposium,* xxix, n. 2, and his notes to the text on pages 46–52. See also Ludwig Edelstein, "The Role of Eryximachus in Plato's *Symposium,*" *Transactions of the American Philological Association,* 76 (1945): 85ff.

19. See Bury, *Symposium,* xxix–xxx, for a thorough discussion of this point. Bury also argues persuasively that the speech is meant to parody medical theories of the time; *Symposium,* xxxi–xxxv, 54ff.

20. Friedländer points out that the association of the three original forms of humans with the sun, earth, and moon, again lifts the discussion to a cosmic level, which will occur again in Diotima's characterization of the function of a daimon. Friedländer, *Plato,* vol. 3, p. 19.

21. M. C. Stokes argues that "Agathon is at bottom obscure, and his obscurity leaves room for doubt of his seriousness of mind and clarity of belief." *Plato's Socratic Conversations: Drama and Dialectic in Three Dialogues* (Baltimore: The Johns Hopkins University Press, 1986), 120.

22. On the recognition of the connection between *erōs* and conflict in Greek culture generally, see Anne Carson, *Eros: The Bittersweet* (Princeton: Princeton University Press, 1986).

23. See Bury, *Symposium,* xxxv–xxxvi, for a detailed comparison.

24. Since love is by definition a positive attitude, the object of love is by definition something one desires as good or beautiful. One may be mistaken in the judgment that the object is good or beautiful, of course. In this sense, that is, under a mistaken judgment, one can love what is bad. A conceptual argument for this claim that one cannot desire what is bad is offered by Socrates in the *Meno* at 77b–78b.

25. A. W. Price gives a perceptive analysis of the complexities and difficulties of this argument; *Love and Friendship in Plato and Aristotle* (Oxford: Clarendon Press, 1989), 17–21. M. C. Stokes does also and shows how well connected it is with what Agathon actually says in his speech. Stokes also discusses the subtle variations made

in this argument when Socrates reports his experience of it with Diotima (*Plato's Socratic Conversations*, 114–46).

26. For a discussion of another example of this technique, see William Cobb, "Plato's Treatment of Immortality in the *Phaedo*," *Southern Journal of Philosophy* 15 (1977): 173–88.

27. Another example of this is the depiction of the young Socrates in the *Parmenides* in comparison to the mature Parmenides.

28. Aristotle's claim that women were actually a sort of subspecies of the human because of their inherently inferior rational capacity probably reflects a common attitude.

29. On the issue of how to interpret the proposal concerning women rulers in the *Republic*, see Julia Annas, *An Introduction to Plato's Republic* (Oxford: Clarendon Press, 1981), 181–85.

30. Santas connects the role of Diotima with the equality of status given to women in the *Republic*. *Plato and Freud: Two Theories of Love*, 51, n. 29.

31. David M. Halperin, "Why Diotima Is a Woman," in David M. Halperin, *One Hundred Years of Homosexuality and Other Essays on Greek Love* (New York: Routledge, 1990), 119–24.

32. *Phaedo* 60a. Phaedo reports that when Xanthippe, Socrates' wife, saw the group of Socrates' friends coming into the prison, "she broke out into the sort of remark you would expect from a woman, 'Oh, Socrates, this is the last time that you and your friends will be able to talk together!'" (60a). Note also his report that when Socrates had drunk the poison and his friends began weeping in earnest, Socrates said, "Really, my friends, what a way to behave! Why, that was my main reason for sending away the women, to prevent this sort of disturbance" (117d). (Hugh Tredennick's translation, from *The Last Days of Socrates*, Penguin Classics, [Baltimore: Penguin Books, 1954]).

33. Halperin, "Why Diotima Is a Woman," 120.

34. For a thorough discussion of various suggestions about the significance of Plato's introduction of Diotima and about whether Diotima represents an actual historical figure, see Halperin, "Why Diotima Is a Woman," 113–51.

35. See *Phaedrus* 242b; *Theages* 128d; and *Apology* 40a.

36. Bury provides a helpful discussion of the antecedents and ancient responses to the elements of this myth (*Symposium*, xl–xlii).

37. Santas defends the view that in Alcibiades' speech "Socrates emerges as the star example of the philosophic lover" described by Diotima (*Plato and Freud: Two Theories of Love*, 15).

38. At this point the personification of love as the god Love is largely dropped, as

Diotima for the most part speaks straightforwardly about the activity or phenomenon of love.

39. In his analysis of Plato's frequent use of sexual imagery, Myles F. Burnyeat offers a useful discussion of the similarities and differences between this metaphor and that of midwifery that Plato develops in the *Theatetus*. He points out that there is a "strange reversal" in Diotima's metaphor: "the pregnancy is the cause, not the consequence, of love; and the birth [rather than the pregnancy] is love's expressive manifestation" (p. 54). On both the physical and spiritual levels of the metaphor, "pregnancy precedes intercourse, because birth and intercourse are imaginatively equated" (p. 55). "Socratic Midwifery, Platonic Inspiration," in *Essays on the Philosophy of Socrates* edited by Hugh H. Benson (Oxford: Oxford University Press, 1992), 53–65.

40. The use of "creativity" (ποίησις, *poiēsis*) at 205b–c to illustrate and support Diotima's claim about the universality of "love" in human life now seems especially appropriate.

41. Brentlinger, for example, sees the culmination of the activity of the lover as Diotima depicts it as consisting in "attaining *possession* of the Good in contemplation." "Cycle," p. 22, emphasis added. This is a misleading characterization of Diotima's view.

42. It is noteworthy that the view of the soul (ψυχή, *psuchē*) Diotima presents here depicts the soul as essentially a collection of changing particular thoughts, feelings, attitudes, etc., with no enduring "owner." Price, however, argues that the fact that Diotima does not explicitly say of the soul, as she does of the body, that it "is only *called* the same over time" (in Price's reading, p. 24) leaves open the possibility that it is only the "contents" of the soul that change while the soul as owner endures (*Love and Friendship in Plato and Aristotle*, 24–25). Price does not mention that Diotima has just denied the possibility of immortality in a literal sense (207c–d). His reading of the text seems implausible.

43. Bury expresses this view well: "Now it may be taken as certain—from passages in the *Phaedrus, Phaedo,* and *Republic*—that personal immortality was a doctrine held and taught by Plato. It is natural, therefore, to expect that this doctrine will be also taught in the *Symposium*....And this is, I believe, the case." *Symposium*, xliv. Bury argues that the *Symposium* suggests the doctrine that it is pure reason alone that is the immortal part of a human being (*Symposium*, xliv–xlv). Price provides an interesting, if rather convoluted, variation on this type of effort to reconcile Diotima's claim with the defense of immortality in other dialogues (*Love and Friendship in Plato and Aristotle*, 30–35).

44. Bury takes this approach, arguing that what is immortal is the pure mind (νοῦς, *nous*). He places special emphasis on Diotima's final remark at 212a, which I discuss below. See *Symposium*, xliv–xlvi.

45. I have argued that a more plausible approach is to see the apparent affirmation of immortality in the other dialogues as ironic, and to take this rejection of immortality in the *Symposium* as the most straightforward analysis of the issue in Plato. See

my "Plato's Treatment of Immortality in the *Phaedo*," *Southern Journal of Philosophy* 15 (1977): 173–88, and "Anamnesis: Platonic Doctrine or Sophistry Absurdity?" *Dialogue: Canadian Philosophical Review* 12 (1973): 604–28.

46. The reader should remember this description when examining Alcibiades' depiction, beginning at 217e, of his intimate encounter with Socrates.

47. Diotima here plays the role of the priestess who leads an initiate into the final rites and mysteries of a religious cult. The motif of a religious initiation also fits the mythical, if not mystical, language she ascends to in this passage.

48. *Fragility*, 165–99. Nussbaum is drawing on Gregory Vlastos' defense of this interpretation of Plato's view of love as of the universal rather than the individual; Gregory Vlastos, "The Individual as Object of Love in Plato's Dialogues," in *Platonic Studies*, 2nd ed. (Princeton: Princeton University Press, 1981, 3–34). A. W. Price attacks this interpretation in "Loving Persons Platonically," *Phronesis* 26 (1981): 25–34, and in *Love and Friendship in Plato and Aristotle*, 45–49.

49. *Symposium*, xlviii–li.

50. "Uniform" translates μονοειδές, *monoeides*, ("homogeneous")

51. There is a helpful, succinct analysis of this passage, including a discussion of the possibility that Plato is influenced by Parmenides, in Henry Teloh, *The Development of Plato's Metaphysics* (University Park: Pennsylvania State University Press, 1981), 91–96).

52. The Greek term is μάθημα, *mathēma*, that which has been learned.

53. The Greek term is γνῷ, *gnō*, a form of the verb meaning "to know" in the sense of recognizing or realizing.

54. See, for example, *Meno* 72a–73c and *Euthyphro* 6d.

55. Dover states that the knowledge acquired at the top of the staircase is "ineffable," although he offers no defense of this claim. See Kenneth Dover, ed., *Plato: Symposium* (Cambridge: Cambridge University Press, 1980), 159.

56. Aristotle, *Metaphysics* XIII.1078b9–32, 1086a37–b5.

57. *Socrates, Ironist and Moral Philosopher*, 72ff.

58. Aristotle, *Metaphysics* VIII.1042a28–29, 1044b12, and *Physics* II.193a30–31, 193b3–5.

59. At *Republic* 532a–b Socrates says, "Whenever someone attempts in a dialectical way through *logos*, without using any of the senses, to start from what each thing is in itself, and not to give up until he grasps in his own thought what the good itself is, he comes upon it at the end of the intelligible realm, just as the prisoner escaping from the cave comes upon the sun at the end of the visible realm." See also *Republic* 534b. There is also a passage at *Phaedo* 99d–e where Socrates seems to suggest that the place to look for the forms is in *logos*.

60. This depiction of Socrates as a lover of *logos* and that of expertise in *logos* are important motifs in the *Phaedrus.*

61. Santas claims that the ultimate lover in the *Symposium* "has only the Form Beauty as the object of his love; he has given up, it seems, all earthly attachments..." (p. 69). He argues that Plato "corrects" this "error" in his theory of *erōs* in the *Phaedrus,* where a passionate involvement in interpersonal relations is characteristic of the best lover (*Plato and Freud: Two Theories of Love*, 69–72). Price points out, against this "exclusive" reading of Diotima's goal, that it is incompatible with the "great sea of beauty" metaphor at 210d (*Love and Friendship in Plato and Aristotle*, 44).

62. Gregory Vlastos ("The Individual as Object of Love in Plato," 33–35) and J. M. E. Moravcsik ("Reason and Eros in the *Symposium*," in *Essays in Ancient Greek Philosophy*, vol. 1, edited by John P. Anton and George L. Kustas, [Albany: State University of New York Press, 1971], 293), take this view.

63. Terence Irwin argues for this interpretation. See *Plato's Moral Theory: The Early and Middle Dialogues* (Oxford: Clarendon Press, 1977), p. 169.

64. Bury asserts that "the purpose [of Alcibiades' speech is that] of vindicating the memory of Socrates from slanderous aspersions and setting in the right light his relations with Alcibiades" (*Symposium*, lii). See also Nussbaum, *Fragility*, 165–99.

65. It is curious that Socrates does not protest Alcibiades' claim at 216d that Socrates "is ignorant about everything and knows nothing," since he had claimed (before Alcibiades arrived at the party) to know what love is. Vlastos takes this characterization of Socrates as disavowing knowledge to be clear evidence that the Socrates of Alcibiades' speech is not the Socrates who defends Diotima's views. *Socrates, Ironist and Moral Philosopher*, 33.

66. Bury argues with regard to Alcibiades' speech that "Its main purpose is to present to us a vivid portrait of *Socrates* as the perfect exemplar of Eros" (*Symposium*, lx). Burnyeat also agrees with this interpretation: "In the *Symposium* the great lover in the spiritual sense is Socrates himself, as we learn from Alcibiades' speech in his praise" ("Socratic Midwifery, Platonic Inspiration," 55).

67. Friedländer claims that the connection with Diotima's speech is crucial: "The pronouncements of the priestess could not be the end of the work. There had to be a concluding part in which the ascent to the heights would be depicted in the reality of actual life. The *Symposium* reaches its climax in the episode involving Alkibiades." *Plato*, vol. 3, p. 28.

68. See John P. Anton, "Some Dionysian References in the Platonic Dialogues," *Classical Journal* 58 (1962): 49–55.

69. The theme of this final conversation in the *Symposium* is intriguing. Friedländer expresses a common view in suggesting that the dialogues, and especially the *Symposium*, are examples of works that are comedic and tragic at the same time (*Plato*, vol. 3, p. 32). However, in the *Republic* Socrates asserts that the same person *cannot* write both tragedy and comedy, and Adimantus agrees (*Republic* 395a). Diskin Clay

examines this issue very thoroughly and argues that it is a major motif in the dialogue as a whole ("The Tragic and Comic Poet of the *Symposium*, " in *Essays in Ancient Greek Philosophy*, vol. 2, edited by John P. Anton and Anthony Preus [Albany: State University of New York Press, 1983], 186–202).

CHAPTER 4. THE PHAEDRUS

1. The term translated as "love" throughout the dialogue is ἔρως (*erōs*). See the discussion of the term in the general introduction.

2. Opposing views about the date of composition and discussions of the internal and external evidence can be found in R. Hackforth, *Plato's Phaedrus* (Cambridge: Cambridge University Press, 1972), 3–7; and C. J. Rowe, *Plato: Phaedrus* (Warminster, England: Aris & Phillips, 1986), 13–14.

3. Phaedrus was actually in exile from Athens between 415 and 404, as a result of his alleged involvement in the infamous destruction of the Herms. Lysias left Athens as a child and did not return until after 411, and Lysias' brother Polemarchus was murdered in 404. Hence, this dialogue could not depict an actual historical conversation, since in the dialogue Lysias is in Athens (227b), Polemarchus is alive (257b), and Phaedrus is not in exile.

4. Hackforth provides a good summary of this controversy; see *Phaedrus*, 16–18.

5. [227a] A famous orator of the time. A number of his speeches are extant.

6. [227a] A well-known physician, the father of Eryximachus who is one of the speakers in the *Symposium*. See 268a ff.

7. [227b] Morychus was a famous bon vivant, and Epicratus was an orator and active in the democratic faction. Both are mentioned in Aristophanes' plays.

8. [227b] Pindar was a major early fifth-century poet in Athens. The quote is from *Isthmians* I.2.

9. [227c] It is tempting to hear in this phrase an echo of Socrates' claim to be an expert in the activities of *erōs* at *Symposium* 177d.

10. [227c] The verb translated as "to gratify" (χαρίζεσθαι, *charizesthai*) is commonly used as a euphemism for giving in to the sexual demands of a lover. The related noun (χάρις, *charis*) I usually translate as "kindness" (see 231a and 233e).

11. [227c] It was common practice for professional orators to construct display speeches on paradoxical themes to demonstrate their skills. A popular theme for such use was a defense of Helen. It seems likely that Lysias' speech is this sort of thing.

12. [227d] A distance of several miles.

13. [227d] Another physician, also mentioned in *Protagoras* 316d.

14. [228b] This oath apparently refers to an Egyptian deity; see *Gorgias* 482b.

15. [228b] The Corybantic rituals were characterized by joyful enthusiasm and associated with possession and madness.

16. [228c] This little speech illustrates the technique of constructing probabilities that Plato later attributes to Tisias (273a ff.).

17. [229a] Though not in the *Symposium* (174a).

18. [229a] A πλάτονος, *platanos*. The modern scientific name of the genus is *Platanus*. The American species, *occidentalis*, is the familiar sycamore. The species that exists in Greece is *orientalis* and is usually called the plane-tree. The Greek name means "broad," probably referring to the shape of the leaves. They were present in the Agora. The wood of the *platanos* is mentioned at *Laws* 705c as useful for the interior of boats.

19. [229b] The story is that Oreithuia was the daughter of Erectheus, one of the legendary kings of Athens. Boreas, the north wind, fell in love with her but was rejected by her father. Boreas then abducted her, and she later bore him two sons. This myth raises the issue of the connection between love and irrational behavior, an important theme in Socrates' second speech. The "wise," whom Socrates refers to below, see in this tale only an accident involving the death of a child. Note that Socrates does not reject this story as untrue. The mythical form of λόγος (*logos*) plays an important role in the *Phaedrus*. (The term μῦθος (*mythos*), from which the English word 'myth' is derived, is translated as "tale.")

20. [229c] Agra was one of the administrative districts or demes of Attica.

21. [229c] The north wind. The Greek word βορέας (*boreas*) refers to the north wind. The Greeks personify many phenomena, using the names of the phenomena as proper names.

22. [229c] "Odd" here and elsewhere translates ἄτοπος (*atopos*) that is, "out of place," a metaphor connected with the situation in the dialogue.

23. [229c] The name of Oreithuia's playmate usually refers to the use of potions for poisoning or witchcraft.

24. [229c] The phrase translated as "a puff of wind" could also be read as "a breath of Boreas."

25. [229d] The Areopagus is the hill in the center of Athens on which the Parthenon and other public buildings are located.

26. [229e] A Centaur is half man and half horse. A Chimaera has a goat's body with a lion's head and a serpent's tail. A Gorgon has snakes for hair; the most famous one is Medusa. A Pegasus is a horse with wings.

27. [229e] Delphi is a center for the worship of Apollo. There was a famous oracle there.

28. [230a] Typhon (Τυφῶν, *Typhōn*) means "vanity" or "arrogance." The root metaphor is smoke, and the idea seems to be that a vain person's true self is obscured by a smoke-screen. The mythical character called Typhon is a hundred-headed monster who challenged the gods but was killed by Zeus; see Hesiod, *Theogony* 820ff. "Agitated" translates a verb based on *typhōn*, ἐπιτυφέσθαι (*epituphesthai*), which means "to be inflamed" and is used by Aristophanes to mean "consumed by lust."

29. [230b] The consort of Zeus.

30. [230b] An ἄγνος (*agnos*). The modern scientific name is *Vitex agnus-castus*. The Greek name refers to the flexible nature of the young shoots. Though often described as willowlike, the chaste tree, as it is commonly called, is not a member of *Salix*, the willow genus. It is a shrubby tree with leaves that are palmately compound, composed of five to seven lanceolate leaflets, so that each leaflet does resemble a willow leaf. The flowers are blue, in showy, upright clusters. Both leaves and flowers have a strong, pungent odor. In ancient Greece it was considered an anti-aphrodisiac, which may be connected with the fact that its name is similar to ἁγνός (*hagnos*), which means "chaste," "pure," or "holy." This latter term occurs in the *Phaedrus* at 254b, where I translate it as "sacred."

31. [230c] Achelous is the primary river god.

32. [230d] "Prescription" translates φάρμακον (*pharmakon*), which means medicine, remedy, or potion, and may be used for good or ill. This is a striking metaphor to use for λόγος, *logos*. The term is also used at 274e and 275a, where I translate it as "magic potion."

33. [232a] A more literal translation in place of this adverb would be "out of friendship with fame and honor."

34. [234a] Literally, this phrase is "will befriend fame and honor in front of everyone."

35. [234d] "Unearthly" translates δαιμόνιον, *daimonion*; see note on 242c.

36. [234d] The feasts and rites associated with the god Bacchus (also called Dionysus) are particularly extravagant and frenzied and are associated with possession and madness.

37. [235c] Sappho and Anacreon are well-known sixth-century poets, particularly famous for their poems about love.

38. [236b] The offering referred to is probably a golden statue of Zeus.

39. [236b] "Darling" translates παιδικά (*paidika*), the standard term for the youthful beloved in a love affair.

40. [236d] A phrase from the poet Pindar. Plato also uses this quotation at *Meno* 76d.

41. [237a] Plato here plays on the name Ligurian and the word λιγύς (*ligus*), which means "clear voiced."

42. [237e] This is an example of the sort of usage of *logos* that is traditionally translated as "reason" or "rational" rather than as "speech." *Logos* can be translated as "speech" here if we think of speech as a gathering of things so as to reveal their nature. Note that *logos* here is being given a certain precedence in the process of human understanding. This usage sheds important light on the relation between *logos* and τὰ ὄντα (*ta onta*), "the things that are," "reality." In the next sentence in the text, the phrase "in a manner contrary to reason" translates the privative adverbial form of *logos.*

43. [238a] I have not found a good translation for the Greek term ὕβρις, *hubris*, in this context. It generally refers to what is outrageous, what violates traditional practice, good sense, or the law. The term "hubris" as used in English has the somewhat different, though related, sense of "arrogance" or "excessive self-confidence." Some choices by other translators are "wantonness" (Hackforth) and "excess" (Rowe). The adjectival form of this term is translated as "hubristic" at 252b, 254c and 254e, and should be understood in the Greek sense. In the *Symposium* the term is translated as "outrageous."

44. [238c] Socrates' conclusion includes an appeal to etymological connections. The "strength" associated here with *erōs* is ῥώμη (*rhōmē*). The etymological play also involves the phrase "is powerfully strengthened," which is ἐρρωμένως ῥωσθεῖσα (*errōmenōs rhōstheisa*), two forms of the verb ῥώννυμι (*rhōnnumi*), which like *rhōmē* and *erōs* involves the radical ρω (*rō*).

45. [238d] Dithyrambic is a metrical style associated with Bacchus (Dionysus) and usually characterized by exaggerated, affected language. Socrates is probably referring to the flamboyant etymology of his final paragraph. Cf. Plato's *Cratylus* 409c.

46. [241b] The reference is to a game played with oyster shells in which the players formed opposing teams and each team ran away or pursued according to which side of a tossed shell fell uppermost.

47. [241e] The epic style in poetry is that of Homer and was rather archaic by Socrates' day. Perhaps he is referring to the bold metaphor in his final line.

48. [242a] Socrates here calls his first *logos* a *mythos*, as he does at 237a.

49. [242a] This phrase apparently refers to the fact that the sun appears to stand still at noon. Phaedrus makes a play on its literal meaning.

50. [242a] "Superhuman" translates δαιμόνιον, *daimonion*; see note on 242c.

51. [242b] Simmias is a major character in the *Phaedo.*

52. [242c] Socrates refers to this phenomenon in *Apology* 31c–d: "Something divine and daimonic comes to me.... This began in my childhood. A certain voice comes, which, whenever it comes, always turns me away from what I was about to do, but it never gives me positive direction." See also *Apology* 40a. The term 'daimonic' (δαιμόνιον, *daimonion*) has special connotations in the *Symposium* because of Diotima's identification of Love as a daimon. Socrates does not refer to his famous sign in

the *Symposium*, and there is no explicit reference to the notion of the daimon as a special intermediary figure in the *Phaedrus* or the *Apology*. In this context the term is probably to be taken as a loose synonym for "divine" (θεῖον, *theion*).

53. [242c] A sixth-century poet.

54. [242d] Aphrodite is the goddess of sexual passion. Plato gives a different account of the genealogy and status of Love (*Erōs*) in Socrates' report of Diotima's views in the *Symposium*. There Love is conceived on the day of Aphrodite's birth, rather than being her son, and is a daimon, rather than a god (*Symposium* 202d–203c).

55. [243a] A seventh-century poet. Plato also refers to this incident at *Republic* 586c.

56. [244a] Some readers find this series of names to be significant. For example, V. Tejera writes: "The reader becomes conscious of the connotations of the name Stesichorus, or 'choral leader,' and of the beautiful meaning of the name of the beautiful youngster [Phaedrus], the 'shining one.' He is the son of the 'fame seeker' (Pythocles) from 'Wreatheville' (Myrrhinous), while the repentant poet is the son of 'Mr. Finespeak' (Euphemos) from 'Longington' (Himera)." *Plato's Dialogues One by One* (New York: Irvington Publishers, 1984), 49.

57. [244a] There was a major shrine and oracle for Apollo at Delphi. Dodona was the site of an oak tree that was sacred to Zeus. The rustling of its leaves was interpreted for inquirers by the priestesses.

58. [244b] A legendary prophetess located in Asia Minor.

59. [245c] Aristotle attributes the claim that what is immortal is always changing to the fifth century Pythagorean thinker Alcmaeon of Crotona (*De Anima* 405a30).

60. [245c] The word translated as "origin" in this passage, ἀρχή (*archē*), is frequently translated as "first principle." The basic notion is what serves as a source, beginning, or point of origin.

61. [245d] This sentence has baffled readers since ancient times. Some scholars change the text to read: "For if an origin comes into being from something, it would not still be an origin." Perhaps the claim is that if origins come into being, they must come from nonorigins or from origins. If the latter, they come from themselves, which is to say that they do not come into being at all. If the former, their "origin" is from what is *not* an origin, which is absurd. Therefore, origins do not come into being.

62. [245e] A similar argument is offered at *Phaedo* 72a–d.

63. [245e] A similar view of the definition of "soul" occurs at *Laws* 895e–896a.

64. [246b] All living things have souls, hence there is a question as to why some of them would be called mortal, the soul having been shown to be immortal.

65. [246d] Literally, this phrase reads: "as is friendly to the god." The reference to "the god" is generic rather than specific, an expression of ordinary piety.

66. [247a] Hestia is the goddess of the hearth. The twelve ruling gods are presumably the traditional gods of Olympus and may also have been associated with the twelve signs of the Zodiac. See *Laws* 828c.

67. [247c] The image is of standing on the outside of a sphere.

68. [248c] Adrasteia is the goddess of that which is inevitable, destiny.

69. [248d] That is, a philosopher, *philosophos.*

70. [249a] Dike is the goddess of justice.

71. [250b] Themis is the goddess of custom or tradition.

72. [252b] The Homericists were special authorities on the works of Homer. Nothing is known of these verses apart from their appearance here. On the question of the sense in which the second line is hubristic, see W. H. Thompson, *The Phaedrus of Plato* (London: Whittaker & Co., 1868), 66–67: "In calling the second line [hubristic] Plato does not refer to any supposed lewd meaning...but simply to the extravagance of the conception and the words in which it is embodied."

73. [252c] Ares is the god of war and destruction.

74. [253b] Apollo, who speaks through the oracle at Delphi, is connected with both prophecy and the arts of music and poetry.

75. [255c] Because of his beauty, Ganymede was abducted to be the wine-server for Zeus. His father Tros was compensated with a gift of marvellous horses. See *Iliad* XX.232–35; and V.265–67. This reference reminds the reader of the earlier story about Oreithuia (229b–d).

76. [255e] Here and in the next paragraph, the term translated as "kiss" is literally "befriend," but it seems here to have the limited sense of "kiss" or "caress."

77. [257b] Polemarchus captures Socrates at the beginning of the *Republic* and that dialogue takes place at his family's home in Piraeus.

78. [257c] That is, his "reputation," φιλοτιμία (*philotimia*).

79. [257e] Several explanations of this remark have been proposed. A plausible one is that the long bend in the Nile which came to be called Pleasant Bend actually is unpleasant because it makes the journey much longer. Socrates' point, then, is that names may be ironic, and Lysias' critic's words should not be taken at face value.

80. [258c] Lycurgus and Solon are held to be the founders of the Spartan and Athenian constitutions respectively. Darius was one of the great kings of Persia. Lycurgus and Solon are also singled out at *Symposium* 209d.

81. [259a] The songs of the Sirens were so enticing that they lured sailors to their deaths on the rocky outcroppings where they sang.

82. [260a] *Iliad* II.361.

83. [260d] This phrase is literally "the art of speeches," ἡ τῶν λόγων τέχνη, *hē tōn logōn technē* (τῶν λόγων is the plural of λόγος in the possessive case). To make the phrase less awkward in English, I add "making" on the assumption that it includes both composing and delivering speeches, as well as spontaneous, responsive interchange.

84. [260e] An "art" (τέχνη, *technē*) involves achieving proper results on the basis of knowledge of the relevant principles. It is a craft or science that requires mastery and expertise. To do something in an "artful" manner is not merely to act gracefully or in an aesthetically pleasing manner, but to act in a way that reflects the understanding of one who has mastered a profession.

85. [260e] The significance of the reference to the Spartan is unclear. It may reflect the Spartans' reputation for blunt, direct speech, or perhaps the unusual word translated as "genuine" (ἔτυμος, *etumos*) is from the Spartan dialect.

86. [261a] Probably a reference to Phaedrus' role in originating speeches. See 242b and *Symposium* 177d.

87. [261b] Nestor is the eloquent elder statesman of the *Iliad* (see *Iliad* I.249). Odysseus is famous for his cleverness and resourcefulness, and Helen says that no one could compete with him as a speaker (*Iliad* III.223). Palamedes, who is famous for his inventions, is identified at 261d with Zeno of Elea, who is famous for his technique of drawing contradictory conclusions from a single premiss (see *Parmenides* 127d–128a).

88. [261c] Gorgias, Thrasymachus, and Theodorus are all famous orators of the time and appear in other Platonic dialogues.

89. [263d] Pan plays the pan-pipe and is associated with shepherding, having goats' legs, ears, and horns. He is also especially amorous. In *Cratylus* 408c–d Socrates identifies him with *logos*. Hermes is the god of change and transformation and hence of good, and bad, luck.

90. [266b] An adaptation of *Odyssey* V.193.

91. [266b] The term is διαλεκτικός, *dialektikos*, which is connected with the term *logos* and refers especially to skill in conversation or dialogue.

92. [266e] Aristotle speaks of Theodorus, along with Tisias and Thrasymachus, as an important contributor to the development of oratory (see *On Sophistical Refutations* 183b32).

93. [267a] Evenus is a poet and Sophist, and is also mentioned in *Apology* 20b and *Phaedo* 60d.

94. [267a] Tisias is the teacher of Gorgias.

95. [267b] The Sophists Prodicus and Hippias are characterized in some detail in the *Protagoras*.

96. [267b] Polus is a pupil of Gorgias and plays a major role in Plato's *Gorgias*.

97. [267c] Aristotle mentions Licymnius as a poet and orator and objects to his superfluous technicalities (see *Rhetoric* 1413b14, 1414b17).

98. [267c] One of the best known of the Sophists. He is a principle character in Plato's *Protagoras*.

99. [267c] Thrasymachus, whose verbal "might" is displayed in the first book of Plato's *Republic*.

100. [268a] Literally, "daimonic." It seems unlikely that Plato intends a connection here either with Socrates' daimonic voice (242b–c above) or with the special view of the daimon in the *Symposium*. See note on 242c.

101. [268a] Eryximachus is one of the speakers in the *Symposium*. He and his father are well-known physicians.

102. [269a] Adrastus is a mythical king of Argos, contemporary with Theseus; the epithet is from the Spartan poet Tyrtaeus. Pericles is the great orator and leader of fifth-century Athens.

103. [269b] Literally, this phrase reads "who do not know how to converse/engage in conversation" (μὴ ἐπιστάμενοι διαλέγεσθαι, *mē epistamenoi dialegesthai*).

104. [270a] A fifth-century Athenian philosopher.

105. [270c] That is, Hippocrates the physician. The god Asclepius is the founder of the art of medicine.

106. [272c] That is, as we would say, to play the devil's advocate.

107. [273c] Plato may be suggesting that the inventor is really Tisias' teacher, Corax, whose name means "crow."

108. [274b] This is a generic reference, an expression of ordinary piety; Socrates need not have any specific deity in mind.

109. [274c] In the Egyptian pantheon, Theuth parallels the Greek Hermes. The story of his inventing writing is also referred to at *Philebus* 18b.

110. [274d] In traditional Greek mythology Prometheus is the inventor of writing.

111. [274e] That is, a *pharmakon*. See note on 230d.

112. [276a] That is, "animated," to use an equivalent term with a Latin root. This term is redundant here, since being alive involves having a soul. Perhaps the claim that this sort of speech has a soul is intended to imply that it can change itself and the person on whose soul it is inscribed, remembering the earlier definition of soul at 245c–246a.

113. [276b] The reference is to the practice of forcing plants into early bloom in shallow pots at the festival commemorating the untimely death of Adonis.

114. [276e] Plato here and throughout this section of the dialogue seems to be making subtle and ironic reference to his own writing.

115. [277a] This form of immortality is like that which Diotima argues for in the *Symposium*.

116. [278d] That is a "philosopher," *philosophos*.

117. [278e] Isocrates (436–388 B.C.E.) was a prominent teacher of rhetoric. A number of his written speeches are extant. Since he was an outspoken critic of Plato and Socrates, it seems likely that the praise of him here is ironic.

118. [279b] See note on 263d.

CHAPTER 5. COMMENTARY ON THE PHAEDRUS

1. Nussbaum's interpretation of the *Phaedrus* is a good example of this approach. She sees it as primarily an expression by Plato of a modification of the view of the role of love in the good life that he has Socrates present in the *Symposium*. In her discussion of the dialogue in *The Fragility of Goodness*, she does not claim to be providing a general interpretation of the dialogue, of course, but it is striking that she has no reservations about treating the discussion of *erōs* as seriously intended by Plato and sees no difficulties in discussing this analysis with little or no reference to the discussion of rhetoric in the latter part of the dialogue. Martha Nussbaum, *The Fragility of Goodness* (Cambridge: Cambridge University Press, 1986), 200–33.

2. C. J. Rowe, trans., *Plato: Phaedrus* (Warminster, England: Aris & Phillips, 1986), 7.

3. James A. Arieti, *Interpreting Plato: The Dialogues As Drama* (Savage, Md.: Rowman & Littlefield, 1991), chapter on the *Phaedrus*. G. E. L. Owen takes a similarly negative view of the philosophical content of the speeches in the first part of the dialogue, seeing their significance in their exemplification of the method of collection and division ("Plato on the Undepictable," in E. N. Lee, A. P. D. Mourelatos, and R. M. Rorty, eds., *Phronesis*, supplementary vol. I [*Exegesis and Argument*], 1973, 349–61).

4. Walter Hamilton, trans., *Plato: Phaedrus and the Seventh and Eighth Letters* (Middlessex, England: Penguin Books, 1973), 9–10.

5. A. W. Price, *Love and Friendship in Plato and Aristotle* (Oxford: Clarendon Press, 1988), 96.

6. R. Hackforth, trans., *Plato's Phaedrus* (Cambridge: Cambridge University Press, 1972), 9–10.

7. Rowe, *Plato: Phaedrus*, 9.

8. Charles L. Griswold, Jr., *Self-Knowledge in Plato's Phaedrus* (New Haven: Yale University Press, 1986), 2–9 and passim.

9. The Greek term is ἐραστής, *erastēs*, which is related to *erōs*. Socrates later calls himself a "friend of speeches/conversations/arguments" (φιλόλογος, *philologos*) (236e).

10. See, for example, 229b.

11. Plato's own name, Πλάτων (*Platōn*) in Greek, has the same root as the name of the plane-tree (πλάτονος, *platonos*); both are based on the word meaning "broad" (πλατύς, *platus*).

12. W. C. Helmbold and W. B. Holther, "The Unity of the *Phaedrus*," *University of California Publications in Classical Philology* 14 (1952): 389, 390. Ferrari provides a thoughtful reflection on the significance of these and other elements of the environment noted in the dialogue (G. R. F. Ferrari, *Listening to the Cicadas: A Study of Plato's Phaedrus* [Cambridge: Cambridge University Press, 1987], 1–36). See also Griswold, *Self-Knowledge*, 33–36.

13. See the *Euthyphro* for the former and the *Apology* for the latter.

14. Rowe provides a detailed discussion of the significance of this comparison (*Phaedrus*, 140–41); as does Griswold (*Self-Knowledge*, 39–42). Ferrari also sees this passage as showing that myth is an important philosophical tool for Socrates (*Listening to the Cicadas*, 11–12).

15. In this sense I agree with Rowe that Plato "is committed to the idea both that gods exist, and that their existence is relevant to human life" (Rowe, *Phaedrus*, 138). Rowe is assuming that the view attributed to Socrates here and in other dialogues can be taken as Plato's own, of course.

16. Note the term μυθολόγημα, *mythologēma*, at 229c—a combination of the term μῦθος, *mythos*, with a term related to *logos*—which I translate as "mythical tale."

17. Griswold defends a similar interpretation of the significance of *mythos* in the *Phaedrus*. He rejects the notion that Plato is using myths in an attempt to "convey something transcending nonmythic rational communication" (p. 143) and argues that, for Plato, "myth (as is especially clear in the *Phaedrus*) is a complex mirror of human experience" (p. 141). *Self-Knowledge*, 140–51.

18. For a wide-ranging and imaginative discussion of the significance of Plato's using pharmakon in the *Phaedrus* and elsewhere, see Jacques Derrida, *Dissemination*, translated by Barbara Johnson (Chicago: University of Chicago Press, 1981); and Walter Brogan, "Plato's *Pharmakon*: Between Two Repetitions," in *Derrida and Deconstruction*, edited by Hugh J. Silverman (New York: Routledge, 1989), 7–23.

19. Hamilton (*Phaedrus*, 26), Rowe (*Phaedrus*, 27), Ferrari (*Listening to the Cicadas*, 13), and Hackforth (*Phaedrus*, 25) all do this. Nussbaum says that in the *Phaedrus*, "Socrates, for the only time in his life, leaves his accustomed urban haunts" (*The Fragility of Goodness*, 204).

20. Kenneth Dorter, "Imagery and Philosophy in Plato's *Phaedrus*," *Journal of the History of Philosophy* 9 (1971): 280.

21. Dover provides a helpful summary of the issues involved in this controversy in *Lysias and the Corpus Lysiacum* (Berkeley: University of California Press, 1968), 69–71.

22. That is, a desire (ἐπιθυμία, *epithumia*) that is "without" *logos*.

23. Socrates' later condemnation of the speech as "irreligious" (ἀσεβῆ, *asebē*) and involving "sinning against the gods"(242c–d) should probably be seen as based on the *content* of the speech, though he does imply that the style is excessive.

24. The speech also follows the structure recommended by Agathon in the *Symposium* (195a) and commended by Socrates in that dialogue (201d).

25. This does not mean that Socrates would disagree with every remark in the speech. The emphasis on the importance of the education of the soul at 241c is a typical Socratic sentiment.

26. Friedländer agrees that this cannot be Socrates' own definition (*Plato*, 223). Although he notes that the psychology in this passage differs in some respects from that found elsewhere in the dialogues, Hackforth nevertheless argues that the view presented here is substantially in agreement with the usual Socratic/Platonic position. He sees Socrates as beginning here an ascent into a divinely inspired "irrationality" that culminates in the second speech. Hackforth, *Phaedrus*, 41–42, 47. Rowe argues that while this view does not conflict with the common understanding of *Plato's* views, it is incompatible with the Socratic rejection of ἀκρασία (*akrasia*, weakness of will). *Phaedrus*, 55–156. See the next note.

27. See, for example, *Meno* 77b–78a. This issue is made more complicated by the fact that it is commonly argued that Plato has Socrates reject this view of the relation between desire and judgment in the *Republic*; see Terence Irwin, *Plato's Moral Theory* (Oxford University Press, 1977), chapter VII. If we assume that Plato is asserting that the highest philosophical/spiritual development involves an irrational (or nonrational) transcendence of understanding, that will also be incompatible with the interpretation of the *Symposium* I have suggested. I would argue that for Plato, throughout the dialogues, *logos* (as speech/reason) is ultimate, both as bearer of the object of knowledge and the determinate of behavior.

28. On this point Griswold argues: "In Socrates' second speech reason will be organically connected with desire, and...winged reason will have the capacity to motivate and control action. This is a crucial element in [the second speech's] view that at least at the highest level reason is erotic, or eros rational." *Self-Knowledge*, 67.

29. Unless one argues, as many commentators do, that Plato, in contrast to the historical Socrates, advocates a type of ultimate irrationality.

30. See *Symposium* 199c, *Meno* 75d, and *Sophist* 218c.

31. There is an unusually sustained etymological play of this sort in the *Minos*. See my "Plato's *Minos*," *Ancient Philosophy* 8 (1988): 187–207.

32. Friedländer asserts that this qualifying phrase "or something divine" is "precisely...a pointer to" the view in the *Symposium* (*Plato,* 511, n. 14). Hackforth says that it is "just possible" that it "is a verbal concession" to that view (*Phaedrus,* 55, n. 1). This seems rather strained to me. Nothing in the context prevents Plato from using the daimon language of the *Symposium.* However, Griswold argues that Socrates is intentionally appealing to ordinary, common views here (*Self-Knowledge,* 256, n. 19).

33. Hackforth (*Phaedrus,* 3–8) provides a general discussion of the evidence. See also Rowe, *Phaedrus,* 14.

34. W. K. C. Guthrie, *A History of Greek Philosophy,* vol. IV (Cambridge: Cambridge University Press, 1975), 401, n. 2.

35. Hackforth is an eloquent defender of this line of interpretation.

36. This reference recalls the claim Socrates makes about the beneficial efforts of Diotima in gaining a postponement of the plague, *Symposium* 201d.

37. For example, *Laches* 199a, *Meno* 99c–d, *Republic* 364b–c, and *Philebus* 67b.

38. Gerasimos Santas argues that, in his second speech, Socrates means that *erōs* is a kind of madness in the sense that it is "the passion of reason" (p. 69), an intense form of desire that is guided by reason and not in conflict with it. *Plato and Freud: Two Theories of Love* (Oxford: Basil Blackwell, 1988), 58–80. Santas also argues, in the same place, that this distinction between a rational and an irrational kind of madness can account for Socrates' claim at *Republic* 403a–b that madness (*mania*) must not be allowed to have anything to do with *erōs.* (This passage in the *Republic* is included in the appendix at the end of this book.)

39. Rowe does this (*Phaedrus,* 169). However, Griswold argues that, although Socrates does say initially (245b–c) that erotic madness "is given by the gods," in his actual depiction of it in 246a–256e the gods are not in fact its source. Griswold claims that it "is not so much sent from gods external to the individual as sparked from a source within him, as is suggested by its association with anamnesis [recollection]." *Self-Knowledge,* 75.

40. Richard Bett, who claims that "Plato intends the argument as a rigorous proof" (p. 2), provides a very thorough analysis of the logic and the assumptions of the argument ("Immortality and the Nature of the Soul in the *Phaedrus,*" *Phronesis* 21 [1986]: 1–26). See also the detailed analysis by Thomas M. Robinson, "The Argument for Immortality in Plato's *Phaedrus,*" in *Essays in Ancient Greek Philosophy,* vol. 1, edited by John P. Anton and George L. Kustas (Albany, New York: State University of New York Press, 1971), 345–53.

41. Hackforth claims that the point here is that for what is self-changing to cease changing itself would be for it "to abandon its own nature, which is inconceivable." Hence, such things cannot come into being (*Phaedrus,* 66).

42. One could argue that this claim that the "essence and definition" (the οὐσία, *ousia,* actual being, and *logos*) of soul consists in its being eternally changing agrees

with the view of Diotima in the *Symposium*, who argues that the soul is a process of changing "experiences and actions" (*Phaedrus* 245c) without any enduring owner. See *Symposium* 207e–208b. Griswold defends this interpretation (*Self-Knowledge*, 81–82).

43. Guthrie, reflecting the traditional view of Plato's development, says, regarding the *Phaedrus*: "It does seem that, as the influence of Socrates recedes, Plato is giving more rein to the poetic side of his own nature; and we must also remember that each dialogue is a separate work of art with its own scene and atmosphere." *Greek Philosophy*, vol. IV, 418.

44. Hackforth argues that while there is much allegory (by which he means an easily translatable symbolic description) in the great myth in Socrates' second speech, much of it is an effort to speak about an "impenetrable mystery" that lies "beyond the limits of pure reason" (*Phaedrus*, 72). An alternative would be to see some elements as directly paralleling aspects of ordinary life and others as either humorous or honorific hyperbole.

45. For a detailed discussion of the view of the soul in the *Phaedrus* and how it relates to views in other dialogues, see Price, *Love and Friendship in Plato and Aristotle*, 67–72.

46. For careful discussions of the details of this and other parts of the myth in Socrates' second speech, including comparisons with the myths in other dialogues, see Hackforth's *Phaedrus*.

47. The forms themselves are "perceived only by the intellect (νοῦς, *nous*), the pilot of the soul" (247c). This would apply straightforwardly to definitions that state the "essence" of things (245e). Perhaps the forms should be understood as linguistic entities, that is, things that are fully grasped only in and by *logos*.

48. Rowe argues that the point here is not that rationality is suspended in the case of the philosopher, but rather that it is increased (*Phaedrus*, 182).

49. For a discussion of the arguments about recollection in the *Meno* and *Phaedo* and of how Plato intends this notion, see my "Anamnesis: Platonic Doctrine or Sophistic Absurdity?" *Dialogue: The Canadian Philosophical Review* 12 (1973): 604–28. For a contrasting interpretation, see T. H. Irwin, "Recollection and Plato's Moral Theory," *Review of Metaphysics* 27 (1974): 752–72; and Gregory Vlastos, "Anamnesis in the *Meno*," *Dialogue: The Canadian Philosophical Review* 4 (1965): 143–67.

50. Gregory Vlastos is surely correct in arguing against virtually everyone that the reference of this passage, as well as the application of the phrase "contrary to nature," is to homosexual and not heterosexual intercourse (*Platonic Studies*, 2nd ed. [Princeton: Princeton University Press, 1981], 25, n. 76, and 424–25. Hackforth takes this as a reference to *heterosexual* love (*Phaedrus*, 98), as does Kenneth Dover (*Greek Homosexuality* [Oxford: Oxford University Press, 1978], 163), but this reflects what is probably a misinterpretation of the metaphor, which seems more plausibly interpreted as referring to homosexual anal intercourse than to heterosexual relations, despite the reputed preference of the ancient Greeks for the position involving the male's

approach from the rear in heterosexual intercourse. Nothing in the text directly supports a sudden departure from the homosexual model that dominates the dialogue.

51. A similar remark occurs at *Laws* 836b–c and 841d. (The first of these passages is included in the appendix at the end of this book.)

52. See especially the *Charmides.*

53. *Phaedrus,* 107–8.

54. A similar view is asserted in *Laws* 837b–d. (This passage in included in the appendix at the end of this book.)

55. The beginning of the *Charmides* is a good example of such ribbing. It is also a significant element in the *Symposium*—and the *Phaedrus,* of course.

56. I take the claim at the end of the *Meno* (99e–100a) to the effect that one acquires virtue only by divinely ordained fate, and without understanding, to be ironic. The whole passage is filled with sarcasm and irony.

57. An "art" (τέχνη, *technē*) is the ability to produce something based on a knowledge of the relevant principles. We might translate the term as "profession." The term is often translated as "craft."

58. See Hackforth for a defence of the former view (*Phaedrus,* 125–26, n. 1), and Rowe for the latter view (*Phaedrus,* 197).

59. Hackforth asserts that it is (*Phaedrus,* 130).

60. In his explanations of the principles of collection and division, Socrates uses his definition of love as an example of the first and his division of madness as an example of the second, which might be seen as implying that he sees these efforts as philosophically sound. However, the qualification he explicitly offers in the first case seems to extend to the second, "whether the definition was stated well or poorly, it did enable the speech to proceed in a manner that was at any rate clear and self-consistent" (265d).

61. The principles of collection and division are used self-consciously in the *Sophist* and throughout the *Statesman.* The suggestion that philosophy is the art of dialectic, the highest use of *logos,* is a major theme in the *Sophist*; see especially 253d. In the *Republic* Socrates says, "Do you call the person who can grasp the *logos* of the reality/being of each thing a dialectician? And the person who cannot do this, who does not have a *logos* to give to himself or another, will you say that to that extent he does not have an understanding of it?" (534b). Compare *Republic* 531e ff. See also *Philebus* 16b–17a.

62. Hackforth argues, with regard to this passage introducing the principles of collection and division, that "there can, I think, be little doubt that the plan of the whole dialogue is centred upon the present section" (*Phaedrus,* 136).

63. This is also the case in the *Sophist.* See my discussion of the divisions in the *Sophist* in my *Plato's "Sophist"* (Savage, Md.: Rowman & Littlefield, 1990), 12–19, 28–31.

64. Hackforth, *Phaedrus*, 133, n. 1.

65. Arieti argues that this is in fact a pervasive aim of the dialogues (*Interpreting Plato*, 7).

66. In describing his early experiences with philosophy, Socrates tells of his disappointment with Anaxagoras' view of the role of intelligence in the universe (*Phaedo* 97c–99c).

67. This is Rowe's view (*Phaedrus*, 204–205). W. H. Thompson argues for a nonironic reading (*The Phaedrus of Plato* [London: Whitaker & Co., 1868], 121–23); as does Hackforth (*Phaedrus*, 149–51). Thompson sees Plato as using terms that are popularly used to denounce philosophy "with a kind of defiance" (p. 121), and de Vries agrees in finding "some self-irony" in this passage (G. J. de Vries, *A Commentary on the Phaedrus of Plato* [Amsterdam, 1969], 233).

68. This point is illustrated in Socrates' analysis of love and madness in his two speeches.

69. Aristotle's famous definition of "human being" by genus and difference, that is usually translated as "rational animal," is literally "animal that possesses *logos*."

70. Rowe discusses the complexities of trying to interpret Socrates' reference in 274b to speeches in an unqualified sense after saying he was going to talk about writing (*Phaedrus*, 207–8). It seems plausible to me to simply assume from the context that Socrates has in mind only *written* speeches, but Rowe shows there are some difficulties in this.

71. There may be a reference here to the notion of recollection that was an element in the myth in Socrates' second speech, though this seems unlikely.

72. Hackforth argues that Plato's depiction of his own writing is partly defensive, because of the comparison with the historical Socrates who was so brilliant at living speech and wrote nothing, and partly a result of the fact that Plato's "profoundest thoughts could not be set down" (*Phaedrus*, 162–64). I have questioned above this assumption that for Plato the truth is ineffable. This passage seems to suggest that the problem is that it cannot be stated in a context-independent or final way, not that it cannot be stated. At the same time, Hackforth accuses Plato of underrating the value of written philosophy (*Phaedrus*, 164).

73. Guthrie has an excellent discussion of the combination of the playful and the serious in the dialogues and of what this passage implies about the kind of texts the dialogues are. See *Greek Philosophy*, vol. IV, 54–66.

74. Griswold provides a helpful analysis of the ways in which the special character of Plato's dialogues enables them to avoid the qualities on which Socrates bases his condemnation of written texts (*Self-Knowledge*, 219–26).

75. Rowe notes the complexity of interpreting the self-referential character of Socrates' remark at 278b, "Then, we've amused [παιδία, *paidia*] ourselves enough

with these issues about making speeches." Plato seems to come close to speaking in his own voice, telling the reader that what this writing says is no more clear or certain than with any other (*Phaedrus*, 214).

76. Guthrie suggests that Plato leaves the reader the task of discovering Plato's own thoughts "through the varied talk of his characters—a rewarding process that leads him far deeper into the human mind than any straightforward theoretical exposition" (*Greek Philosophy*, vol. IV, 412).

77. There is a similar play on the terms *sophos* and *sophistēs* at the end of the *Sophist* at 268b–c. However, in this case the visiting stranger is saying that one who is accurately called *sophistēs* must be truly *sophos*.

78. Thompson has a helpful discussion of the history and usage of these terms (*Phaedrus*, 145–46).

79. The Greek word for "poet" is ποιητής, *poiētēs*, which is based on the verb 'to make' or 'to produce.' In the Athenian dialect the term was applied especially to those who practiced the literary arts. This point is exploited at *Symposium* 205b–c.

80. Hackforth, *Phaedrus*, 167–68. For a thorough discussion of the views of Isocrates and the interpretation of Plato's intention in this and other passages in his dialogues that can be connected with Isocrates, see Thompson, *Phaedrus*, 170–83, and de Vries, *Phaedrus*, 15–18. A. E. Taylor argues for the accuracy of the ancient view that Plato and Isocrates were not enemies and suggests that this praise of Isocrates is intended to show that the *Phaedrus* is not an attack on him (*Plato: The Man and His Work*, 7th ed. [London: Methuen & Co. Ltd., 1960], 318–19.

81. Rowe, *Phaedrus*, 215–16.

82. *Cratylus* 408c–d.

83. Plato offers a similar sentiment in more detail at *Critias* 120e–121c.

84. The Greek is κοινὰ γὰρ τὰ τῶν φίλων, *koina gar ta tōn philōn*. The proverb is used several times by Plato, see *Republic* 424a and 449c, *Lysis* 207c, *Laws* 739c.

Select Bibliography

Arieti, James. *Interpreting Plato: The Dialogues As Drama*. Savage, Md.: Rowman & Littlefield, 1991.

Bury, R. G., ed. *The Symposium of Plato*, 2nd ed. Cambridge: W. Heffer and Sons, Ltd., 1973.

Dover, K. J., ed. *Plato: Symposium*. Cambridge Greek and Latin Classics. Cambridge: Cambridge University Press, 1980.

Ferrari, G. R. F. *Listening to the Cicadas: A Study of Plato's Phaedrus*. Cambridge: Cambridge University Press, 1987.

Friedländer, Paul. *Plato*. Three volumes. Bollingen Series LIX. Princeton: Princeton University Press, 1969.

Griswold, Charles L., Jr., ed. *Platonic Writings: Platonic Readings*. New York: Routledge, 1988.

———. *Self-Knowledge in Plato's Phaedrus*. New Haven: Yale University Press, 1986.

Guthrie, W. K. C. *A History of Greek Philosophy*. Volume IV. Cambridge: Cambridge University Press, 1975.

Hackforth, R., trans. *Plato's Phaedrus*. Cambridge: Cambridge University Press, 1972.

Halperin, David M. "Platonic *Eros* and What Men Call Love." *Ancient Philosophy* 5 (1985): 161–204.

———. "Why Diotima Is a Woman." In David M. Halperin, *One Hundred Years of Homosexuality and Other Essays on Greek Love*. New York: Routledge, 1990.

Nussbaum, Martha C. *The Fragility of Goodness*. Cambridge: Cambridge University Press, 1986.

Price, A. W. *Love and Friendship in Plato and Aristotle*. Oxford: Clarendon Press, 1989.

Rowe, C. J., ed. and trans. *Plato: Phaedrus.* Warminster, England: Aris & Phillips, 1986.

Santas, Gerasimos. *Plato and Freud: Two Theories of Love.* Oxford: Basil Blackwell, 1988.

Stokes, M. C. *Plato's Socratic Conversations: Drama and Dialectic in Three Dialogues.* Baltimore: The Johns Hopkins Unviersity Press, 1986.

Taylor, A. E. *Plato: The Man and His Work*, 7th ed. London: Methuen & Co. Ltd., 1960.

Vlastos, Gregory. "The Individual as Object of Love in Plato." In *Platonic Studies*, 2nd ed. Princeton: Princeton University Press, 1981.

INDEX

Printed in the United States
835100003B